ANXIETY AND DEPRESSION IN ADULTS AND CHILDREN

For information address:

SAGE Publications, Inc.
2455 Teller Road
Thousand Oaks, California 91320

SAGE Publications Ltd.
6 Bonhill Street
London EC2A 4PU
United Kingdom

SAGE Publications India Pvt. Ltd.
M-32 Market
Greater Kailash I
New Delhi 110048 India

Printed in the United States of America

Library of Congress Cataloging-in-Publication Data

Anxiety and depression in adults and children / [edited by] Kenneth D.
 Craig, Keith S. Dobson.
     p. cm.—(Banff international behavioral sciences series)
   Includes bibliographical references and index.
   ISBN 0-8039-7020-X (cloth).—ISBN 0-8039-7021-8 (pbk.)
   1. Anxiety. 2. Depression, Mental. I. Craig, Kennth D., 1937-
   II. Dobson, Keith S. III. Series.
 RC531.A566 1995
 616.85'223—dc20   94-40361

95 96 97 98 10 9 8 7 6 5 4 3 2 1

Sage Production Editor: Diane S. Foster

ANXIETY AND DEPRESSION IN ADULTS AND CHILDREN

Kenneth D. Craig
Keith S. Dobson
editors

Bᴀɴꜰꜰ Iɴᴛᴇʀɴᴀᴛɪᴏɴᴀʟ Bᴇʜᴀᴠɪᴏʀᴀʟ Sᴄɪᴇɴᴄᴇ ꜱᴇʀɪᴇꜱ

SAGE Publications
International Educational and Professional Publisher
Thousand Oaks   London   New Delhi

BANFF INTERNATIONAL BEHAVIORAL SCIENCE Series

SERIES EDITORS

Kenneth D. Craig, *University of British Columbia*
Keith S. Dobson, *University of Calgary*
Robert J. McMahon, *University of Washington*
Ray DeV. Peters, *Queen's University*

Volumes in the **Banff International Behavioral Science** Series take the behavioral science perspective on important basic and applied challenges that confront practitioners working in the fields of the social, psychological, and health services. The editors invite leading investigators and practitioners to contribute because of their expertise on emergent issues and topics. Contributions to the volumes integrate information on themes and key issues relating to current research and professional practice. The chapters reflect the authors' personal, critical analysis of the topics, the current scientific and professional literature, and discussions and deliberations with other experts and practitioners. It is our intention to have this continuing series of publications provide an "expressive" early indicator of the developing nature and composition of the behavioral sciences and scientific applications to human problems and issues. The volumes should appeal to practitioners, scientists, and students interested in the interface between professional practice and research advances.

- *Anxiety and Depression in Adults and Children* Edited by Kenneth D. Craig and Keith S. Dobson

Forthcoming:

- *Cognitive/Behavioral Therapies: State of the Art* Edited by Keith S. Dobson and Kenneth D. Craig
- *Childhood Disorders, Substance Abuse and Delinquency: Prevention and Early Intervention Approaches* Edited by Ray DeV. Peters and Robert J. McMahon

Contents

Preface

This volume is one of a continuing series of publications sponsored by the Banff International Conferences on Behavioral Science. We are pleased to join Sage Publications in bringing this series to an audience of practitioners, investigators, and students. The publications arise from conferences held each spring since 1969 in Banff, Alberta, Canada, with the papers representing the product of deliberations on themes and key issues. The conferences serve the purpose of bringing together outstanding behavioral scientists and professionals in a forum where they can present and discuss data related to emergent issues and topics. As a continuing event, the Banff International Conferences have served as an expressive "early indicator" of the developing nature and composition of the behavioral sciences and scientific applications to human problems and issues.

Because distance, schedules, and restricted audience preclude wide attendance at the conferences, the resulting publications have equal status with the conferences proper. Presenters at each Banff Conference are required to write a chapter specifically for the forthcoming book, separate from their presentation and discussion at the conference itself. Consequently this volume is not a set of conference proceedings. Rather it is an integrated volume of chapters contributed by leading researchers and practitioners who have had the unique opportunity of spending several days together presenting and discussing ideas prior to preparing their chapters.

We are pleased to present this volume focusing upon anxiety and depression in adults and children. A primary consideration in the selection of contributors was a concern for life span development. The papers in this volume bridge different age ranges and demonstrate continuity between early development and adult emotional challenges. We were pleased that the leading contributors in the fields of anxiety and depression with this orientation accepted our invitation to participate.

This conference represented the 25th Banff International Conference on Behavioural Science. This silver anniversary achievement reflected the dedicated efforts of a large number of organizers, scientists, practitioners, and students of the field to advance our understanding of the important basic and applied challenges that confront our society. We are truly grateful for their outstanding work over 25 years. Our "conference of colleagues" format provides for formal and informal interactions among all participants through invited addresses, workshops, poster presentations, and conversation hours. When combined with sight-seeing expeditions, cross-country and downhill skiing, and other recreations in the spectacular Canadian Rockies, the conferences have generated great enthusiasm and satisfaction among participants. The Banff Centre, our venue for the conferences for many years, has contributed immeasurably to the success of these meetings through its very comfortable accommodation, dining, and conference facilities. The following documents conference themes over the 25 years. We look forward to the next 25!

1969: I. Ideal Mental Health Services

1970: II. Services and Programs for Exceptional Children and Youth

1971: III. Implementing Behavioral Programs for Schools and Clinics

1972: IV. Behavior Change: Methodology, Concepts, and Practice

1973: V. Evaluation of Behavioral Programs in Community, Residential, and School Settings

1974: VI. Behavior Modification and Families and Behavioral Approaches to Parenting

1975: VII. The Behavioral Management of Anxiety, Depression, and Pain

1976: VIII. Behavioral Self-Management Strategies, Techniques, and Outcomes

1977: IX. Behavioral Systems for the Developmentally Disabled

    A. School and Family Environments

    B. Institutional, Clinic, and Community Environments

1978: X. Behavioral Medicine: Changing Health Lifestyles

KENNETH D. CRAIG
KEITH S. DOBSON

Introduction

PERSPECTIVES ON ANXIETY AND
DEPRESSION IN ADULTS AND CHILDREN

KENNETH D. CRAIG

KEITH S. DOBSON

Human life cannot be contemplated without consideration of the emotional and mood states that the terms *anxiety* and *depression* evoke. The words have commonplace meanings that make them readily accessible to people describing the inevitable uncertainties, demands, and disappointments of daily life. As well, the labels have highly technical and restrictive meanings that are often applied to the clinical needs of clients requiring professional intervention. Although people using the vernacular and professional language may differ in the meanings they assign to the terms, both usages signal the emphasis we attach to these salient qualities of conscious experience.

There is little doubt that these emotional states play an extremely important role in people's lives. An examination of the relative balance and importance of human feelings, thoughts, and behavior leads to the conclusion that it is moods and emotional states, ranging between despair or agony and joy or elation, that add pleasant or unpleasant significance and meaning to our experiences. The rich variations in emotional reactions, sometimes subtle but often strong, accompany every moment of human existence. Appropriately, practitioners addressing health problems attach major importance to excessive or inappropriate emotional reactions, and changing dysfunctional anxiety and depression is a commonplace therapeutic objective for practitioners in psychology, medicine, and other professions.

Unfortunately, there is conceptual confusion concerning the nature of anxiety and depression, giving rise to very different formal conceptions. Although the unpleasant feelings of fear and apprehension associated with anxiety and the sadness and debilitating impact of depression are very real, theoretical models attempting to explain these states encompass the broad range of biological, psychoanalytic, cognitive-behavioral, and phenomenological domains. Recognizing feeling states as ongoing components of experience has given rise to quantitative approaches that favor dimensional analyses and emphasize the continuities of experience between everyday and extraordinary states. In turn, the qualitative perspective has led to an appreciation for the rich nuances of experience and categorization of common types of experience into psychiatric syndromes.

The prevalence, centrality, and importance of these emotional states to the human experience have led to considerable recent basic and applied research. The following represent a number of the emergent issues and challenges being confronted.

1. *Communication of subjective experiences.* Although most people know anxiety and depression all too well, anxiety and depression as private experiences cannot be observed directly by others and can be known to observers through inference. Even verbal report of these experiences can be complex and ambiguous. Conscious experience is made up of a highly plastic, dynamic flow of intimate feelings, images, and thoughts that are sometimes turbulent, confusing, and very private. People often have difficulty articulating their experiences, not infrequently failing at it, and carefully monitor the social context to ensure socially correct behavior. It is little wonder that our language often fails to capture the essence of affective states and oversimplifies these experiences in the interests of communication (Nisbett & Wilson, 1977; Zajonc, 1980), or that the best contemporary measuring instruments have difficulty discriminating anxiety and depression (Feldman, 1993). Efforts to assess these internal states have led to many ingenious operational definitions that have varied in their focus upon self-report, behavioral manifestations, and physiological concomitants.

2. *Issues of definition.* Despite frequent use of the terms *anxiety* and *depression* and their psychological importance, there remains considerable uncertainty as to their precise meaning. In part, the challenge of providing clear definitions derives from the highly personal and subjective nature of these experiences. The confusion is also reflected in the different meanings attached to these terms when used by the lay public and professionals. The terms can be used to describe what appear to be necessary and inevitable vicissitudes of everyday life, on the one hand, and probably unnecessary and destructive pathological states, on the other. Similarly, the focus can be upon cognitive, behavioral, or somatic dimensions of anxiety. Given different perspectives, it is not surprising that terms with widespread common meanings are understood differently by scientists and practitioners. Increasingly, we conceptualize both anxiety and depression as multifaceted and multidimensional phenomena.

3. *Conceptual clarity of the concepts of anxiety and depression.* Surprisingly, a long history of research has not led to tighter definitions or understandings of anxiety and depression as conceptually and empirically distinct phenomena. Most people have considered them to be distinct emotional experiences, and different traditions of theoretical explanation and psychological intervention for these apparently separate feeling states have emerged over time. However, we increasingly recognize they are not separate psychological states, but have overlapping qualities (e.g., Clark & Watson, 1991; Feldman, 1993). Data-based studies of anxiety and depression demonstrate substantial overlap in the subjective experiences, physiological correlates, and behavioral manifestations that characterize them. Similarly, when either anxiety or depression occurs to a pathological extreme, there is a high probability that the other will also be observed. As several chapters in this volume attest, the proposition that anxiety and depression are separate distinct phenomena is breaking down. Concomitant with this change in conceptualization has been an increasing interest in organizing constructs, such as negative affectivity, that comprise the fundamental essences of both anxiety and depression (see Ingram & Malcarne, this volume).

4. *Interactions among feeling states, cognition, and behavior.* One can appreciate the complexities of anxiety and depression by considering the interactions among feeling states, cognition, and behavior. Each aspect of this triad can be formulated as either a consequence or a determinant of the others. Emotions can color or filter our understanding and reactions to our thoughts and the external world, just as our thoughts and external events give

rise to powerful emotions. Thus some theories of human behavior attach importance to how overwhelming emotions drive specific thoughts and actions, and other theories emphasize how emotions arise from certain thoughts, other cognitive states, or. behavior. The several theories and methodologies described in the following chapters reflect different approaches to the interactions among these interrelated processes.

5. *Individual differences.* Contributing to the complexities of understanding, assessing, and intervening with clinical distress, reports of anxious or depressed experiences often reflect striking individual differences. These varied patterns are most evident when one examines different people's reactions to what appear to be highly comparable events: People often dramatically vary in their responses to a broad range of social, personal, and physical threats. The focus upon individual differences has also brought attention to the highly heterogeneous nature of these experiences. One person's anxiety is unlikely to be the same as another person's, and comparing them is a considerable challenge. The quantitative and qualitative variations also may include temporal variations. For some people, anxiety and depression are transitory experiences, but for others they have an enduring and pervasive impact.

6. *An emergent developmental perspective.* Clinicians confronted with the challenge of explaining an adult's pathological fears or depression have recognized for a long time that important causal events can be discovered in the life history of the individual. They are accustomed to looking at the biological and personal history of the individual to determine whether formative influences are associated with the person's unique characteristics. Although proponents of the psychodynamic perspective have long recognized the role of developmental factors, only recently has the broader cognitive-behavioral perspective been brought to bear upon the contributions of biological and life history factors to individual differences in these emotional processes. Similarly, we have come to appreciate the necessity of developmental sensitivity; these formative influences have an impact on children whose reactions are based upon emerging stages of cognitive and social development. Understanding the course and discontinuities of development best allows one to appreciate the experience of the child or adult. Not only do maturity, health, and experiences dictate that children differ from adults in their reactions to situations, but prior experiences ultimately determine how an adult will react to situations.

7. *Biological/experiential interactions.* A bioevolutionary perspective clarifies the adaptive properties of emotional processes. In the course of evolution these would have emerged to fulfill activation, directive, and organizing purposes, with their current role reflecting the long-term biological imperatives. A complete understanding of anxiety and depression will require an appreciation of associated biological inheritance and the manner in which maturation and life experiences in family and social contexts interact to produce these experiences at any given stage of life.

This volume brings together essays addressing anxiety and depression from three perspectives: (a) our conceptual foundations—just what have we accomplished in trying to understand these problems and where should we be going, (b) assessment strategies—we can help people only if we can assess what is problematic, and (c) treatment interventions—despite limitations of our conceptual understanding and assessment tools, recently developed interventions have been proven remarkably effective.

Part I of this volume provides four chapters addressing current important conceptual issues. Kendall and Brady (Chapter 1) open the volume by examining the problem of comorbidity, or the likelihood that clients with one diagnosis will satisfy criteria for other diagnoses, among other definitions carefully explored. This allows a wide-ranging discussion of important issues. Substantial overlaps between mood and anxiety disorders are demonstrated for both children and adults, suggesting overlapping and distinctive features for these emotional states. Theoretical viewpoints delineating the nature of the interrelationship between anxiety and depression are also described. The ramifications of comorbidity are examined for understanding the nature and validity of current diagnostic categories, for the etiology of the disorders, and for assessment and treatment. Given the substantial comorbidity that is readily demonstrated, it would seem that current diagnostic efforts often oversimplify clients' problems and that prescriptive therapies for any given client will have to address more than one problem.

Given the dominant role cognition has assumed in both the experimental and the clinical behavioral sciences in recent years, and the emergence of cognitive-behavioral interventions as prominent strategies for addressing emotional problems, it is appropriate that Ingram and Malcarne (Chapter 2) should address theoretical and empirical findings on commonalities and differences in cognitive processes that accompany depression and anxiety. A broad conceptual model of psychopathology encompassing conceptual and empirical distinctions between cognitive structures and processes is applied to organize and contrast models of anxiety and depression. The important concept of negative affectivity is examined in detail. It is suggested that people who are high on both depression and anxiety are predisposed to negative affectivity because of increased negative cognition, but the area of negative affectivity is largely unexplored from the cognitive perspective.

Chapter 3 by Alden, Bieling, and Meleshko examines depression and anxiety from an interpersonal perspective to determine whether these conditions are associated with distinctive cognitive and behavioral reactions to interpersonal situations. Depressed and socially anxious people tend to share a common characteristic: Interpersonal interactions exacerbate rather than alleviate emotional problems. Cognitive and behavioral theories and empirical literature that address interpersonal aspects of depression and social anxiety are examined, with a primary focus upon distinctive cognitive-behavioral patterns in the ways that depressed and anxious people process social information. Negative and dysfunctional cognitions are described for both groups, including some that are shared and others that appear relatively unique to specific emotional problems. A less consistent pattern emerges from studies of social behavior in depressed and anxious people, with both groups tending toward displays of limited social skills and behavioral inhibition, and depressed people engaging in high levels of negative verbal behavior. It is interesting that subtypes of depression and anxiety may be identified in terms of specific interpersonal deficits and excesses.

Hammen (Chapter 4) pursues the argument that models of depression must take broad contextual factors into account, rather than relying on simple intraindividual factors, whether neuroendocrinological or cognitive. She proposes a "cognitive-interpersonal model of depression," suggesting it may be more aptly described as "a multifactorial, transactional, transgenerational cognitive/life stress/interpersonal model of depression," thereby effectively delineating the domains it encompasses. As in Chapter 3, an emphasis is placed upon interpersonal functioning, with three propositions, examined in detail, capturing essential elements of the model: (a) depression runs in families; (b) depression risk is mediated by dysfunctional schemata about the self and others and by maladaptive interpersonal skills, especially those related to social problem solving; and (c) vulnerability to depression in part consists of stressful environments to which the person is exposed and creates. This focus upon risk factors contributes substantially to the prospects of primary and secondary prevention.

Part II examines the assessment and management of anxiety. Ollendick (Chapter 5) examines the problem-solving strategies involved in child behavioral assessment of "internalizing" disorders, specifically clinical anxiety and phobic disorders. The broad range of behavioral interviews, self- and other-reports, self-monitoring, physiological recording, and behavioral observation is examined. Two major criteria dictated the selection of instruments: They had to have evidence of empirical validation and had to be developmentally sensitive to the discontinuities and stabilities of growth. A "multimethod, multimodal" case example is provided to illustrate the principle that assessment requires a range of procedures needed to explore and test hypotheses about a specific child and to formulate specific interventions.

Rachman (Chapter 6) turns to a pervasive problem in the management of anxiety disorders: the recurrence of fears in the absence of further aversive events. He proposes that a theory of "emotional processing" can accommodate a number of disparate findings in the anxiety management literature, including the return of fear, recurrent nightmares, verbal preoccupation with unpleasant events, obsessional ideas and images, and flashback experiences of terror. As well, it is a unifying construct that may account for the equal effectiveness of many cognitive and exposure strategies in reducing anxiety.

Bakal, Hesson, and Demjen (Chapter 7) shift the focus to the role of somatic factors in anxiety disorders. The majority of somatic complaints presented during anxiety disorders correspond in character to primary symptoms of major medical disorders, yet they are presented in the absence of physical diagnoses, often leading to considerable practitioner and patient dissatisfaction. This chapter provides a framework for understanding the somatic complaints associated with anxiety and the development of a therapeutic approach incorporating somatic awareness into cognitive-behavioral treatment. Rather than conceptualizing somatic symptoms as a substitute for psychological distress, as in psychodynamic formulations, the authors see them as biological reactions to distress, in proportion to the distress experienced. Theoretical, data-based, and practical observations are made for integration of somatic awareness training as an emotional processing strategy.

In Chapter 8, the author of the therapeutic approach of anxiety management training, Richard Suinn, provides both its theoretical and research foundations and a summary of the therapeutic methodology. There are similarities to Rachman's concepts of emotional processing and Bakal, Hesson, and Demjen's approach to somatic awareness, but a full range of therapeutic techniques is described. Clients are taught to pay attention to

anxiety symptoms with a coping method; relaxation is then taught to eliminate anxiety once precipitated. Core characteristics of the method are guided
imagery, anxiety arousal, and relaxation for self-control. Support for applications of the therapeutic approach to both anxiety and depression is provided through a review of the numerous research investigations. Treatment
procedures for both individual and group anxiety management training are
also provided.

Part III examines the assessment and management of depression. In
Chapter 8, Rehm provides a state-of-the-art review of therapy programs for
depression that have been empirically studied and validated, a field of study
and development that has developed dramatically in recent years and led to
interventions that yield clinically significant improvements. The chapter
describes rationale and procedures; summarizes the research, highlighting
particular and unexpected findings; integrates the findings to provide a
statement about effective therapy for depression; and suggests directions for
future innovation and research. The review also provides a primer on research design in that it systematically examines studies using no therapy
control groups (i.e., waiting lists, delayed therapy, etc.), the use of placebo
therapies, and comparisons among therapies, including pharmacotherapy.

Swallow and Segal (Chapter 10) provide a more specific analysis of the
increasingly popular and highly effective cognitive-behavioral therapy for
unipolar depression, encompassing both theory and practice. The chapter
examines theoretical foundations, procedures for assessing depression and
planning treatment, some defining characteristics, specific intervention strategies, and guidelines for identifying patients for whom the strategy works
optimally. The integration of research with details on assessment strategies
and representative intervention techniques demonstrates the effective interplay between research and treatment innovation. Identifying depression as a
prevalent and perhaps the most significant problem for adolescents, along
with the comorbid problems of anxiety, substance abuse, and disruptive
behavior, Hops and Lewinsohn (Chapter 11) have adapted their well-established
treatment program for this age group. The Coping With Depression Course
for Adolescents is described here in terms of its conceptual and treatment
antecedents, the components of the program and adaptations that were
necessary to make it appropriate for adolescents, and details on a long-term,
longitudinal study assessing its effectiveness. The chapter provides an excellent model for therapy development in that it combines conceptual innovation with empirical validation, demonstrating that theoretically sound planning

can lead to demonstrably effective treatment and inspiration for additional development.

REFERENCES

Clark, L. A., & Watson, D. (1991). Tripartite model of anxiety and depression. Psychometric evidence and taxonomic implications. *Journal of Abnormal Psychology, 100,* 316-336.

Feldman, L. A. (1993). Distinguishing depression and anxiety in self-report: Evidence from confirmatory factor analysis on nonclinical and clinical samples. *Journal of Consulting and Clinical Psychology, 61,* 631-638.

Nisbett, R. N., & Wilson, T. D. (1977). Telling more than we can know: Verbal reports on mental processes. *Psychological Review, 84,* 231-259.

Zajonc, R. B. (1980). Feeling and thinking: Preferences need no inferences. *American Psychologist, 35,* 151-175.

PART I

Conceptual Advances

1

Comorbidity in the Anxiety Disorders of Childhood

IMPLICATIONS FOR VALIDITY AND CLINICAL SIGNIFICANCE

PHILIP C. KENDALL

ERIKA U. BRADY

Anxiety disorders in adult populations have been the focus of considerable research, particularly in the last decade (Barlow, 1988). For example, studies have examined their course, outcome, or response to treatment (e.g., Coryell et al., 1988; Stein & Hoover, 1989), patterns of comorbidity among anxiety disorders (e.g., Brown & Barlow, 1992; Sanderson, DiNardo, Rapee, & Barlow, 1990), and the relationship of anxiety to other emotional disorders or depression (e.g., Akiskal, 1985; Breier, Charney, & Heninger, 1985; Kendall & Watson, 1989; Watson, Clark, & Carey, 1988).

Relative to adult anxiety disorders, anxiety disorders in childhood have received little empirical attention, despite the fact that a significant number of children suffer from anxiety. Two initial studies reporting the prevalence of *DSM-III* disorders in children provide data on the anxiety disorders.

Anderson, Williams, McGee, and Silva (1987) reported a prevalence rate for anxiety disorders of 7.4% in their sample of 11-year-olds from the general population. In a sample of children visiting their primary care pediatrician for a variety of routine medical procedures, Costello et al. (1988) found the prevalence rate for anxiety disorders to be 21.7%. In both studies, anxiety disorders were among the most frequently diagnosed disorders in children.

It is surprising that this area has been relatively overlooked, given the evidence that childhood anxiety may have both immediate and long-term implications for an individual's functioning. Anxiety in children has an immediate negative impact on schoolwork and social adjustment (Dweck & Wortman, 1982; Strauss, Lease, Last, & Francis, 1988). Data supporting the idea of long-term consequences come from studies indicating that a large number of anxiety-disordered adults report suffering from anxiety problems as children (Last, Hersen, Kazdin, Francis, & Grubb, 1987; Last, Phillips, & Statfield, 1987; Weissman, Leckman, Merikangas, Gammon, & Prusoff, 1985). Moreover, reports so far indicate that older children exhibit greater levels of anxiety than younger children with the same disorder, suggesting that symptoms worsen over time (Strauss, Lease, et al., 1988).

Researchers in the field of psychopathology have focused increased attention on the area of comorbidity. For example, a recent issue of the *Journal of Consulting and Clinical Psychology* was devoted to the topic of comorbidity (e.g., Brown & Barlow, 1992; Kendall, Kortlander, Chansky, & Brady, 1992). Comorbidity may have important implications for the nature and validity of diagnostic categories, for the etiology of disorders, and for treatment.

Within the discipline of psychological treatment, appropriate therapeutic interventions would be markedly simplified and conceivably more potent if each disorder had a set of nonoverlapping symptoms that could be reliably assessed and if specific treatment procedures were known to remediate each identified disorder (Kendall & Clarkin, 1992). What have been aptly labeled *targeted* or *prescriptive* therapies require, in part, that there be specific discernible and homogeneous diagnostic categories to which identified and validated treatments can be applied. This goal, though meritorious, is far from being realized because the diagnostic situation, though recently improved, remains much more complicated than preferred. Indeed, most mental health professionals are all too familiar with the error variance that exists within diagnostic classification systems and the limitations of cross-diagnostic decisions when clients meet the criteria for more than one disorder. The legitimate aspiration for prescriptiveness in psychotherapy requires that the issue of comorbidity be thoroughly addressed.

This chapter reviews the literature on comorbidity in the childhood anxiety disorders. The term comorbidity is defined, and diagnostic issues relevant to childhood anxiety are explored. The validity of the three *DSM-III-R* childhood anxiety disorders is discussed in reference to the overlap among these disorders. Implications for the validity of the childhood anxiety disorders are also reviewed with regard to the relationship of anxiety and depression. Several theoretical viewpoints that delineate the nature of the interrelationship of anxiety and depression are presented. Studies are reviewed that explore the use of rating scales to differentiate the two constructs. Data on comorbidity between childhood anxiety and depressive disorders are discussed. Finally, differences between anxiety- and depressive-disordered children in terms of family history and descriptive variables are also reviewed.

COMORBIDITY: DEFINITIONAL PERSPECTIVE

The term *comorbidity* most commonly refers to the presence of any additional disorder in a patient with a particular index disorder (Feinstein, 1970). In some cases, however, researchers have used the term to refer to the extent to which symptoms or symptom clusters co-occur (Brown & Barlow, 1992; Moras & Barlow, 1992). This approach is useful because the presence of subclinical disorders or symptom clusters not meeting an additional diagnosis can also have etiological and predictive value. Another consideration when studying comorbidity is the difference between interepisode or lifetime comorbidity and intraepisode comorbidity (Klerman, 1990). Discussions and studies of comorbidity must consider the question, Which is the primary diagnosis? In some cases, the distinction between primary and secondary diagnoses is made temporally on the basis of which disorder appeared first. In other cases, clinical severity is the distinguishing factor. And in still other cases, the causal relationship between two disorders is examined, and the primary disorder is held to be the one that causes the other disorder (Klerman, 1990).

Another factor that is important in studying comorbidity is the presence of hierarchical exclusionary criteria in the classification system. One change with the advent of *DSM-III-R* and *DSM-IV* was the suspension of some of the hierarchical exclusionary rules that were present in *DSM-III*. This change helped spur recent interest in studying comorbidity. Hierarchical exclusionary rules state that one disorder cannot be diagnosed if it occurs only in the presence of another disorder. This system had great impact on the anxiety disorders because other disorders were higher in the hierarchy. The *DSM-III-R*, for example, stipulates that Generalized Anxiety Disorder and its childhood equivalent, Overanxious Disorder, should not be diagnosed if they occur only during the course of a mood disorder. Researchers studying comorbidity often suspend hierarchial rules because they give a misleading picture about the extent of overlap between mood disorders and anxiety disorders.

DIAGNOSTIC ISSUES

The prevailing classification system used in the United States, the *Diagnostic and Statistical Manual of Mental Disorders* (*DSM*, American Psychiatric Association [APA], 1987, 1994), recognizes two classes of anxiety disorders: those originating in infancy through adolescence, and ones that can develop at any age but commonly occur in adulthood. Children and adolescents can receive diagnoses from either class of disorders. There is considerable debate as to the validity and the diagnostic reliability that can be achieved with a categorical system such as the *DSM*, especially regarding the classification of child and adolescent disorders. The precursor to the *DSM-III-R*, the *DSM-III*, did not have a research or theoretical basis for many of the child and adolescent disorders it described (Achenbach, Connors, Quay, Verhulst, & Howell, 1989). The *DSM-III-R* classifies anxiety and depressive disorders as separate categories in both children and adults. The *DSM* is a manual that continues to be in a process of revision, however. The *DSM-IV* (APA, 1994) includes things that greatly affect the anxiety disorders. These revisions will be discussed later in this section. The focus of this chapter will be on the *DSM-III-R* anxiety disorders because, as yet no studies have been published based on *DSM-IV* criteria.

The three *DSM-III-R* childhood anxiety disorders are separation anxiety disorder (SAD), overanxious disorder (OAD), and avoidant disorder. None of these disorders has received much empirical attention until recently, but there has been support for SAD and OAD in the clinical literature (Bowlby, 1973). Of the three childhood anxiety disorders, avoidant disorder has received the least attention, and there is considerable debate about its validity. Separation anxiety has long been recognized as a normal developmental phenomenon that most children experience. As a disorder, it is defined as excessive anxiety about separation from a major attachment figure, beyond what would be expected from the child's developmental level. Overanxious disorder is a more generalized disorder, comparable to generalized anxiety disorder (GAD). It is characterized by excessive or unrealistic anxiety not focused on any one specific situation or stimulus. Avoidant disorder is characterized by excessive shrinking from unfamiliar people that interferes with the child's life.

In the past 5 years, Last and colleagues have published a number of reports regarding the reliability and validity of diagnoses of these childhood anxiety disorders. They have demonstrated that with the use of structured interviews, these disorders can be reliably diagnosed (Last, Hersen, Kazdin, Finkelstein, & Strauss, 1987; Last, Perrin, Hersen, & Kazdin, 1992; Last, Strauss, & Francis, 1987; Strauss, Last, Hersen, & Kazdin, 1988). They have documented differences between children diagnosed with SAD and those with OAD. Children with SAD tend to be younger and come from families with lower socioeconomic status, and children with OAD are more likely to have a comorbid anxiety disorder. On the basis of this study the authors concluded that the results supported the distinction between SAD and OAD as described in the *DSM-III-R* (Last et al., 1987). Beidel (1991) reported findings that also support the category of OAD in her comparison of children with OAD, social phobia, and normal controls. She found that children with social phobia could be distinguished from the other two groups on the basis of self-report inventories, anxiety self-monitoring, and psychophysiological measures.

Reports by Last and colleagues have indicated that avoidant disorder is one of the least frequent disorders diagnosed in anxious children (Last et al., 1992). Francis, Last, and Strauss (1992) examined the diagnostic category of avoidant disorder. Prior to this study, no data specific to children with this disorder had been reported. The study's purpose was to compare avoidant disorder and social phobia. *Social phobia* is defined as a persistent fear of one or more situations involving scrutiny by others because of the possibility of doing something embarrassing or humiliating. In some cases, the person fears only one social situation (e.g., eating in public or public speaking), but often he or she fears several social situations or even most social events. Children and adolescents can be diagnosed with social phobia provided that the symptoms do not meet the criteria for avoidant disorder. Francis et al. (1992) pointed out that the criteria for both disorders showed considerable overlap, and that previously there had been no data on their discrimination. They compared three groups of children: those with avoidant disorder, those with social phobia, and those with both disorders. They found that the groups were similar in all respects except age at intake. From this finding they concluded that social phobia and avoidant disorder may not be distinct disorders, and that instead avoidant disorder (essentially fear of strangers) may be a type of social phobia that is more common in younger children. They describe this as a developmental phenomenon in that in normal development fear of strangers predates social-evaluative fears. Data from the Temple Child and Adolescent Anxiety Disorders Clinic similarly suggest that it is difficult to distinguish avoidant disorder and generalized social phobia.

As mentioned earlier, the childhood anxiety disorders section of the *DSM-III-R* has undergone major revision in the *DSM-IV*. These changes reflect the data collected on the reliability and validity of the *DSM-III-R* categories. Specifically, avoidant disorder and overanxious disorder have been eliminated as separate categories and are included in the adult equivalents of these two disorders. Thus avoidant disorder is now classified as "social phobia—generalized," and overanxious disorder as "generalized anxiety disorder." Specific age-related features are indicated in the description of the disorders. The separation anxiety disorder category remains essentially the same, with the addition of minor clarifications to individual symptom criteria.

Diagnostic Overlap Among Childhood Anxiety Disorders

Information about the validity of the childhood anxiety disorders can come from data on the comorbidity among these disorders. Do children with one childhood anxiety disorder have another coexisting anxiety disorder, or are these three disorders mutually exclusive? Data from studies on adults with anxiety disorders show a high degree of comorbidity. Sanderson et al. (1990), for example, found that social phobia and simple phobia each coexisted in about a third of their patients with another principal anxiety disorder. Overall, approximately 37% of the anxiety-disordered patients had a comorbid anxiety disorder. Brown and Barlow (1992) found that about a third (approximately 32%) of the patients in their study had a coexisting anxiety disorder, with GAD being the most common additional anxiety disorder (23%). De Ruiter, Rijken, Garssen, van Schaik, and Kraaimaat

(1989) found comparably high rates of comorbidity in their sample of Dutch anxiety-disordered individuals. Brown and Barlow proposed that the high rates of comorbidity in their study and previous studies lend support to the idea that the anxiety disorders share a basic process of overarousal and anxious apprehension that are characterological or temperamental in nature, and that these basic processes form a vulnerability to emotional disorders. Thus they recommend that a classification system that incorporates dimensional scaling of symptoms would lend itself better to treatment planning.

Data on the comorbidity among childhood anxiety disorders show similarly high rates among the childhood anxiety disorders. Figure 1.1 shows the diagnostic overlap among the childhood anxiety disorders from a sample of 106 consecutive cases accepted for treatment at the Temple Child and Adolescent Anxiety Disorders Clinic (CAADC). Children ranged in age from 9 to 13, with the mean age being 11.4 years. There were 67 males and 39 females. The children were primarily Caucasian ($n = 88$), with 10 African Americans, 3 Asians, 2 Hispanics, and 3 children whose race was designated as "other." Only 36 of the 106 children had only one childhood anxiety disorder. OAD was by far the most common diagnosis, present as a primary or comorbid disorder in all but nine cases. Approximately 80% of children with primary avoidant disorder or SAD had comorbid OAD. For children with primary OAD, about 45% had comorbid avoidant disorder, and just over 20% also had SAD. Simple phobias were common in all three groups, ranging in prevalence from 40% for children with primary avoidant disorder to about 82% of children with SAD. Figure 1.2 displays the prevalence of comorbid diagnoses. At this clinic two thirds of the children have two or more childhood anxiety disorders. This finding suggests that the categorical system that classifies child anxiety may be misleading in that it is relatively infrequent for children to have only one of these disorders.

Bernstein (1992) reported data from a clinic for children with school-refusing problems. This clinic serves children with anxiety disorders, depressive disorders, both anxiety and depressive disorders, and neither anxiety nor depressive disorder. The assessment process at this clinic and the chart review for diagnostic assignment focused on separation anxiety disorder and overanxious disorder, so the prevalence rate of other anxiety disorders (e.g., avoidant disorder) may be underestimated. In a sample of 96 children evaluated at this clinic, 27 had only anxiety disorders. Of these 27.4 (14.8%) had both SAD and OAD, and 1 (3.7%) had separation anxiety disorder and avoidant disorder.

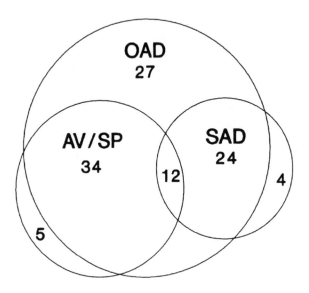

OAD=overanxious disorder
AV/SP=avoidant disorder/social phobia
SAD=separation anxiety disorder
n = 106

Figure 1.1. Comorbidity among the childhood anxiety disorders.

Last and colleagues at the Western Psychiatric Institute and Clinic in Pittsburgh have also reported data on comorbidity among the childhood anxiety disorders (Last et al., 1992; Last, Strauss, & Francis, 1987). Their Child and Adolescent Anxiety Clinic served children between the ages of 5 and 18 with anxiety disorders. Last, Strauss, and Francis (1987) reported data on 73 consecutively evaluated children. The most common diagnosis was SAD (*n* = 24), followed by OAD (*n* = 11). Only one child had primary avoidant disorder. Among children with primary SAD, 58.3% had no additional anxiety disorders. Among children with primary OAD, 45.4% had no additional anxiety disorder. About one third of the children in either diagnostic group were comorbid for the other disorder. Three children (12.5%) with SAD also had avoidant disorder, as did three children (27.3%) with

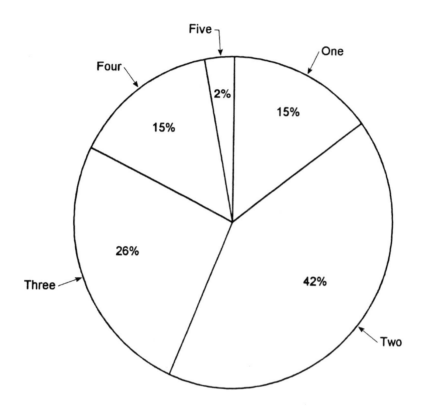

Figure 1.2. Prevalence of comorbidity in children with anxiety disorders:
Number of additional diagnoses.

OAD. These rates of comorbidity are slightly lower than those found at the
Temple clinic, but they are nevertheless still high.

The most recent report from the Pittsburgh clinic reported on 188 consecutive admissions covering a 3-year span. In this article the authors (Last
et al., 1992) reported lifetime prevalence of disorders. All children had an
intake interview in which information about current and past disorders was
obtained. Some children also participated in follow-up interviews at 12 and
24 months after intake. Lifetime prevalence was ascertained on the basis of
the information from the last available assessment. Diagnoses were based on
DSM-III-R criteria as determined from a modified version of the Schedule
for Affective Disorders and Schizophrenia for School-Age Children (K-SADS).

Again, of the childhood anxiety disorders, SAD was the most frequent primary diagnosis ($n = 51$, 27.1%; lifetime $n = 84$, 44.7%), followed by OAD ($n = 25$, 13.3%; lifetime $n = 51$, 27.1%) and avoidant disorder ($n = 5$, 2.7%; lifetime $n = 20$, 10.6%). The majority of children in all three diagnostic groups had an additional anxiety disorder at some point, with the prevalence ranging from 65.5% of children with SAD, 90.0% of children with avoidant disorder, and 96.1% of children with OAD. When each disorder was considered separately, of the children with avoidant disorder, 60% had a lifetime history of OAD and 35% had a history of SAD. Of the children with OAD, 23.5% had a history of avoidant disorder and 37.3% had a history of SAD. Finally, 8.3% of the children with SAD had a history of avoidant disorder and 22.6% had a history of OAD. Children with SAD had the lowest rates of comorbidity, a finding that may be due in part to the fact that they were younger than the other two groups, with a mean age at intake of 10.3 compared to 13.6 for children with OAD and 12.7 for children with avoidant disorder. These data are not directly comparable to those of the other studies cited here because they report on lifetime comorbidity rather than concurrent comorbidity. However, the fact that lifetime rates are higher than concurrent rates lends support to the idea that the anxiety disorders are alike in sharing hyperarousal but that the content of the anxiety differs and perhaps changes over the course of development.

RELATIONSHIP OF ANXIETY AND DEPRESSION

Theoretical Viewpoints

Both anxiety and depression have multiple levels of meaning. Some of the confusion surrounding their relationship results from lack of clarity regarding which level is being discussed. Anxiety and depression are symptoms, syndromes, or diagnostic entities. Both also have affective, cognitive, behavioral, and physiological components (see Clark, 1989; Kendall, Cantwell, & Kazdin, 1989; Maser & Cloninger, 1990). Different theoretical viewpoints have examined the relationship of anxiety and depression from different standpoints.

From an affective point of view, several theories have addressed the nature of the distinction between anxiety and depression. Emotion theorists posit that there are a small number of specific and discrete emotions that form the core of human affective expression (see Blumberg & Izard, 1986; Ekman, 1982; Plutchik, 1980). For example, Izard's differential emotions theory states that there are 10 basic emotions. Anxiety and depression are complex combinations of the basic emotions; they overlap in their composition, but they are differentiated by a predominant emotion. In anxiety, fear predominates, and in depression, sadness predominates (Blumberg & Izard, 1986; Izard, 1972).

An alternative affective theory of the relationship between anxiety and depression is the idea of negative affectivity. Watson and Clark (1984) have defined *negative affectivity* as a construct that encompasses a broad category of self-reported negative emotional features. Both anxious patients and depressed patients score high on measures of negative affectivity. Watson and Tellegen (1985) developed a two-dimensional model of affect with two orthogonal factors: positive affect and negative affect. High positive affectivity is characterized by adjectives such as *active, enthusiastic,* and *excited.* Negative affectivity is not the absence of positive affectivity but rather a state of unpleasant arousal characterized by adjectives such as *nervous, hostile, fearful,* and *distressed.* Both of these mood factors have state and trait features. According to this model, both anxiety and depression are characterized by high negative affectivity. However, the two disorders are differentiable in that only depression is characterized by low positive affectivity. This theory of affective structure is a hierarchical model that posits that each of these higher order mood constructs is composed of several correlated yet ultimately distinct emotional states (Watson & Clark, 1992). Watson and Clark (1992) presented results from four studies that support their hierarchical model. Clark and Watson (1991) reviewed the literature specific to the relationship of depressive and anxiety disorders and concluded that a tripartite model best captures the relationship of these disorders. They found that there is a large component of general affective distress shared by the two disorders but that there are factors specific to each. According to this model, high negative affectivity is the shared component, low positive affectivity is specific to depression, and physiological tension and hyperarousal are specific to anxiety. Much of the research on positive and negative affectivity has focused on adults, but because these are conceptualized as trait as well as state constructs, this model can easily be applied to the relationship of anxiety and depression in children.

Beck (Beck & Emery, 1985; Clark & Beck, 1989) has proposed a cognitive model of anxiety and depressive disorders. Central to his theory are schemata, or cognitive organizations of information. Schemata function to direct the processing of environmental stimuli. They serve to economize the processing of information by selectively elaborating and encoding schema-consistent information while ignoring schema-inconsistent information (Greenberg, Vazquez, & Alloy, 1988). This selective processing can introduce systematic errors in the information-processing system, thereby distorting the perception of information. According to Beck, it is this distortion of information that is the primary cognitive dysfunction in anxiety and depression (Clark & Beck, 1989). What differentiates anxiety and depression is the specific content of the maladaptive schemata. In anxiety, the distorted cognitions revolve around thoughts of threat, danger, or harm. In depression, thoughts of loss and failure predominate (Alloy, Kelly, Mineka, & Clements, 1990; Beck, Brown, Steer, Eidelson, & Riskind, 1987; Beck & Emery, 1985; Beck & Stewart, 1990; Clark & Beck, 1989).

An alternate cognitive-behavioral perspective on the relationship of anxiety and depression is that of helplessness-hopelessness (Alloy et al., 1990). This viewpoint is based on the hopelessness theory of depression, which in turn is based on the reformulated learned helplessness theory of depression (Abramson, Alloy, & Metalsky, 1988; Abramson, Metalsky, & Alloy, 1989; Abramson, Seligman, & Teasdale, 1978; Alloy et al., 1990). This theory is a causal model of a particular type of depression called *hopelessness depression.* Hopelessness is considered a proximal sufficient cause of depression. It is defined as negative expectations about the occurrence of highly desired outcomes coupled with feelings of helplessness about being able to change the likelihood of these outcomes' occurrence and feelings of certainty about the negative expectations and accompanying helplessness (Alloy et al., 1990). Thus, according to this conceptualization, hopelessness is a cause of depression and must precede the depression. Hopelessness depression is hypothesized to have characteristic symptoms including sad affect, low energy, apathy, retarded initiation of voluntary responses, psychomotor retardation, suicidal acts and ideation, sleep disturbance, and difficulty with concentration. Some of these symptoms overlap the *DSM-III-R* symptoms of a depressive episode (sad affect, psychomotor retardation, lack of energy, difficulty with concentration, suicidality). However, some of the symptoms listed in the *DSM-III-R* are not typical of hopelessness depression. These symptoms are anhedonia, appetite disturbances, and feelings of worthlessness (Abramson, Alloy, & Metalsky, 1988; Abramson, Metalsky, & Alloy, 1989; Alloy et al., 1990).

According to the hopelessness theory of depression, hopelessness is mediated by perceived negative life events and the attributions made for them. Attributing negative events to stable, internal, global causes and perceiving the events to be uncontrollable increase the likelihood of experiencing hopelessness. Individuals vary in their typical attributional and control patterns, with some people exhibiting a depressogenic attributional style (Abramson et al., 1978; Alloy, Clements, & Kolden, 1985; Alloy et al., 1990).

The helplessness-hopelessness theory may also account for some types of anxiety syndromes. Anxiety can be characterized by helplessness, but differs from depression because there is less certainty about the helplessness. An individual who has expectations of helplessness and the occurrence of negative events but who is uncertain about his or her helplessness will experience pure anxiety. Such an anxiety syndrome is characterized by anxious arousal that facilitates attention to control relevant cues and by activity geared toward gaining control. In contrast, an individual who believes he or she is helpless but is uncertain about the occurrence of aversive events will experience a mixed anxious and depressed syndrome. This syndrome is characterized by a decrease in arousal and activity but continued anxiety about possible future outcomes (Alloy et al., 1990).

These differing theoretical viewpoints of the relationship of anxiety and depression all try to account for shared elements and distinguishing features. Each of these theoretical stances acknowledges that anxiety and depression share certain factors but claims that the two constructs can be meaningfully distinguished (see also Kendall & Watson, 1989). Only the hopelessness-helplessness perspective posits a causal and temporal relationship between anxiety and depression.

ASSESSMENT

Measures

Much attention has focused on the assessment of anxiety and depression in adults through the use of self-report measures. A number of studies have reported high correlations between self-report measures of anxiety and depression in a variety of populations, with a range extending from .40 to .70 (e.g., Dobson, 1985; Gotlib & Cane, 1987; Zurawski & Smith, 1987). More recently, correlations between children's self-report scales of anxiety and depression have been reported. Because most of the children's self-report

measures have been adapted from the corresponding adult scales, the similarity between correlations of anxiety and depression measures in these two
different populations would suggest continuity from childhood to adulthood
in the relationship of anxiety and depression.

The three most widely used scales of children's self-report anxiety and
depression are Reynolds and Richmond's (1978) Revised Children's Manifest Anxiety Scale (RCMAS), Spielberger's (1973) State-Trait Anxiety Inventory for Children (STAIC), and Kovacs' (1980/1981) Children's
Depression Inventory (CDI). Data on reliability and validity of each of these
scales have been reported elsewhere (for review, see Finch, Lipovsky, &
Casat, 1989; Kendall, Cantwell, & Kazdin, 1989; Kendall & Ronan, 1990).
The RCMAS provides a total anxiety score as well as three factor scores
reflecting physiological anxiety, concentration anxiety, and worry and oversen-
sitivity. It also has a lie scale. The STAIC has two scales, one assessing trait
anxiety (STAIC-T) and the other measuring transitory state anxiety (STAIC-S).
The Children's Depression Inventory has two factors: one measuring self-
deprecation and self-criticism, and the other measuring dysphoric mood
(Saylor, Finch, Spirito, & Bennett, 1984).

Another method of assessing anxiety and depression in the young is through
behavioral rating scales. The most notable and widely used is the Child Behavior
Checklist (Achenbach & Edelbrock, 1983, 1986, 1987). The authors devised
three separate inventories designed to assess behavioral problems and emotional functioning. The three forms are the Youth Self-Report (CBCL-Y),
the Parent Report (CBCL-P), and the Teacher Report (TRF). Each scale
yields a behavior profile that is divided into Internalizing and Externalizing
scales. Each scale is further broken down into subscales that vary depending
on the age and sex of the child. The checklist yields T scores for each of the
factor scales that reflect norms for the various age and sex groupings. The
scoring profiles for the three forms of the CBCL have been modified recently
so that the subscales have been standardized across age and sex groupings.
This change makes direct comparisons across these groupings possible.

An alternative method of assessment is the use of interview schedules and
clinician rating scales. Interview schedules useful in identifying symptoms
and generating diagnoses include the Schedule for Affective Disorders and
Schizophrenia for school-age children (K-SADS; Puig-Antich & Chambers,
1978), the Interview Schedule for Children (Kovacs, 1978), the Anxiety
Disorders Interview Schedule for Children (ADIS-C; Silverman, 1987), the
Diagnostic Interview for Children and Adolescents (Herjanic & Reich, 1982),
and the Diagnostic Interview Schedule for Children (Costello, Edelbrock,

Kalas, Kessler, & Klaric, 1982). A new instrument, the Child and Adolescent Psychiatric Assessment (CAPA) provides a structural diagnostic interview to assess *DSM-IV* disorders present in children and adolescents. All of these interview schedules establish diagnosis according to prevailing classification systems such as the *DSM* or the Research Diagnostic Criteria (Spitzer, Endicott, & Robins, 1978). Reliability and validity of the schedules vary across instruments; a review of these data is beyond the scope of this chapter (see Chambers et al., 1985). Examples of clinician rating scales are the Brief Psychiatric Rating Scale for Children (Overall & Pfefferbaum, 1981) and the Children's Depression Rating Scale (Poznanski, Cook, & Carroll, 1979).

Discriminant Validity of Rating Scales

Discriminant Validity at the Symptom Level

Finch and his colleagues have made several efforts to examine the question of intercorrelations between rating scales of depression and anxiety. Eason, Finch, Brasted, and Saylor (1985) studied a group of hospitalized pediatric patients, using as their measures the CDI, the RCMAS, the STAIC, and the Children's Depression Rating Scale. In addition, they devised two measures, the Children's Anxiety Rating Scale and the Anxiety Rating Scale for Children, for the study. Both of these scales are clinician rating scales of symptoms of anxiety in children. The study sample consisted of 44 children between the ages of 7 and 14 with various medical problems. Eason et al. found that the measures they used were all highly correlated and thus displayed a lack of discriminant validity. From this, they concluded that the measures they employed assessed a unitary trait they termed *general level of emotional distress*—a concept paralleling negative affectivity. The authors offered two possible explanations for their results: Their sample of children may have exhibited only vague symptoms of emotional distress that could not be differentiated, or the assessment instruments may have lacked the specificity necessary for differentiation of symptoms. Also, the two mood states may in fact overlap.

Wolfe et al. (1987) conducted another recent study that reported relationships between measures of anxiety and depression in children. The measures they used included the Children's Depression Inventory, the RCMAS, the STAIC, and the Child Behavior Checklist-Teacher Report. Their sample of 102 children and adolescents were psychiatry inpatients who ranged in age from 6.5 to 16 years. The *DSM-III* diagnoses of the participants included conduct disorder (38%), adjustment disorder (15%), affective disorder (11%), anxiety disorder (7%), psychosis (5%), and "other" (12%). The authors found moderate and significant intercorrelations between the self-report measures of anxiety and depression and the Child Behavior Checklist-Teacher Report Depression and Social Withdrawal Scale and the Anxiety Scale. They also performed a multiple regression analysis that revealed that the combination of anxiety self-report measures and the Children's Depression Inventory significantly predicted the Child Behavior Checklist-Teacher Report Internalizing Scale score, whereas none of the self-report measures predicted the Externalizing Scale score. They concluded that these measures assessed the Watson and Clark (1984) broad-band construct of negative affectivity rather than the separate constructs of anxiety and depression.

Ollendick and Yule (1990) examined the relationship of depression with anxiety and fear in a sample of 327 British and 336 American children. They administered the CDI, the RCMAS, and the Fear Survey Schedule for Children-Revised. They found moderately high, significant correlations between the anxiety and depression measures. The correlation between depression and fear was also significant but more modest in size. Children identified with high levels of depression (CDI score > 19) also reported high levels of anxiety and high levels of social-evaluative fears, but not high levels of specific fears. The authors state that poor construct validity exists for the depression and anxiety measures, perhaps because of genuine covariation of anxiety and depressive symptoms, or perhaps because of item overlap on the measures.

Similarly, Norvell, Brophy, and Finch (1985) investigated the relationship between children's self-report measures of anxiety and depression. Their sample, like the Wolfe et al. sample, consisted of psychiatry inpatients and had a mean age of 11.5 years. The diagnoses of the 30 children and adolescents who participated included dysthymic disorder (30%), conduct disorder (10%), overanxious disorder (7%), attention deficit disorder (7%), and "other" (46%). The CDI was significantly correlated with the RCMAS and the STAIC. The authors analyzed the two factors of the CDI separately and found that only the dysphoric mood factor correlated significantly with the RCMAS overall anxiety score and its three factor scores. With a stepwise regression analysis, they found that two factors of the RCMAS, Physiological and Concentration, predicted total CDI score and the Dysphoric mood factor. The authors acknowledged that the results suggested a significant relationship between anxiety and depression. However, they also concluded that depression is a multidimensional trait and that high correlations between scales may reflect item overlap rather than construct overlap.

The meaningful correlations between children's and adolescents' self-report measures of anxiety and depression, like those reported in the adult literature, indicate that anxiety and depressive symptoms overlap to a large degree in children and that self-report measures, as well as behavioral and observation rating scales, lack adequate discriminant validity. One problem with the various rating scales of anxiety and depression is that anxiety and depression have common symptoms, which the scales tap. Similar items appear on the RCMAS, the STAIC, and the CDI. An approach to boost discriminant validity would be to eliminate shared symptoms on each scale and just include symptoms specific to anxiety on the anxiety scales and symptoms specific to depression on the depression measures. Conversely, given the high intercorrelations and overlapping symptoms, another approach would be to combine anxiety and depression into a single construct such as negative affectivity.

Discriminant Validity at the Disorder Level

The studies in the above section all investigated the relationship of anxiety and depressive symptoms, but they did not address the relationship of anxiety and depression specific to children with anxiety and/or depressive disorders. The question that remains is whether the assessment measures previously discussed can differentiate children with anxiety disorders from children with depressive disorders.

Bernstein and Garfinkel (1986) studied a group of 26 chronic school refusers who ranged in age from 9 to 17.5 years. They used the Diagnostic Interview for Children and Adolescents to determine *DSM-III* diagnoses. In addition, anxiety symptoms were assessed with the RCMAS and two scales designed specifically for their study. The first scale was the Anxiety Rating for Children (ARC), a clinician rating scale based on the Hamilton Anxiety Scale for adults. The second scale, the ARC/CMAS, included two subscales from the ARC and 12 questions from the RCMAS that did not overlap with depressive symptoms. They identified four diagnostic groups: affective disordered only, anxiety disordered only, affective and anxiety disordered, and neither affective nor anxiety disordered. The group with both affective and anxiety disorders scored highest on all rating scales of anxiety and depression but did not differ significantly from the depressive-disordered-only group. This group was significantly different from the anxiety-only group and the group with neither anxiety nor an affective disorder on anxiety and depression ratings. The groups with anxiety only and neither anxiety nor an affective disorder did not differ significantly on any measure. Finally, the school refusers were divided into high- (>8) and low- (<7) anxiety groups on the basis of the ARC/CMAS. The high-anxiety group was significantly higher than the low-anxiety group on the Children's Depression Rating Scale and on the Children's Depression Scale but not on the CDI.

Specific symptoms from the Children's Depression Rating Scale (depressed affect, anhedonia, low self-esteem, and suicidal ideation) and specific scales on the Children's Depression Scale (anhedonia and low self-esteem) differentiated the two groups. This finding is not surprising, however, given that each member of the high-anxiety group had a diagnosed depressive disorder but only 6 of the 14 low-anxiety children had a depressive diagnosis. The authors concluded that anxious children generally do not report depression and that high-anxiety children do endorse specific depressive symptoms, conclusions that seem to contradict their data because 13 of the 16 anxiety disorder patients reported enough depressive symptoms to meet diagnostic criteria for depression. Because of the restricted composition of their sample, the findings are not readily generalizable to the overall population of children with anxiety and depressive disorders.

More recently, Bernstein (1992) replicated the Bernstein and Garfinkel (1986) study with a larger group of 96 school refusers. The age range extended from 7 years, 8 months, to 17 years, 7 months, with a mean age of 13.5. The children and adolescents were again grouped by diagnosis into four groups: anxiety disorder only, depressive disorder only, both anxiety and depressive disorders, and neither anxiety nor depressive disorder (mainly disruptive behavior disorders such as conduct disorder or oppositional defiant disorder). Bernstein administered measures similar to those used in her earlier study. The instruments included the ARC, the RCMAS, the Revised Form of the Children's Depression Rating Scale, the CDI, and the Children's Depression Scale. She found significant differences between the four groups on all of these rating scales. The anxiety- and depressive-disordered group scored highest on all scales, and the group with neither anxiety nor depressive disorder scored the lowest. The anxiety-disordered-only and depressive-disordered-only groups were psychometrically similar and were intermediate between the other two groups. Bernstein found significant differences in the mean age in the four diagnostic groups, with the anxiety-disorders-only group having the lowest mean age, 11.3 years. The other three groups had mean ages as follows: The group with both anxiety and depressive disorders had a mean of 13.9 years, the group with neither anxiety nor depressive disorders had a mean age of 14.3, and the group with depressive disorders had a mean of only 14.6 years.

Hershberg, Carlson, Cantwell, and Strober (1982) administered a semis-tructured interview, a parental report, and the CDI to examine the relation-ship of anxiety and depression in children and adolescents between the ages of 7 to 17. From a sample of 102 randomly selected youths referred for psychiatric evaluation, they identified 28 individuals meeting *DSM-III* cri-teria for depression and 14 who met criteria for an anxiety disorder. They found that children with depressive disorders rarely had an accompanying anxiety diagnosis and that children with an anxiety disorder rarely had a depressive disorder. It was unclear whether any of the study participants had both an anxiety and a depressive disorder or if children or adolescents with both disorders were excluded from participation. The authors found that four symptoms assessed in the interview (dysphoric mood, low self-esteem, anhedonia, and suicidal ideation) were significantly more frequent in the depressed group and that this group also had significantly higher overall ratings of depression from the interview and significantly higher CDI scores. There were no significant differences between the groups on anxiety symp-toms except that the anxiety-disordered group more frequently reported situ-ation-specific anxiety. Limitations of their study that the authors noted included lack of standardized instruments, especially for assessing anxiety, and the fact that the interview used to gather information on symptoms did not examine anxiety symptoms as exhaustively as they did depressive symptoms.

Carey, Finch, and Imm (1989) studied 50 child and adolescent psychiatric inpatients. They divided their sample into three diagnostic groups on the basis of the *DSM-III-R*. The groups were depressive disordered ($n = 13$), depressive and anxiety disordered ($n = 16$), and any other nonpsychotic disordered ($n = 21$). The measures used to compare the diagnostic groups were the Child Assessment Schedule, the RCMAS, the Child Behavior Checklist-Youth Report (CBCL-Y), the Differential Emotions Scale, and the Suicide Ideation Questionnaire. The authors did not administer a depression measure, which would have been useful to determine if the groups differed in self-reported depression. The three groups differed significantly on the RCMAS overall score and its three subscales and on the CBCL-Y. The depres-sive- and anxiety-disordered group reported higher levels of dysfunction than did the depressive-disordered group or the other group; the latter two groups did not differ from each other. The groups also differed on the Suicide Ideation Questionnaire and on certain emotions from the Differential Emotions Scale (surprise, sadness, disgust, shame, and hostility). The pattern of differences was the same, with the depressive- and anxiety-disordered group scoring significantly higher than the remaining two groups, who did not differ from one another. The authors concluded that the depressive- and anxiety-disordered youth differed quantitatively from youth with depressive disorders or youth with other nonpsychotic disorders. The authors did not address the issue of why the depressive-disordered group was not distinguishable from the group with other nonpsychotic disorders. This finding may have been the result of the composition of the other group, which they did not specify. Alternatively, inpatient psychiatrically disordered children and adolescents may all share a nonspecific general distress factor.

Mitchell, McCauley, Burke, and Moss (1988) examined the phenomenology of depression in a sample of 125 children and adolescents who were psychiatrically referred with presenting symptoms of depressed mood, school refusal, or suicidal behavior. Diagnoses were determined through the use of the K-SADS. Most of the sample (95 of 125) were diagnosed with a current or recent episode of major depression. The authors found that 43 of the 95 depressed children had a comorbid anxiety disorder. The authors separated the youths by age, forming two groups: children and adolescents. The depressive- and anxiety-disordered children reported significantly more hypersomnia. The depressive- and anxiety-disordered adolescents more frequently reported hypersomnia, agitation, weight gain or loss, increased appetite or anorexia, and guilt. Furthermore, the depressive- and anxiety-disordered youth, especially the adolescents, rated their symptoms as more severe than the depressive-disordered-only group.

Strauss, Last, et al. (1988) examined the relationship between anxiety and depression in a sample of 106 patients from an outpatient anxiety clinic. They divided their sample into two groups on the basis of diagnostic status as determined by the Interview Schedule for Children. The two groups were children with both a depressive and an anxiety disorder and children with only anxiety disorders. They also had a control group of other unspecified psychopathology. Mean scores on three self-report measures of anxiety, the RCMAS, the STAIC, and the Fear Survey Schedule for Children, were compared across all three groups, and mean scores on the CDI were compared across the anxiety-disordered and control groups. The latter two groups were compared on symptom ratings of depression from the Interview Schedule for Children. The depressive- and anxiety-disordered group was excluded from these comparisons because by definition it was composed of children with clinically significant depression. Results indicated that the depressive- and anxiety-disordered group consistently reported themselves as more anxious and as having more fears than the anxiety-disordered or control groups. The only difference between the anxiety-disordered group and the control group was on their mean STAIC-State scale, with the anxiety-disordered group reporting more state anxiety. The authors offered two possible explanations for the fact that the self-report measures of anxiety did not differentiate the anxiety-disordered and control groups. The first explanation is that self-report instruments may provide a global measure of distress but not be useful in measuring specific symptoms. The other possibility is that anxiety disorders in children may not be meaningful clinical syndromes unless they are accompanied by depression.

The final report to be reviewed here was conducted by Stavrakaki, Vargo, Boodoosingh, and Roberts (1987). They had a sample of 84 children ranging in age from 6 to 16 who had sought psychiatric treatment as either outpatients or day patients. The children had either a *DSM-III* anxiety disorder or a depressive disorder. The children were assessed with the CDI, RCMAS, CBCL-P, and Brief Psychiatric Rating Scale for Children. The authors developed four factors from the CBCL-P for use in this study: Anxiety, Depression, Conduct, and Somaticism. These factors were designed so that items that measured symptoms that overlapped between anxiety and depression were excluded. The authors performed a discriminant function analysis and found that the profiles of scores on the Brief Psychiatric Rating Scale for Children and CBCL-P reports of depression were significantly different for the two groups, with the depressive-disordered group rated as more depressed than the anxiety-disordered group. None of the anxiety measures discriminated between the two groups. Stavrakaki et al. concluded that anxiety disorder and depressive disorder in children are distinct entities that can be separated on the basis of severity of depressive symptoms as rated by parents and clinicians. However, this conclusion does not address why the anxiety measures failed to discriminate between the two groups. It might be the result of discriminant validity on the anxiety measures or the result of anxiety symptoms' being equally prevalent in both groups.

Diagnostic Overlap Between Anxiety and Depression

Just as studying patterns of comorbidity among the childhood anxiety disorders can yield important information regarding the validity of the diagnostic system and clinical implications of syndrome overlap, examining the pattern of relationship between childhood anxiety and depression can help us begin to understand the nature of the relationship between these disorders. Research in this area has been hampered by hierarchical exclusionary rules, but a growing number of studies have reported rates of comorbidity. Table 1.1 summarizes the findings of recent studies that reported diagnostic data.

Two studies have looked at the prevalence rates of psychiatric disorders in nonreferred children. Anderson et al. (1987) investigated the prevalence of *DSM-III* disorders in the general population. They sampled a cross-section of 11-year-olds and identified 63 children with an anxiety or depressive disorder. A total of 10 children had both an anxiety and a depressive disorder. The prevalence rates and extent of comorbidity may change as a function of age, a possibility that cannot be explored with their cross-sectional data.

The second study on nonpsychiatrically referred children examined the rates of *DSM-III* disorders in a group of children aged 7 to 11 years who visited their primary care physician for varying medical reasons. Costello et al. (1988) interviewed a sample of 300 of the 789 children and their parents with the Diagnostic Interview Schedule for Children. The prevalence rate of anxiety and simple phobias was 21.7%, and the prevalence rate for depression/dysthymia was 1.7%. Comorbidity of anxiety and depression occurred in just 0.8% of the sample.

Two studies examined the concomitant presence of anxiety disorders in children and adolescents diagnosed with a depressive illness (Carey et al., 1989; Kovacs, Gatsonis, Paulauskas, & Richards, 1989). Carey et al. found that 55.2% of the 29 depressive-disordered inpatients in their sample had a comorbid anxiety disorder. In a sample of 104 outpatients, Kovacs et al. found the rate of comorbidity to be 31.5%. The difference in reported rates of comorbidity in these four studies may result from the different samples and may reflect the degree of disturbance in the sample. Children with comorbid anxiety and depression tend to be more symptomatic than children with depression only or anxiety only. Thus it is not surprising that the highest rates of comorbidity are reported in the inpatient sample and the lowest rates in the nonreferred sample.

Table 1.1   Comorbidity of Anxiety and Depressive Disorders in Children

Sample	Authors	Results
Nonreferred (Pediatric primary care patients)	Costello et al. (1988)	172 anxiety disordered 13 depressive disordered 3 anxiety and depressive disordered (0.8%)
Nonreferred (Representative sample of 11-year-olds from the general population)	Anderson, Williams, McGee, & Silva (1987)	49 anxiety disordered 4 depressive disordered 10 anxiety and depressive disordered (15.9%)
Nonreferred, high risk (Children of probands with affective disorders or of normal controls)	Weissman, Leckman, Merikangas, Gammon, & Prusoff (1985)	5 anxiety disordered 9 depressive disordered 8 anxiety and depressive disordered (36.4%)
Anxiety disorders clinic (Outpatients)	Strauss, Last, Hersen, & Kazdin (1988)	76 anxiety disordered 30 anxiety and depressive disordered (28.3%)
Anxiety disorders clinic (Outpatients)	Last, Perrin, Hersen, & Kazdin (1992)	155 anxious (OAD, SAD, or AD) 57 anxiety and depressive disordered (36.8%)
School refusal clinic (Outpatients)	Bernstein (1991)	27 anxiety disordered 27 depressive disordered 24 anxiety and depressive disordered (30.8%)
School refusal clinic (Outpatients)	Bernstein & Garfinkel (1986)	3 anxiety disordered 5 depressive disordered 13 anxiety and depressive disordered (61%)
Depressive disordered (Outpatients)	Kovacs, Gatsonis, Paulauskas, & Richards (1989)	85 depressive disordered 39 anxiety and depressive disordered (31.5%)
Depressive disordered (Inpatients)	Carey, Finch, & Imm (1989)	13 depressive disordered 16 anxiety and depressive disordered (55.2%) 13 anxiety and depressive disordered (61%)
Depressive disordered (Outpatients)	Kovacs, Gatsonis, Paulauskas, & Richards (1989)	85 depressive disordered 39 anxiety and depressive disordered (31.5%)
Depressive disordered (Inpatients)	Carey, Finch, & Imm (1989)	13 depressive disordered 16 anxiety and depressive disordered (55.2%)

Last and colleagues have published several reports, based on the children in their outpatient anxiety clinic, that have documented comorbidity with depression (Last et al., 1992; Strauss, Last, et al., 1988). Strauss, Last, et al. (1988) found that 28.3% of the 106 anxiety-disordered outpatients also had diagnosable depression, a rate comparable to the rate reported by Kovacs et al. (1989) in their outpatient depressive-disordered children. Last et al. (1992) reported data on 188 children and adolescents from the same outpatient anxiety clinic and found rates of comorbidity with depression to be 29.8% for children with SAD, 35.0% for children with avoidant disorder, and 49.0% for children with OAD. These comorbidity figures reflect lifetime comorbidity, not just concurrent comorbidity.

Bernstein and Garfinkel (1986) found that 61.9% of their sample of school refusers had concomitant depressive and anxiety disorders. The high rate may be due to the severity of illness in the sample of chronic school refusers, many of whom had had prior treatment without any success. In a replication of this study with a larger sample, Bernstein (1992) found that 30.8% of the 96 school refusers in her sample had coexisting depressive and anxiety disorders.

Finally, Weissman et al. (1985) studied the children of adult probands with depressive disorders and the children of normal controls. Of the 22 depressive- or anxiety-disordered children in their sample, 36.4% had comorbid anxiety and depressive disorders. In summary, the percentage of each sample that met criteria for both a depressive and an anxiety disorder ranges from 0.8% to 61.9%. It is not surprising that the results are so discrepant, given the variety of samples that were studied.

These studies all reported concurrent anxiety and depressive disorders with comorbidity rates that suggest that the relationship is not just coincidental overlap. However, Hershberg et al. (1982) did not find comorbidity in their sample. As discussed earlier, there has been a lack of consistent criteria for assigning diagnoses when symptoms from both disorders are present. One convention holds that only a primary diagnosis based on those symptoms that are most prominent should be given. The *DSM-III* and *DSM-III-R* give guidelines that allow for multiple diagnoses with the exception of certain hierarchical exclusionary rules. Researchers in the area of comorbidity between anxiety and depression generally suspend the hierarchical exclusionary rules because the rules obscure information. The problem with this inconsistency is that sometimes the approach to classification is not clear.

The data from these studies suggest that there are differences between children who are anxiety disordered only, depressive disordered only, or depressive and anxiety disordered, as assessed by self-report, behavioral observation, and clinician ratings. In general, anxiety measures are not useful in discriminating groups, but ratings from depression measures tend to be higher for depressive-disordered and depressive- and anxiety-disordered children. However, it is difficult to summarize results across studies because of the variability in subject samples. In some cases, the studies focused on the relationship of anxiety and depression in children with anxiety disorders, and in other cases their purpose was to examine the relationship of the two constructs in children with depressive disorders. To address this area more systematically, future studies need to focus equally on anxiety and depression and to include (a) an alternate psychopathology control group, (b) children who are dually diagnosed with anxiety and depression, (c) children with depression only, and (d) children with anxiety only. The issue of specificity to anxiety/depression and questions of symptom overlap will not be fully answered until there are sufficient data that are based on comparisons of these groups.

Family History

An alternate method to investigate the relationship of anxiety and depression in children centers on information about family history of psychological disorder. There is evidence based on family history and twin studies of familial factors in both anxiety and depressive disorders (e.g., Crowe, 1985; Slater & Shields, 1969). Recently, Torgersen (1990) presented data on the concordance of anxiety and depression in twin pairs. Torgersen examined lifetime comorbidity of depressive and anxiety disorders in his twin sample. He found a relationship between mixed anxiety and depression and depression only. There was no relationship between depression only or mixed anxiety and depression and anxiety only. These relationships were significant for monozygotic twins only, suggesting a genetic basis. In contrast, Kendler, Neale, Kessler, Heath, and Eaves (1992) found in their twin studies that the same genetic factors influenced major depression and generalized anxiety disorder. The discrepancy between these studies might be a result of different types of anxiety disorders. Torgersen found that if he analyzed his data by separating out panic disorder, the relationship between mixed anxiety and depression and depression only was strengthened.

If anxiety and depression are distinct disorders, then different patterns of family history should be expected. However, if the two disorders are part of a broader, unitary phenomenon, the family history patterns should not be clearly distinguishable. Recent research in this area is beginning to provide information about the similarities and differences in the pattern of family history in depressed versus anxious groups of children.

Puig-Antich et al. (unpublished, as reported by Puig-Antich & Rabinovich, 1986) conducted a family history study of prepubertal major depression in which they compared family history of psychiatric disorder in children with major depression, children with nondepressed emotional disorders, and normal controls. They found that there was significant familial aggregation of major depression as well as significantly higher rates of alcoholism in the relatives of children with major depression as compared to families of normal controls. The families of children who had nondepressed emotion disorders did not differ significantly in rate of major depression from the families of children with major depression or the families of normal controls. These families did have a significantly lower morbidity risk for alcoholism than the families of children with major depression but did not differ from the families of normal controls. The significance of the increased alcoholism in the families of depressed children is not clear, but one explanation is that alcoholism and depression are alternate expressions of the same underlying pathology. Another explanation is that the presence of alcoholism in the family affects children in such a way that they are more likely to become depressed. The prevalence of "other psychiatric disorders" (a category that encompasses mainly anxiety disorders) in the adult relatives of depressed and nondepressed children was equivalent and was significantly higher than the morbidity risk found in the families of normal controls. This study suggests that depressed children did not have an increased prevalence of depressive disorders in their families as compared with nondepressed emotionally disordered children but that both of these groups had higher rates of other psychiatric disorders. A limitation of this study was that the particular disorders of the children with nondepressed emotional disorders were not specified, nor was it clear exactly which disorders constituted the "other psychiatric disorder" category.

Stavrakaki et al. (1987) also looked at family pathology in their sample of anxiety- and depressive-disordered children. They classified family history of psychopathology into four categories: emotional, behavioral, multiple, and none/other. The problem with this classification system is that it lacks adequate specificity. Despite this limitation, the authors did find differences in family pathology. The anxious children had relatives characterized by multiple psychological problems, whereas the depressed children had family psychopathology most frequently classified as emotional.

Livingston, Nugent, Rader, and Smith (1985) studied the family histories of 12 anxious and 11 depressed children who were psychiatric inpatients. They found few differences in the family histories of the two groups. The one difference they found was that depressed children had a greater prevalence of alcoholism in their nonparent relatives. It is unclear what significance this finding has, particularly given the limitations of this study such as small sample size and the fact that the anxiety-disordered youngsters may not be representative of most anxiety-disordered children because such children generally do not require hospitalization.

Two studies have examined psychopathology in the offspring of psychologically disordered adults. Weissman et al. (1985) compared the prevalence of psychological disorders in children of probands with major depression, children of probands with major depression and an anxiety disorder, and matched normal controls. The rates of *DSM-III* disorders were highest for the children of probands with both depressive and anxiety disorders. Children of probands with depression only did not display any anxiety disorders. Two characteristics of the probands increased the risk of *DSM-III* disorders in their children: (a) the number of depressive episodes and (b) the number of first-degree relatives with major depression or anxiety disorder.

Turner, Beidel, and Costello (1987) assessed 16 children of anxiety-disordered patients as compared with children with dysthymic disorder, children of nondisordered parents, and normal school children. They found that the rate of *DSM-III* disorders was greater in the offspring of anxiety-disordered parents and dysthymic-disordered parents than in the offspring of normal parents and the sample of normal children.

Family history studies can contribute to our understanding of the distinctive and overlapping features of anxiety and depression in youth. An important question that is still unanswered is whether heredity or family environment confers a risk for a specific disorder or whether a general predisposition to negative affectivity is experienced. Therefore studies would benefit from greater direct focus on this issue to delineate more clearly differences in family psychopathology for depressed, anxious, and comorbid anxious and depressed children.

Descriptive and Developmental Variables

Another area from which useful information could emerge about differences and similarities in affective- and anxiety-disordered children and adolescents concerns descriptive and developmental factors. Although there are few studies of this type, they typically assess differences in symptoms through different rating scales or clinical interviews. However, one powerful impetus for studying the relationship of anxiety and depression is to gain knowledge that is applicable to devising improved treatment strategies. Questions such as duration and course of the disorder, response to treatment, presenting problems, and age at onset are all directly relevant to this aim but generally have not been addressed adequately.

The most consistent finding is that there seems to be a temporal relationship between the disorders. Children with depression or depression and an anxiety disorder are older than children with just an anxiety disorder (Hershberg et al., 1982; Stavrakaki et al., 1987; Strauss, Last, et al., 1988; Strauss, Lease, et al., 1988). Kovacs et al. (1989) presented longitudinal data that supported the idea that anxiety usually predated depression in children with both disorders. They also found that children with secondary depression and primary anxiety had longer depressive episodes than children with primary depression and secondary anxiety.

CONCLUSIONS

The anxiety disorders of childhood as conceptualized by the *DSM-III-R* have been questioned in terms of their validity and usefulness as distinct categories in the classification system. Data to date indicate that avoidant disorder is relatively indistinguishable from social phobia, and this category has been eliminated from the *DSM-IV.* Although empirical evidence supports the validity of SAD and to some degree OAD, the extent of comorbidity among the childhood anxiety disorders indicates that thinking of these disorders as discrete categories may be erroneous. The tripartite model of anxiety and depression is useful here in capturing the high trait negative affectivity and generalized hyperarousal characterized by anxious children and adults. What differentiates anxious patients is the focus of worry. In many cases, there are multiple areas of worry that result in the current picture of high diagnostic overlap. Future research needs to address whether the DSM-IV changes reduce comorbidity among anxiety disorders in children.

Past classification of childhood anxiety made the implicit assumption that the childhood disorders were equivalent to adult disorders. Thus agoraphobia was the adult equivalent of SAD, and GAD is the adult equivalent of OAD. The *DSM-IV* makes the relationship between the child and adult forms of the disorders more explicit by eliminating separate child categories for avoidant disorder, which is classified as generalized social phobia, and overanxious disorder, which is classified as generalized anxiety disorder. Currently, data that support this assumption are retrospective. What is needed are prospective, longitudinal studies to determine the relationship between childhood and adult anxiety disorders.

The current classification scheme for childhood anxiety can also be questioned on the basis of empirical studies of anxiety and depression showing that there is a significant and meaningful relationship between anxiety and depression in youth. However, the data do not indicate that the two disorders are indistinguishable at the syndromal level. Given that some researchers can identify children who are primarily anxious, others who are primarily depressed, and still others who meet criteria for both disorders, the mandate for future research should be on determining the differences between these three populations and the clinically relevant implications of the differences (see also Kendall & Watson, 1989). In this area, too, the *DSM-IV* may contain changes that reflect data collected to date. It contains a category called "mixed anxiety and depression" to capture those cases that do not meet full criteria for either disorder but present with an array of symptoms from both disorders.

Research in this area needs to be guided by theory. Several such viewpoints were reviewed, including Differential Emotions Theory, Beck's cognitive model, the helplessness-hopelessness model, and the tripartite model proposed by Clark and Watson (1991). These theoretical viewpoints can guide researchers in gathering data that will help to clarify the nature of the relationship and differentiating aspects of the disorders. Most of the research reviewed here can only indirectly support or disconfirm the different theories. For example, the helplessness-hopelessness model makes several predictions about comorbidity, including the temporal relation between the disorders. Data do indicate that as this model proposes, anxiety often predates depression.

The area of assessment would greatly benefit from an increased theoretical emphasis. Current measures of anxiety and depression lack adequate discriminant validity. Measures based on the separation of negative and positive affectivity have greater discriminant validity. For example, the measurement of positive affectivity adds to the discriminability of depressive and anxiety disorders. Similarly, measures could assess cognitive differences or attributional differences. This approach is being used in research with adults, but research with children has tended to lag behind.

A major concern yet to be addressed is treatment outcome. If depression and anxiety are part of a generalized negative affectivity syndrome, should treatment approaches be similar, or do they require differential intervention (Kendall et al., 1992)? Do children with depression and children with anxiety respond to the same treatments? Comparative studies of treatment strategies guided by the various theories and attention to differential outcome would clarify the relationship among the childhood anxiety disorders and between anxiety and depression.

REFERENCES

Abramson, L. Y., Alloy, L. B., & Metalsky, G. L. (1988). The cognitive diathesis-stress theories of depression: Toward an adequate evaluation of the theories' validities. In L. B. Alloy (Ed.), *Cognitive processes in depression* (pp. 3-30). New York: Guilford.

Abramson, L. Y., Metalsky, G. L., & Alloy, L. B. (1989). The hopelessness theory of depression: Does the research test the theory? In L. Y. Abramson (Ed.), *Social cognition and clinical psychology: A synthesis.* New York: Guilford.

Abramson, L. Y., Seligman, M. E. P., & Teasdale, J. D. (1978). Learned helplessness in humans: Critique and reformulation. *Journal of Abnormal Psychology, 87,* 49-74.

Achenbach, T. M., Connors, C. K., Quay, H. C., Verhulst, F. C., & Howell, C. T. (1989). Replication of empirically derived syndromes as a basis for taxonomy of child/adolescent psychopathology. *Journal of Abnormal Child Psychology, 17,* 299-323.

Achenbach, T. M., & Edelbrock, C. S. (1983). *Manual for the Child Behavior Checklist and Revised Child Behavior Profile.* Burlington, VT: University Associates in Psychiatry.

Achenbach, T. M., & Edelbrock, C. S. (1986). *Manual for the Teacher's Report Form and Teacher Revision of the Child Behavior Profile.* Burlington, VT: University Associates in Psychiatry.

Achenbach, T. M., & Edelbrock, C. S. (1987). *Manual for the Youth Self-Report Form and Self-Report Version of the Child Behavior Profile.* Burlington, VT: University Associates in Psychiatry.

Akiskal, H. S. (1985). Anxiety: Definition, relationship to depression, and proposal for an integrative model. In A. H. Tuma & J. D. Maser (Eds.), *Anxiety and the anxiety disorders* (pp. 787-797). Hillsdale, NJ: Lawrence Erlbaum.

Alloy, L. B., Clements, C., & Kolden, G. (1985). The cognitive diathesis-stress theories of depression: Therapeutic implications. In S. Reiss & R. R. Bootzin (Eds.), *Theoretical issues in behavior therapy* (pp. 379-410). Orlando, FL: Academic Press.

Alloy, L. B., Kelly, K. A., Mineka, S., & Clements, C. M. (1990). Comorbidity of anxiety and depressive disorders: A helplessness-hopelessness perspective. In J. D. Maser & C. R. Cloninger (Eds.), *Comorbidity of mood and anxiety disorders* (pp. 499-543). Washington, DC: American Psychiatric Press.

American Psychiatric Association. (1987). *Diagnostic and statistical manual of mental disorders* (3rd ed., rev.). Washington, DC: Author.

Anderson, J. C., Williams, S., McGee, R., & Silva, P. A. (1987). DSM-III disorders in preadolescent children. *Archives of General Psychiatry, 44,* 69-76.

Barlow, D. H. (1988). *Anxiety and its disorders: The nature and treatment of anxiety and panic.* New York: Guilford.

Beck, A. T., Brown, G., Steer, R. A., Eidelson, J. I., & Riskind, J. H. (1987). Differentiating anxiety and depression: A test of the cognitive content-specificity hypothesis. *Journal of Abnormal Psychology, 96,* 179-183.

Beck, A. T., & Emery, G. (1985). *Anxiety disorders and phobias: A cognitive perspective.* New York: Basic Books.

Beidel, D. C. (1991). Social phobia and overanxious disorder in school-age children. *Journal of the American Academy of Child and Adolescent Psychiatry, 30,* 545-552.

Bernstein, G. A. (1991). Comorbidity and severity of anxiety and depressive disorders in a clinic sample. *Journal of the American Academy of Child and Adolescent Psychiatry, 30,* 43-50.

Bernstein, G. A., & Garfinkel, B. D. (1986). School phobia: The overlap of affective and anxiety disorders. *Journal of the American Academy of Child Psychiatry, 25,* 235-241.

Blumberg, S. H., & Izard, C. E. (1986). Discriminating patterns of emotions in 10- and 11-year-old children's anxiety and depression. *Journal of Personality and Social Psychology, 51,* 852-857.

Bowlby, J. (1973). *Separation: Anxiety and anger.* New York: Basic Books.

Breier, A., Charney, D. S., & Heninger, G. R. (1985). The diagnostic validity of anxiety disorders and their relationship to depressive illness. *American Journal of Psychiatry, 142,* 787-797.

Brown, T. A., & Barlow, D. H. (1992). Comorbidity among anxiety disorders: Implications for treatment and DSM-IV. *Journal of Consulting and Clinical Psychology, 60,* 835-844.

Carey, M. P., Finch, A. J., & Imm, P. (1989, November). *Differentiating depressive and anxiety disorders from other child psychiatric disorders: The role of overt behavior, cognition, and emotions.* Paper presented at the Association for the Advancement of Behavior Therapy, Washington, DC.

Chambers, W. J., Puig-Antich, J., Hirsch, M., Paez, P., Ambrosini, P. J., Tabrizi, M. A., & Davies, M. (1985). The assessment of affective disorders in children and adolescents by semistructured interview: Test-retest reliability. *Archives of General Psychiatry, 42,* 696-702.

Clark, D. A., & Beck, A. T. (1989). Cognitive theory and therapy of anxiety and depression. In P. C. Kendall & D. Watson (Eds.), *Anxiety and depression: Distinctive and overlapping features* (pp. 379-411). San Diego: Academic Press.

Clark, D. A., Beck, A. T., & Stewart, B. (1990). Cognitive specificity and positive-negative affectivity: Complementary or contradictory views on anxiety and depression? *Journal of Abnormal Psychology, 99,* 148-155.

Clark, L. A. (1989). The anxiety and depressive disorders: Descriptive psychopathology and differential diagnosis. In P. C. Kendall & D. Watson (Eds.), *Anxiety and depression: Distinctive and overlapping features* (pp. 83-130). San Diego: Academic Press.

Clark, L. A., & Watson, D. (1991). Tripartite model of anxiety and depression: Psychometric evidence and taxonomic implications. *Journal of Abnormal Psychology, 100,* 316-336.

Coryell, W., Endicott, J., Andreasen, N. C., Keller, M. B., Clayton, P. J., Hirschfeld, R. M. A., Scheftner, W. A., & Winokur, G. (1988). Depression and panic attacks: The significance of overlap as reflected in follow-up and family study data. *American Journal of Psychiatry, 145,* 293-300.

Costello, A. J., Edelbrock, C., Kalas, R., Kessler, M. D., & Klaric, S. (1982). *The NIMH Diagnostic Interview Schedule for Children (DISC).* Pittsburgh: Author.

Costello, E. J., Costello, A. J., Edelbrock, C., Burns, B. J., Dulcan, M. K., Brent, D., & Janiszewski, S. (1988). Psychiatric disorders in pediatric primary care. *Archives of General Psychiatry, 45,* 1107-1116.

Crowe, R. R. (1985). The genetics of panic disorder and agoraphobia. *Psychiatric Developments, 2,* 171-186.

de Ruiter, C., Rijken, H., Garssen, B., van Schaik, A., & Kraaimaat, F. (1989). Comorbidity among the anxiety disorders. *Journal of Anxiety Disorders, 3,* 57-68.

Dobson, K. S. (1985). The relationship between anxiety and depression. *Clinical Psychology Review, 5,* 307-324.

Dweck, C., & Wortman, C. (1982). Learned helplessness, anxiety, and achievement. In H. Krone & L. Laux (Eds.), *Achievement, stress and anxiety* (pp. 93-125). New York: Hemisphere.

Eason, L. J., Finch, A. J., Brasted, W., & Saylor, C. F. (1985). The assessment of depression and anxiety in hospitalized pediatric patients. *Child Psychiatry and Human Development, 16,* 57-64.

Ekman, P. (Ed.). (1982). *Emotion in the human face* (2nd ed.). Cambridge, UK: Cambridge University Press.

Feinstein, A. R. (1970). The pre-theraputic classification of co-morbidity in chronic disease. *The Journal of Chronic Diseases, 23,* 455-468.

Finch, A. J., Lipovsky, J. A., & Casat, C. D. (1989). Anxiety and depression in children and adolescents: Negative affectivity or separate constructs? In P. C. Kendall & D. Watson (Eds.), *Anxiety and depression: Distinctive and overlapping features* (pp. 171-197). San Diego: Academic Press.

Gotlib, I. H., & Cane, D. B. (1987). Construct accessibility and clinical depression: A longitudinal investigation. *Journal of Abnormal Psychology, 96,* 199-204.

Greenberg, M. S., Vazquez, C. V., & Alloy, L. B. (1988). Depression versus anxiety: Difference in self and other schemata. In L. B. Alloy (Ed.), *Cognitive processes in depression.* New York: Guilford.

Herjanic, B., & Reich, W. (1982). Development of a structured psychiatric interview for children: Agreement between child and parent on individual symptoms. *Journal of Abnormal Psychology, 10,* 307-334.

Hershberg, S. G., Carlson, G. A., Cantwell, D. P., & Strober, M. (1982). Anxiety and depressive disorders in psychiatrically disturbed children. *Journal of Clinical Psychiatry, 43,* 358-361.

Izard, C. E. (1972). *Patterns of emotions: A new analysis of anxiety and depression.* San Diego: Academic Press.

Kendall, P. C., Cantwell, D. P., & Kazdin, A. E. (1989). Depression in children and adolescents: Assessment issues and recommendations. *Cognitive Therapy and Research, 13,* 109-146.

Kendall, P. C., & Clarkin, J. F. (1992). Introduction to special section: Comorbidity and treatment implications. *Journal of Consulting and Clinical Psychology, 60,* 833-835.

Kendall, P. C., Kortlander, E., Chansky, T. E., & Brady, E. U. (1992). Comorbidity of anxiety and depression in youth: Treatment implications. *Journal of Consulting and Clinical Psychology, 60,* 869-880.

Kendall, P. C., & Ronan, K. R. (1990). Assessment of children's anxieties, fears, and phobias: Cognitive-behavioral models and methods. In C. R. Reynolds & R. W. Kamphaus (Eds.), *Handbook of psychological and educational assessment of children.* New York: Guilford.

Kendall, P. C., & Watson, D. (Eds.). (1989). *Anxiety and depression: Distinctive and overlapping features.* New York: Academic Press.

Kendler, K. S., Neale, M. C., Kessler, R. C., Heath, A. C., & Eaves, L. J. (1992). Major depression and generalized anxiety disorder: Same genes, (partly) different environments? *Archives of General Psychiatry, 49,* 716-722.

Klerman, G. L. (1990). Approaches to the phenomena of comorbidity. In J. D. Maser & C. R. Cloninger (Eds.). *Comorbidity of mood and anxiety disorders.* Washington, DC: American Psychiatric Press.

Kovacs, M. (1978). *Interview Schedule for Children (ISC)* (10th rev. ed.). Pittsburgh, PA: University of Pittsburgh School of Medicine.

Kovacs, M. (1980/1981). Rating scales to assess depression in school-aged children. *Acta Paedopsychiatrica, 46,* 305-331.

Kovacs, M., Gatsonis, C., Paulauskas, S. L., & Richards, C. (1989). Depressive disorders in childhood. *Archives of General Psychiatry, 46,* 776-782.

Last, C. G., Hersen, M., Kazdin, A. E., Finkelstein, R., & Strauss, C. C. (1987). Comparisons of *DSM-III* separation anxiety and overanxious disorders: Demographic characteristics and patterns of comorbidity. *Journal of American Academy of Child Adolescent Psychiatry, 26,* 527-531.

Last, C. G., Hersen, M., Kazdin, A., Francis, G., & Grubb, H. (1987). Psychiatric illness in mothers of anxious children. *American Journal of Psychiatry, 144,* 1580-1583.

Last, C. G., Perrin, S., Hersen, M., & Kazdin, A. E. (1992). DSM-III-R anxiety disorders in children: Sociodemographic and clinical characteristics. *Journal of the American Academy of Child and Adolescent Psychiatry, 31,* 1070-1076.

Last, C. G., Phillips, K. A., & Statfield, E. (1987). Childhood anxiety disorders in mothers and their children. *Child Psychiatry and Human Development, 18,* 103-112.

Last, C. G. Strauss, C. C. (1992). Avoident disorder and social phobia in children and adolescence. *Journal of the American Academy of Child and Adolescent Psychiatry, 31,* 1086-1089.

Last, C. G., Strauss, C. C., & Francis, G. (1987). Comorbidity among childhood anxiety disorders. *Journal of Nervous and Mental Disorders, 175,* 726-730.

Last, C. G., Strauss, C. C. (1992). Avoidant disorder and social phobia in children and adolescence. *Journal of the American Academy of Child and Adolescent Psychiatry, 31,* 1086-1089.

Livingston, R., Nugent, H., Rader, L., & Smith, G. R. (1985). Family histories of depressed and severely anxious children. *American Journal of Psychiatry, 142,* 1497-1499.

Maser, J. D., & Cloninger, C. R. (Eds.). (1990). Comorbidity of mood and anxiety disorders. Washington, DC: American Psychiatric Press.

Mitchell, J., McCauley, E., Burke, P. M., & Moss, S. J. (1988). Phenomenology of depression in children and adolescents. *American Academy of Child and Adolescent Psychiatry, 27,* 12-20.

Moras, K., & Barlow, D. H. (1992). Dimensional approaches to diagnosis and the problem of anxiety and depression (pp. 27-33). In W. Fiegenbaum, A. Ehlers, J. Margraf, & I. Florin (Eds.), *Perspectives and promises of clinical psychology.*

Norvell, N., Brophy, C., & Finch, A. J. (1985). The relationship of anxiety to childhood depression. *Journal of Personality Assessment, 49,* 150-153.

Ollendick, T. H., & Yule, W. (1990). Depression in British and American children and its relation to anxiety and fear. *Journal of Consulting and Clinical Psychology, 58,* 126-129.

Overall, J. E., & Pfefferbaum, B. (1981). *The Brief Psychiatric Rating Scale for Children.* Houston: University of Texas Medical School.

Plutchik, R. (1980). *Emotion: A psychoevolutionary synthesis.* New York: Harper & Row.

Poznanski, E., Cook,. S., & Carroll, B. (1979). A depression rating scale for children. *Pediatrics, 64,* 442-450.

Puig-Antich, J., & Chambers, W. (1978). *The Schedule for Affective Disorders and Schizophrenia for School-Age Children (K-SADS).* Pittsburgh, PA: Western Psychiatric Institute and Clinic.

Puig-Antich, J., & Rabinovich, H. (1986). Relationship between affective and anxiety disorders in childhood. In R. Gittelman (Ed.), *Anxiety disorders of childhood* (pp. 136-156). New York: Guilford.

Reynolds, C. R., & Richmond, B. O. (1978). What I think and feel: A revised measure of children's manifest anxiety. *Journal of Abnormal Child Psychology, 6,* 271-280.

Sanderson, W. C., DiNardo, P. A., Rapee, R. M., & Barlow, D. H. (1990). Syndrome comorbidity in patients diagnosed with a DSM-III-R anxiety disorder. *Journal of Abnormal Psychology, 99,* 308-312.

Saylor, C. F., Finch, A. J., Spirito, A., & Bennett, B. (1984). The Children's Depression Inventory: A systematic evaluation of psychometric properties. *Journal of Consulting and Clinical Psychology, 52,* 955-967.

Silverman, W. K. (1987). *Anxiety Disorders Interview Schedule for Children (ADIS-C).* Albany, NY: Center for Stress and Anxiety Disorders.

Slater, E., & Shields, J. (1969). Genetic aspects of anxiety. In M. H. Lader (Ed.), *Studies of anxiety.* Ashford, UK: Headley Brothers.

Spielberger, C. D. (1973). *Preliminary manual for the State-Trait Anxiety Inventory for Children ("How I Feel Questionnaire").* Palo Alto, CA: Consulting Psychologists Press.

Spitzer, R. L., Endicott, J., & Robins, E. (1978). Research diagnostic criteria: Rationale and reliability. *Archives of General Psychiatry, 35,* 773-782.

Stavrakaki, C., Vargo, B., Boodoosingh, L., & Roberts, N. (1987). The relationship between anxiety and depression in children: Rating scales and clinical variables. *Canadian Journal of Psychiatry, 32,* 433-439.

Stein, P. A., & Hoover, J. H. (1989). Manifest anxiety in children with learning disabilities. *Journal of Learning Disabilities, 22,* 66-71.

Strauss, C. C., Last, C. G., Hersen, M., & Kazdin, A. E. (1988). Association between anxiety and depression in children and adolescents with anxiety disorders. *Journal of Abnormal Child Psychology, 16,* 57-68.

Strauss, C. C., Lease, C. A., Last, C. G., & Francis, G. (1988). Overanxious disorder: An examination of developmental differences. *Journal of Abnormal Child Psychology, 16,* 433-443.

Torgersen, S. (1990). Comorbidity of major depression and anxiety disorders in twin pairs. *American Journal of Psychiatry, 147,* 1199-1202.

Turner, S. M., Beidel, D. C., & Costello, A. (1987). Psychopathology in the offspring of anxiety disorder patients. *Journal of Consulting and Clinical Psychology, 55,* 229-235.

Watson, D., & Clark, L. A. (1984). Negative affectivity: The disposition to experience aversive emotional states. *Psychological Bulletin, 96,* 455-490.

Watson, D., & Clark, L. A. (1992). Affects separable and inseparable: On the hierarchical arrangement of the negative affects. *Journal of Personality and Social Psychology, 62*(3), 489-505.

Watson, D., Clark, L. A., & Carey, G. (1988). Positive and negative affectivity and their relation to anxiety and depressive disorders. *Journal of Abnormal Psychology, 97,* 346-353.

Watson, D., & Tellegen, A. (1985). Toward a consensual structure of mood. *Psychological Bulletin, 98,* 219-235.

Weissman, M. M., Leckman, J. F., Merikangas, K. R., Gammon, G. D., & Prusoff, B. A. (1985). Depression and anxiety disorders in parents and children. *Archives of General Psychiatry, 41,* 845-852.

Wolfe, V. V., Finch, A. J., Jr., Saylor, C. F., Blount, R. L., Pallmeyer, T. P., & Carek, D. J. (1987). Negative affectivity in children: A multitrait-multimethod investigation. *Journal of Consulting and Clinical Psychology, 55,* 245-250.

Zurawski, R. M., & Smith, T. W. (1987). Assessing irrational beliefs and emotional distress: Evidence and implications of limited discriminant validity. *Journal of Counseling Psychology, 34,* 224-227.

2

Cognition in Depression and Anxiety

SAME, DIFFERENT, OR A LITTLE OF BOTH?

RICK E. INGRAM

VANESSA L. MALCARNE

Depression and anxiety are among the most common and most troubling emotional conditions. Cognitive models that distinguish between depression and anxiety assume that these affective states are brought about by cognitive factors that are relatively unique to either depression or anxiety. As is evident from the title of this chapter, our focus here will be on the cognitive similarities and distinctions between these affective states. Specifically, we will examine current data on cognitive processes in depression and anxiety, present a model for conceptualizing unique and overlapping cognitive factors in depression and anxiety, and finally address cognition in combined depressive and anxious states.

Before we examine these issues, two caveats are important to note. First, although the target of this chapter is cognition, this should not be taken to imply that we view cognitive variables as the only determinants of depression and anxiety. A number of conceptual approaches that range across considerably diverse levels of analysis recognize a variety of factors that shape behavior in important ways. Despite the significant contributions of these approaches to understanding numerous aspects of both functional and dysfunctional behavior, it is clear that no single perspective can account for all aspects of functioning, and cognitive perspectives are no exception. Ideally, our understanding of functioning should include knowledge not only of cognitive contributions but also of biological, neurological, genetic, interpersonal, and sociological determinants and, most important, of how these various factors interact. Although we have not yet attained the conceptual development or empirical sophistication necessary to achieve such a goal, it is clear that an understanding of cognitive functioning will be an important component of such an eventual integration.

A second caveat refers to the nature of the depression and anxiety constructs themselves, specifically whether the appropriate focus of this chapter is clinical depression and anxiety or subclinical depression or anxiety, or perhaps even variations in normal depressive and anxious mood states. These are clearly important issues that deserve attention, but there is insufficient time and space to examine them here. Thus the constructs we will address are depressive and anxious states that are sufficiently maladaptive to interfere with people's functioning, whether or not these states might meet some criterion or another of being called a disorder. Although this definition may narrow the topic somewhat, it still covers a wide range of affective conditions from which people suffer.

COGNITION IN DEPRESSION AND ANXIETY

The number and diversity of cognitive variables that have been studied in depression and anxiety are truly remarkable. A sampling of cognitive variables that have been studied in depression includes cognitive bias (Krantz & Hammen, 1979), cognitive distortion (Hammen, 1978; Hammen & Krantz, 1976), underestimates of reinforcements (Hammen & Glas, 1975; Nelson & Craighead, 1977; Roth & Rehm, 1980), negative automatic thoughts (Dobson & Breiter, 1983; Harrell & Ryon, 1983; Hollon & Kendall, 1980), negative response bias (Rabin, 1985; Zuroff, Colussy, & Wielgus, 1983), task-distracting cognitions (Vredenburg & Krames, 1983), task recall deficiencies (Johnson, Petzel, Hartney, & Morgan, 1983), overestimates of negative event frequency (Kuiper & MacDonald, 1983), negative content information processing (Derry & Kuiper, 1981; Kuiper & Derry, 1982), stability of negative schematic processing (Dobson & Shaw, 1987; Ingram, Smith, & Brehm, 1983), self-schema consistency (Kuiper, Olinger, & MacDonald, 1988; Ross & Mueller, 1983), overestimates of depressive parameters (Kuiper et al., 1988), dysfunctional thoughts (Lam, Brewin, Woods, & Bebbington, 1987), negative inaccuracies in interpersonal feedback recall (Gotlib, 1983), negative construct accessibility (Gotlib & Cane, 1987; Gotlib & McCann, 1984), and irrational beliefs (Cook & Peterson, 1986).

For anxiety disorders, the list includes distorted cognition (Gormally, Sipps, Raphael, Edwin, & Varvil-Weld, 1981), negative attributional patterns (Alden, 1987), negative information processing (Mueller & Thompson, 1984), negative self-statements (Kendall & Hollon, 1989), increased other-referent information processing (Smith, Ingram, & Brehm, 1983), enhanced encoding of anxiety information (McNally & Foa, 1987), irrational beliefs (Deffenbacher, 1986; Mizes, Landolf-Fritsche, & Grossman-McKee, 1987), dysfunctional interpretations of ambiguous information (McNally & Foa, 1987), overestimates of risk judgments (Butler & Mathews, 1983, 1987), and increased environmental vigilance (MacLeod, Mathews, & Tata, 1986).

Although some of these variables may evidence considerable conceptual overlap and may therefore differ more in terminology than in theoretical formulation, by any count a substantial array of various cognitive dysfunctions have been employed to describe the cognitive pathology and consequent affective and behavioral features of these presumably different clinical syndromes.

Many of these studies emanate from conceptual models emphasizing cognitive structures that are theorized to organize the processing of information in a dysfunctional fashion. For example, Teasdale (1983, 1988) and Ingram (1984) have independently proposed network models of depression that have been derived from associative network concepts (e.g., Bower, 1981; Collins & Loftus, 1975; Norman, 1981, 1986). In the case of depression, each has suggested that information processing in depressed people is structured by activated networks of negative self-referent propositions that are organized around negative emotion structures. Through spreading activation processes, these structures facilitate the selective processing and encoding of negative self-referent information.

Of course, the most widely known structural approach to cognition in depression is Beck's (1967, 1987) negative self-schema theory. Beck's model is structurally quite similar to network formulations and suggests that the negative self-schema that is active in depression reflects self-representations revolving around themes of loss and personal inadequacy. This schema is thought, among other things, to serve as a filter that precipitates negatively biased, and hence dysfunctional, information processing.

At least some cognitive models of anxiety share very similar assumptions. For instance, Beck (1987; Beck & Emery, 1985) suggests that depressed individuals deploy cognitive structures characterized by pessimistic and self-degrading content that perpetuates depressive affect, whereas the cognitive schemata of anxious individuals are characterized by propositions of fear and apprehension. Consequently, whereas depressed people should evidence a sensitivity to self-devaluative information and thus process this type of information more effortlessly and efficiently, individuals with anxiety schemata should evidence a vigilance for information that is threatening to their safety. This information can come from external sources, as in the case of social phobia when another person's yawn may be readily perceived and interpreted as social disapproval. Alternatively, information can also come from internal sources, as in the example of a person who misperceives bodily sensations as the sign of a heart attack, which then precipitates a panic episode.

These models of depression and anxiety clearly evidence theoretical discriminant validity. That is, they highlight different cognitive variables that are presumed to be unique and specific to each state. Thus, as these models are evaluated in particular, and as the veracity of the cognitive approach is more generally evaluated, we would expect to find evidence of specific cognitive factors in depression and anxiety. To the extent that depression and anxiety represent sufficiently distinct pathological syndromes, some demonstrable cognitive differences should exist. Indeed, proof that specific cognitive factors are differentially linked to particular psychopathological states is consistent with the assumption that these factors are causally related to these conditions, although questions of causality cannot be answered on the basis of specificity alone (Garber & Hollon, 1991).

Alternatively, a lack of cognitive specificity raises potentially troublesome issues. Preservation of the causal integrity of cognitive models of depression and anxiety requires at least some demonstrable cognitive differences between the two states. That is, given that there are recognized differences in depression and anxiety, an inability to find any cognitive specificity calls into some question the ultimate contribution of cognitive conceptualizations of maladaptive behavior and affect. Hence if there are genuine differences in psychopathological states but not in the cognitive dysfunctions associated with these states, then it is reasonable to question the causal meaningfulness of current cognitive conceptualizations of maladaptive states. It should be noted, however, that just as specificity does not guarantee that cognitive variables are meaningful, neither does a lack of specificity completely rule out important cognitive contributions. As Garber and Hollon (1991) have recently noted, a lack of specificity for a given cognitive variable only rules out that variable as a sufficient cause of the disorder.

THE METACONSTRUCT MODEL:
A GUIDING CONCEPTUAL FRAMEWORK
FOR COGNITIVE SPECIFICITY

Extant empirical data on cognitive specificity in depression and anxiety suggest that there are indeed some cognitive variables that appear to be unique to depression and anxiety, respectively, but also that some are common to both states. Before examining these data, however, it is important to consider how to make theoretical sense out of data indicating the presence of cognitive features that are unique to these affective states while also showing that some cognitive features are jointly associated with both depression *and* anxiety. Specifically, it is useful to consider conceptual frameworks that broadly organize the different varieties of cognitive factors. Ingram (1983, 1990b), Ingram and Kendall (1986, 1987), Ingram and Wisnicki (1991), and Kendall and Ingram (1987) have proposed a conceptual framework for classifying the diverse cognitive variables that have been applied to various disorders. This framework, referred to as a *metaconstruct model of psychopathology* (Ingram, 1990b), is based on previous work on the conceptual and empirical distinctions between cognitive structures and processes that have been proposed by both cognitive-experimental (see Bower, 1981) and cognitive-clinical researchers (Goldfried & Robins, 1983; Hollon & Kriss, 1984; Kihlstrom & Nasby, 1981). The metaconstruct model is viewed as a generalized model of psychopathology aimed at describing and classifying various levels of cognitive analysis. The model incorporates two theoretical approaches to the description of different psychological functioning: a components approach to psychopathological variance and a cognitive taxonomy.

Taxonomy refers to the science of classification that underlies virtually all systematic descriptions of naturally occurring phenomena. As such a phenomenon, cognition is a construct that can undoubtedly be broken down and classified into constituent elements. Employing such a taxonomical approach, we refer to the first part of this framework as a *cognitive* taxonomy that attempts to provide guidelines for the classification of various categories of cognitive constructs that are presumably linked to maladaptive functioning. This taxonomy suggests that there are important distinctions between different cognitive variables and their corresponding measures: For example, selective attention processes and attributions, although both clearly cognitive and related at some level, are relevant to different types or categories of cognition. Hence these variables should be able to be classified according to specified cognitive categories; selective attention and causal attributions would fall into fundamentally different cognitive categories.

What is referred to as *cognition,* of course, is an integrated series of mechanisms, and it is not possible to isolate pure cognitive variables in either theoretical conceptualizations or empirical methodologies. Thus any attempt at cognitive classification represents a matter of emphasis rather than of mutual exclusion. The cognitive taxonomy idea is intended to provide broad categories as an initial step in differentiating various aspects of the cognitive system.

Cognitive Taxonomy Elements

We suggest four categories into which cognitive constructs can fall: *structural, propositional* (stored content), *operational* (processes), and *product* variables (Ingram & Kendall, 1986, 1987; Kendall & Ingram, 1987). Although these categories are proposed to be distinct in a conceptual sense, constructs within each category are presumed to operate jointly to produce what is typically referred to as *cognition.*

Cognitive Structural Constructs. Structural concepts refer broadly to the "architecture" of the cognitive system in that these variables describe mechanisms encompassing how information is stored and organized. Concepts such as short- and long-term memory are noteworthy examples of variables that focus upon the structural aspects of information processing.

Cognitive Propositional Constructs. Structural mechanisms are by definition "contentless"; *propositions* refer to the content of information that is stored and organized within a structure. Episodic knowledge and semantic knowledge represent illustrations of propositional variables. Because this category describes the stored content of the cognitive system, it could easily be labeled *cognitive content*. But because *content* is used in different ways to describe different phenomena (e.g., the content of self-statements, the content of beliefs), the term *propositions* was chosen to decrease ambiguity between classes of cognitive variables.

Cognitive Operational Constructs. Operations consist of the processes by which the system works. Some examples of cognitive operations variables include information encoding, retrieval, and attentional processes. Cognitive operations could also be referred to as cognitive processes. As with *content,* however, because *processes* has been used to describe cognitive variables spanning all four categories, the term *operations* was chosen instead.

Cognitive Product Constructs. Products are defined as the end result of the operation of the cognitive system to process information; these are the cognitions or thoughts that the individual experiences as a result of the interaction of incoming information with cognitive structures, propositions, and operations. Examples include constructs such as attributions. Because an attribution is an individual's causal explanation of a prior behavioral event, it results from (is a product of) cognitive processing of related content.

Components Model of Psychopathology Elements

The second part of the metaconstruct framework is a *components model of psychopathology* that seeks to examine the cognitive features that are unique to a particular disorder as well as those that appear to be generalized across disorders (Ingram & Kendall, 1987; Kendall & Ingram, 1987). It is probably unrealistic to assume that all or most cognitive variables are unique to a particular psychological disorder. A useful metaphor for understanding how these variables relate to different disorders is incorporated into a model that views the variance in psychopathology much as variance is conceptualized in experimental research. Specifically, we propose that the variance in psychopathology can be conceptually "partitioned" in much the same way that experimental variance is partitioned by an ANOVA.[1] Hence the ultimate symptomatic expression of a disorder is a function of several converging and identifiable sources of variance. For example, a two-way ANOVA would partition an experimental result into components represented as Effect = A + B + AB + E, where A equals the unique variance due to the first factor, B equals the unique variance due to the second factor, AB equals the common or shared variance resulting from the interaction of the factors, and E represents the error variance. In a similar fashion, the expression of a particular psychopathology can be conceptualized as the result of the confluence of "critical psychopathological features," "common psychopathological features," and unpredictable error variance.

Critical Features. These features represent variance that is uniquely characteristic of a particular disorder and thus describe variables specific to a given psychopathology. Hence critical features are defined as those that not only differentiate disorder from nondisorder but also differentiate one disorder from another.

Common Features. In contrast to critical psychopathological features, common features are those that are generally characteristic of all or most disorders and are therefore conceptualized as common or shared psychopathological variance. But although these features do not differentiate particular disorders, they are defined as differentiating disorder from nondisorder. That is, although common features are not unique to a given disorder, they are "unique" to psychopathology in general and thus broadly separate adaptive from maladaptive functioning.

Error Variance. Finally, *error variance* represents the unpredictable variance in psychopathology that is due to nonsystematic factors. Although the majority of variance in the expression of psychopathology can most likely be accounted for by critical and common features, the precise symptoms and characteristics of the disorder will also be influenced to some degree by the factors unique to the particular person involved. Any psychopathological state will thus be a function of variance unique to that state, variance characteristic of generalized psychopathology, and error variance. However, because error variance is by definition unpredictable, it will not be discussed further.

What this framework suggests, among other things, is that even variables that are nonspecific can have some causal status in various disorders. It is well known, for example, that there is a significant degree of overlap in depressive and anxious states. A variance partitioning approach evokes the

| Cognitive Taxonomy | Psychopathological Variance | |
Categories	Critical Features	Common Features
Structural	—	—
Propositional	—	—
Operational	—	—
Products	—	—

Figure 2.1. Structure of the Metaconstruct Model

possibility that nonspecific variables may account for some of the considerable overlap in symptoms of depression and anxiety; overlapping variables may account for overlapping symptoms.

The metaconstruct model proposes a structure for organizing both the taxonomy and the components model into broad conceptual categories that encompass both similar and different psychopathological features. The combination of these approaches is illustrated in Figure 2.1. The task for empirical research is to generate data that will fill in the slots within this framework.

Although only a limited number of studies have specifically assessed cognitive specificity in depression and anxiety, data from these studies have indicated some patterns of uniqueness and overlap. For instance, reviews of much of these data by Clark and Beck (1989), Malcarne and Ingram (1994), and Kendall and Ingram (1987, 1989) have suggested that depression is uniquely characterized by cognitive structures representing themes of negativity toward the self and personal loss, cognitive processing that encompasses negative appraisals of information that are pervasive, absolute, and past oriented, and cognitions involving thoughts of loss and failure. Alternatively, anxiety appears to be characterized by cognitive structures exemplifying themes of physical or psychological threat to the self, negative appraisals that are specific, tentative, and future oriented, and cognitions involving threat and danger.

The data also show evidence of cognitive overlap. For example, research has suggested that both depression and anxiety evidence an increased accessibility of maladaptive cognitive processing structures and a dysfunctionally high level of self-focused attention. Figure 2.2 illustrates how these presumably unique and overlapping cognitive features are conceptualized within the metaconstruct framework.

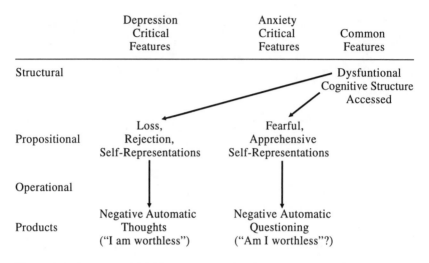

	Depression Critical Features	Anxiety Critical Features	Common Features
Structural			Dysfuntional Cognitive Structure Accessed
Propositional	Loss, Rejection, Self-Representations	Fearful, Apprehensive Self-Representations	
Operational			
Products	Negative Automatic Thoughts ("I am worthless")	Negative Automatic Questioning ("Am I worthless"?)	

Figure 2.2. Structure of the Metaconstruct Model

Although these data are generally consistent with schema or network models of depression and anxiety, some investigators have argued that other data are at least somewhat inconsistent with these models, and further suggest a different pattern of cognitive specificity. On the basis of several studies, for example, Williams and Oaksford (1992) have suggested that greater cognitive resources in anxiety are devoted to the possible detection of threatening information in the environment and an avoidance of further elaborating this information. This avoidance in turn leads to an impoverished encoding of anxiety-relevant information. They suggest that in depression cognitive resources are devoted less to the detection of depression-relevant external information and more toward the enhanced elaboration and encoding of negative material. A key cognitive difference between depressed and anxious individuals is thus how they deploy their cognitive resources.

Somewhat contrary to this depiction of cognitive differences, however, data have been reported indicating that both depressed and anxious people are apt to show a sensitivity to external information that reinforces their specific perceived inadequacies, and that they are also particularly likely to encode this information effectively (e.g., Greenberg & Beck, 1989; Ingram, Kendall, Smith, Donnell, & Ronan, 1987). Williams and Oaksford's (1992) distinctions may be valuable but may point more to a *relative* emphasis than to an absolute difference in how depressed and anxious individuals allocate their cognitive resources.

ARE DEPRESSION AND
ANXIETY DISTINCT DISORDERS?
NEGATIVE AFFECTIVITY

The preceding placement of cognitive features within the metaconstruct framework is, of course, tentative and subject to revision as additional data emerge. The discussion of this theoretical organization, however, presupposes that depression and anxiety are separate affective disorders. Up until now the question of whether depression and anxiety really are different states or are perhaps instead different aspects of the same affective condition has not been addressed.

To be sure, there are data that suggest these states are, or at least can be, meaningfully differentiated. Indeed, *DSM-IV* has recognized depression and anxiety as discrete nosological entities. By the same token, there are also data that point to significant overlap between what we call depression and anxiety. Indeed, much of the question of unique versus general affective states has its origin in data demonstrating moderate to high correlations between measures of depression and anxiety in both children and adults (see Finch, Lipovsky, & Casat, 1989; Gotlib, 1984; Kendall, this volume; King, Ollendick, & Gullone, 1991; Ollendick & Hersen, 1989; Smith & Rhodewalt, 1991). Figures vary in different studies, but few studies show correlations between depression and anxiety of less than .5. Although it can be noted that even a correlation of .7 will leave 50% of the variance unaccounted for, by any estimate there is a significant degree of overlap in depressive and anxious states.

A number of investigators (e.g., Dobson, 1985) have provided excellent reviews of the literature on depression and anxiety overlap. In a recent review, Watson and Kendall (1989) presented self-report, symptom and diagnostic, and biological and genetic evidence that consistently shows positive correlations between depression and anxiety. On the basis of findings such as these, several researchers have argued that we cannot rule out that depression and anxiety may represent different aspects of the same construct (e.g., Clark & Watson, 1991; Dobson, 1985; Malcarne & Ingram, 1994; Watson & Clark, 1984). This view is not without controversy, but there are considerable data that argue for the existence of such a multidimensional but nevertheless singular construct. This singular construct has been referred to as *negative affectivity* (NA).

The construct of negative affectivity was first introduced by Watson and Clark (1984), although it has earlier theoretical roots in work by Tellegen (1982) and Eysenck and Eysenck (1968, 1975). Eysenck and Eysenck (1968, 1975), for example, have described a broad and pervasive personality dimension that they designated originally as *neuroticism* (Eysenck & Eysenck, 1968) and more recently as *emotionality* (Eysenck & Eysenck, 1975). Watson and Clark (1984) argue that negative affectivity represents a preferable conceptualization, although they acknowledge that it is similar in a number of respects to these constructs.

Watson and Clark (1984) define negative affectivity in this way:

> We view Negative Affectivity as a mood-dispositional dimension. It reflects pervasive individual differences in negative emotionality and self-concept: High-NA individuals tend to be distressed and upset and have a negative view of self, whereas those low on the dimension are relatively content and secure and satisfied with themselves. . . . The negative mood states experienced by persons high in NA include subjective feelings of nervousness, tension and worry; thus NA has as one of its central features what others have called "trait anxiety." . . . However, this is too narrow a labeling of the construct: NA represents a more general negative condition. It also includes such affective states as anger, scorn, revulsion, guilt, self-dissatisfaction, a sense of rejection, and to some extent, sadness. In contrast, NA is unrelated to an individual's experience of positive emotions; that is, a high-NA level does not necessarily imply a lack of joy, excitement, or enthusiasm. Fearfulness also seems to be an unrelated disposition. (p. 465)

It is easy to see how this definition encompasses the constructs of depression and anxiety.

Cognition in Negative Affectivity

What do extant data suggest about the relationship between cognition and negative affectivity? Although a number of studies have examined the affective characteristics of negative affectivity, we are aware of only one published study that has specifically attempted to assess cognition in negative affectivity. Clark, Beck, and Stewart (1990) found that depressive cognitions for mixed depressed and anxious patients were more frequent than for anxiety-only patients and that anxious cognitions for mixed patients were more frequent than for depressed-only patients. In addition, sociotropic beliefs, that is, beliefs about potentially disrupted interpersonal relations, were somewhat higher for mixed patients than for patients with depression only or anxiety only.

Although Clark et al. (1990) is the only study that has specifically sought to assess cognition in negative affectivity, cognitive specificity studies may also provide some intriguing clues about cognition in negative affectivity; although the focus of these studies is on contrasting depression and anxiety, they typically also include subjects who are both depressed and anxious. To the extent that a high score on measures of both depression and anxiety, or a clinical diagnosis of depression *and* anxiety, is a reasonable operationalization of the construct, these studies may be informative about the cognitive processing patterns that are characteristic of negative affectivity. For example, Ingram et al. (1987) found that subjects high in both depression and anxiety reported more negative self-referent thoughts and cognitive interference than either purely depressed or purely anxious subjects. This was the case even though the respective depression and anxiety levels were roughly the same; depressed and anxious subjects reported no more depression than the depressed group and no more anxiety than the anxious group, but they had a much more negative cognitive profile.

A similar pattern is found in two additional cognitive specificity studies reported by Ingram (1989, 1990a). In these studies, depressed and anxious subjects reported somewhat more negative automatic thoughts and somewhat fewer positive automatic thoughts, denied more positive things about themselves, and acknowledged more negative things than either depressed or anxious subjects. Again, this was the case even though there were roughly equal levels of affective distress. Finally, some very recently collected data show similar findings: McKellar, Ingram, and Malcarne (1993) found that individuals high in negative affectivity reported more negative automatic thoughts than individuals who are either depressed only or anxious only. This was the case even though there were no mood differences between these groups.

On the basis of these data, it therefore appears that individuals who evidence both depression *and* anxiety consistently have a more negative cognitive profile than those who experience only depression or anxiety, even though the degree of depression and anxiety is roughly the same. Although clearly much more work needs to be done in this arena, what can be made of these early cognitive returns? Watson and Clark (1984) argue that negative affectivity represents a pervasive, negative personality disposition. If it can be ventured that this disposition is accompanied by a very negative cognitive profile, or in accordance with schema models, diffusely negative associative networks or schemata, it is intriguing to speculate that these negative cognitive patterns might predispose people to experience life and interact with others in ways that produce the features of negative affectivity: distress, increased emotionality, anger, scorn, revulsion, guilt, self-dissatisfaction, a sense of rejection, and subjective feelings of sadness, nervousness, tension, and worry. That is, this negative cognitive profile may mediate the behavioral and affective features that are seen in negative affectivity. Whether such a cognitive profile is causally linked to negative affectivity or is instead a consequence of the negative affect is unclear and merits serious research consideration. Nevertheless, it does seem clear that cognitive profiles may be able to differentiate to some degree the various aspects of the different affective syndromes. Causal or not, such cognitive differences, if they can be confirmed by additional research, may eventually be useful in making diagnostic discriminations between various affective syndromes.

In a number of respects, this type of cognitive personality conceptualization of negative affectivity is reminiscent of Beck's recent work on cognitive schemata in personality disorders. Beck and Freeman (1990) have suggested that individuals with personality disorders possess and employ cognitive schemata that structure processing in a manner consistent with the disorder. One particularly illuminating example provided by Beck and Freeman (1990) is the case of dependent personality disorder. Beck argues that these individuals have self-schemata that embody constructs such as weakness, neediness, helplessness, and incompetence and are thus prepared to process information about the self that fits these characteristics. Such information processing is apt to reinforce the person's perceived inadequacies and thus helps maintain the dysfunction. Negative affectivity may be a personality dimension that cognitively functions in a very similar way.

Such a personality dimension interpretation must remain tenuous at present because there are competing explanations for the increased cognitive negativity that occurs with the joint existence of depressive and anxious states. Data show, for instance, that certain categories of life events are predictive of anxiety states, whereas others are more uniquely associated with depression (Smith & Allred, 1989). Given that negative life events are rarely so discrete in real life, it is conceivable that the occurrence of these life events produces more negative cognition and both the depression and the anxiety that look like negative affectivity. Life events would thus serve as a third variable that may account for the relationship between increased negative cognition and what appears to be NA in the form of heightened depression and anxiety.

There may well also be other explanations for the observed relationship. Nevertheless, the prospect that people who are high on both depression and anxiety are predisposed to negative affectivity because of increased negative cognition is, at the very least, intriguing. But what is to be made of the fact that depression and anxiety can be discretely identified by at least diagnostic and perhaps other standards? Assuming the existence of NA, it seems appropriate to speculate, as do Clark and Watson (1991), that NA may coexist with, or possibly underlie, these other syndromes. Clark and Watson (1991) have proposed a tripartite model of depression and anxiety that assumes that a general distress factor (NA) will always be present in depression and anxiety. They argue that although elevated NA in and of itself may constitute a disorder and be the underlying feature of mixed depression and anxiety disorders, separate depression disorders exist and are differentiated by a lack of positive affect, whereas separate anxiety disorders are differentiated by the presence of psychophysiological arousal. Specifically, Clark and Watson (1991) argue that

> anxious and depressed syndromes share a significant nonspecific component that encompasses general affective distress and other common symptoms, whereas these syndromes are distinguished by physiological hyperarousal (specific to anxiety) versus the absence of [positive affect] (specific to depression). This tripartite view implies that a complete description of the affective domain requires assessing both the common and unique elements of the syndromes: general distress, the physiological tension and hyperarousal of anxiety, and the pervasive anhedonia of depression. Neither general distress alone nor the syndrome-specific symptom clusters can completely describe these syndromes; rather they jointly define the domain. (p. 331)

Many aspects of the tripartite model are consistent with the metaconstruct framework, particularly inasmuch as Clark and Watson (1991) have suggested that negative affectivity may represent a distinct syndrome in addition to being a generalized distress factor. Whereas the critical affective component of depression may be the absence of positive affect, cognition specific to depression may comprise self-representations of personal negativity and loss, negative appraisals of self-related information that are pervasive, absolute, and past oriented, and intrusive thoughts of loss and failure. Similarly, whereas the specific affective factor in anxiety may be hyperarousal, the specific cognitive features of anxiety may comprise themes of physical or psychological threat to the self, persistent thoughts of threat and danger, and negative self-appraisals that are specific, tentative, and future oriented. It is probably too early to tell what the cognitive features of the negative affective or mixed depression and anxiety syndrome will look like, other than that the features appear to be more severely negative and hence dysfunctional. Whether these cognitive features differ only in quantity—for example, whether there is simply a greater frequency of negative thoughts or whether these negative thoughts differ in quality—is also unclear. What is clear, however, is that the area of negative affectivity is largely unexplored from a cognitive perspective and thus deserves immediate empirical attention. It is doubtful that our understanding of the cognitive factors operating in affective states will be complete until we have begun to explore the implications of cognition within the construct of negative affectivity.

REFERENCES

Alden, L. (1987). Attributional responses of anxious individuals to different patterns of social feedback: Nothing succeeds like improvement. *Journal of Personality and Social Psychology, 52,* 100-106.

Beck, A. T. (1967). *Cognitive therapy and the emotional disorders.* New York: International University Press.

Beck, A. T. (1987). Cognitive models of depression. *Journal of Cognitive Psychotherapy: An International Quarterly, 1,* 5-37.

Beck, A. T., & Emery, G. (1985). *Anxiety disorders and phobias: A cognitive perspective.* New York: Basic Books.

Beck, A. T., & Freeman, A. (1990). *Cognitive therapy of personality disorders.* New York: Guilford.

Bower, G. H. (1981). Mood and memory. *American Psychologist, 36,* 129-148.

Butler, G., & Mathews, A. (1983). Cognitive processes in anxiety. *Advances in Behavior Therapy and Research, 5,* 51-62.

Butler, G., & Mathews, A. (1987). Anticipatory anxiety and risk perception. *Cognitive Therapy and Research, 11,* 551-566.

Clark, D. A., & Beck, A. T. (1989). Cognitive theory and therapy of anxiety and depression. In P. C. Kendall & D. Watson (Eds.), *Anxiety and depression: Distinctive and overlapping features* (pp. 379-412). New York: Academic Press.

Clark, D. A., Beck, A. T., & Stewart, B. (1990). Cognitive specificity and positive-negative affectivity: Complementary or contradictory views on anxiety and depression? *Journal of Abnormal Psychology, 99,* 148-155.

Clark, L., & Watson, D. (1991). Tripartite model of anxiety and depression: Psychometric evidence and taxonomic implications. *Journal of Abnormal Psychology, 100,* 316-336.

Collins, A. M., & Loftus, E. F. (1975). A spreading activation theory of semantic processing. *Psychological Review, 82,* 407-428.

Cook, M. L., & Peterson, C. (1986). Depressive irrationality. *Cognitive Therapy and Research, 10,* 293-298.

Deffenbacher, J. L. (1986). Cognitive and physiological components of test anxiety in real life exams. *Cognitive Therapy and Research, 10,* 635-644.

Derry, P. A., & Kuiper, N. A. (1981). Schematic processing and self-reference in clinical depression. *Journal of Abnormal Psychology, 90,* 286-297.

Dobson, K. S. (1985). Relationship between anxiety and depression. *Clinical Psychology Review, 5,* 305-324.

Dobson, K. S., & Breiter, H. J. (1983). Cognitive assessment of depression: Reliability and validity of three measures. *Journal of Abnormal Psychology, 92,* 107-109.

Dobson, K. S., & Shaw, B. F. (1987). Specificity and stability of self-referent encoding in clinical depression. *Journal of Abnormal Psychology, 96,* 34-40.

Eysenck, H., & Eysenck, S. B. G. (1968). *Manual for the Eysenck Personality Inventory.* San Diego: Educational and Industrial Testing Service.

Eysenck, H., & Eysenck, S. B. G. (1975). *Eysenck Personality Questionnaire.* San Diego: Educational and Industrial Testing Service.

Finch, A. J., Jr., Lipovsky, J. A., & Casat, J. D. (1989). Anxiety and depression in children and adolescents: Negative affectivity or separate constructs. In P. C. Kendall & D. Watson (Eds.), *Anxiety and depression: Distinctive and overlapping features* (pp. 171-202). San Diego: Academic Press.

Garber, J., & Hollon, S. D. (1991). What can specificity designs say about causality in psychopathology research? *Psychological Bulletin, 110,* 129-136.

Goldfried, M. R., & Robins, C. (1983). Self-schema, cognitive bias, and the processing of therapeutic experiences. In P. C. Kendall (Ed.), *Advances in cognitive-behavioral research and therapy.* (Vol. 2, pp. 33-80). New York: Academic Press.

Gormally, J., Sipps, G., Raphael, R., Edwin, D., & Varvil-Weld, D. (1981). The relationship between maladaptive cognitions and social anxiety. *Journal of Consulting and Clinical Psychology, 49,* 300-301.

Gotlib, I. H. (1983). Perception and recall of interpersonal feedback: Negative bias in depression. *Cognitive Therapy and Research, 7,* 399-412.

Gotlib, I. H. (1984). Depression and general psychopathology in university students. *Journal of Abnormal Psychology, 93,* 19-30.

Gotlib, I. H., & Cane, D. B. (1987). Construct accessibility and clinical depression: A longitudinal investigation. *Journal of Abnormal Psychology, 96,* 199-204.

Gotlib, I. H., & McCann, C. D. (1984). Construct accessibility and depression: An examination of cognitive and affective factors. *Journal of Personality and Social Psychology, 47,* 427-439.

Greenberg, M. S., & Beck, A. T. (1989). Depression versus anxiety: A test of the content specificity hypothesis. *Journal of Abnormal Psychology, 98,* 9-13.

Hammen, C. L. (1978). Depression, distortion, and life stress in college students. *Cognitive Therapy and Research, 2,* 189-192.

Hammen, C. L., & Glas, D. R. (1975). Depression, activity, and evaluation of reinforcement. *Journal of Abnormal Psychology, 84,* 718-721.

Hammen, C. L., & Krantz, S. (1976). Effect of success and failure on depressive cognitions. *Journal of Abnormal Psychology, 85,* 577-586.

Harrell, T. H., & Ryon, N. B. (1983). Cognitive-behavioral assessment of depression: Clinical validation of the automatic thoughts questionnaire. *Journal of Consulting and Clinical Psychology, 51,* 721-725.

Hollon, S. D., & Kendall, P. C. (1980). Cognitive self-statements in depression: Development of an automatic thoughts questionnaire. *Cognitive Therapy and Research, 4,* 383-395.

Hollon, S. D., & Kriss, M. (1984). Cognitive factors in clinical research and practice. *Clinical Psychology Review, 4,* 35-76.

Ingram, R. E. (1983, August). Content and process distinctions in depressive self-schemata. In L. B. Alloy (chair), *Depression and schemata.* Symposium presented at the meeting of the American Psychological Association, Anaheim, CA.

Ingram, R. E. (1984). Toward an information processing analysis of depression. *Cognitive Therapy and Research, 8,* 443-477.

Ingram, R. E. (1989). Unique and shared cognitive factors in social anxiety and depression. *Journal of Social and Clinical Psychology, 8,* 198-208.

Ingram, R. E. (1990a). Attentional non-specificity in depressive and generalized anxious affective states. *Cognitive Therapy and Research, 14,* 25-35.

Ingram, R. E. (1990b). Self-focused attention in clinical disorders: Review and a conceptual model. *Psychological Bulletin, 107,* 156-176.

Ingram, R. E., & Kendall, P. C. (1986). Cognitive clinical psychology: Implications of an information processing perspective. In R. E. Ingram (Ed.), *Information processing approaches to clinical psychology* (pp. 3-21). Orlando, FL: Academic Press.

Ingram, R. E., & Kendall, P. C. (1987). The cognitive side of anxiety. *Cognitive Therapy and Research, 11,* 523-536.

Ingram, R. E., Kendall, P. C., Smith, T. W., Donnell, C., & Ronan, K. (1987). Cognitive specificity in emotional distress. *Journal of Personality and Social Psychology, 53,* 734-742.

Ingram, R. E., Smith, T. W., & Brehm, S. S. (1983). Depression and information processing: Self-schemata and the encoding of self-referent information. *Journal of Personality and Social Psychology, 45,* 412-420.

Ingram, R. E., & Wisnicki, K. S. (1991). Cognition in depression. In P. A. Magaro (Ed.), *Annual review of psychopathology* (pp. 187-230). Newbury Park, CA: Sage.

Johnson, J. E., Petzel, T. P., Hartney, L. M., & Morgan, R. A. (1983). Recall of importance ratings of completed and uncompleted tasks as a function of depression. *Cognitive Therapy and Research, 7,* 51-56.

Kendall, P. C., & Hollon, S. D. (1989). Anxious self-talk: Development of the anxious self-statements questionnaire. *Cognitive Therapy and Research, 13,* 81-93.

Kendall, P. C., & Ingram, R. E. (1987). The future for cognitive assessment of anxiety: Let's get specific. In L. Michelson & M. Ascher (Eds.), *Anxiety and stress disorders: Cognitive-behavioral assessment and treatment* (pp. 89-104). New York: Guilford.

Kendall, P. C., & Ingram, R. E. (1989). Cognitive-behavioral perspectives: Theory and research on negative affective states. In P. C. Kendall & D. Watson (Eds.), *Negative affective conditions* (pp. 27-53). San Diego: Academic Press.

Kihlstrom, J. F., & Nasby, W. (1981). Cognitive tasks in clinical assessment: An exercise in applied psychology. In P. C. Kendall & S. D. Hollon (Eds.), *Assessment strategies for cognitive-behavioral interventions* (pp. 287-317). New York: Academic Press.

King, N. J., Ollendick, T. H., & Gullone, E. (1991). Negative affectivity in children and adolescents: Relations between anxiety and depression. *Clinical Psychology Review, 11,* 441-460.

Krantz, S., & Hammen, C. (1979). Assessment of cognitive bias in depression. *Journal of Abnormal Psychology, 88,* 611-619.

Kuiper, N. A., & Derry, P. A. (1982). Depressed and nondepressed content self-reference in mild depressives. *Journal of Personality, 50,* 67-80.

Kuiper, N. A., & MacDonald, M. R. (1983). Schematic processing in depression: The self-based consensus bias. *Cognitive Therapy and Research, 7,* 469-484.

Kuiper, N. A., Olinger, L. J., & MacDonald, M. (1988). Vulnerability and episodic cognitions in a self-worth contingency model of depression. In L. B. Alloy (Ed.), *Cognitive process in depression.* (pp. 289-309). New York: Guilford.

Lam, D. H., Brewin, C. R., Woods, R. T., & Bebbington, P. E. (1987). Cognition and social adversity in the depressed elderly. *Journal of Abnormal Psychology, 96,* 23-26.

MacLeod, C., Mathews, A., & Tata, P. (1986). Attentional bias in emotional disorders. *Journal of Abnormal Psychology, 95,* 15-20.

Malcarne, V. L., & Ingram, R. E. (1994). Cognition and negative affectivity. In T. Ollendick & R. Prinz (Eds.), *Advances in child clinical psychology* (pp. 141-176). New York: Plenum.

McKellar, J. D., Ingram, R. E., & Malcarne, V. L. (1993, November). *Cognitive processing and negative affectivity.* Paper submitted for presentation at the meeting of the Association for the Advancement of Behavior Therapy, Atlanta.

McNally, R. J., & Foa, E. B. (1987). Cognition and agoraphobia: Bias in the interpretation of threat. *Cognitive Therapy and Research, 11,* 567-582.

Mizes, J. S., Landolf-Fritsche, B., & Grossman-McKee, D. (1987). Patterns of distorted cognitions in phobic disorders: An investigation of clinically severe simple phobics, social phobics, and agoraphobics. *Cognitive Therapy and Research, 11,* 583-592.

Mueller, J. H., & Thompson, W. B. (1984). Test anxiety and distinctiveness of personal information. In H. M. van der Ploeg, R. Schwarzer, & C. D. Spielberger (Eds.), *Advances in test anxiety research* (Vol. 3, pp. 21-37). Hillsdale, NJ: Lawrence Erlbaum.

Nelson, R. E., & Craighead, W. E. (1977). Selective recall of positive and negative feedback, self-control behaviors, and depression. *Journal of Abnormal Psychology, 86,* 379-388.

Norman, D. A. (1981). Categorization of action slips. *Psychological Review, 88,* 1-15.

Norman, D. A. (1986). Toward a theory of memory and attention. *Psychological Review, 75,* 522-536.

Ollendick, T. H., & Hersen, M. (Eds.). (1989). *Handbook of child psychopathology* (2nd ed.). New York: Plenum.

Rabin, A. S. (1985, November). *Selective memory in depression: Memory deficits or response bias?* Paper presented at the meeting of the Association for the Advancement of Behavior Therapy, Houston.

Ross, M. J., & Mueller, J. H. (1983, May). *Consistency of the self-schema in depression.* Paper presented at the meeting of the Midwestern Psychological Association, Chicago.

Roth, D., & Rehm, L. P. (1980). Relationships among self-monitoring processes, memory and depression. *Cognitive Therapy and Research, 4,* 149-157.

Smith, T. W., & Allred, K. D. (1989). Major life events in anxiety and depression. In P. C. Kendall & D. Watson (Eds.), *Anxiety and depression: Distinctive and overlapping features* (pp. 205-223). San Diego: Academic Press.

Smith, T. W., Ingram, R. E., & Brehm, S. S. (1983). Social anxiety, anxious self-preoccupation, and recall of self-relevant information. *Journal of Personality and Social Psychology, 44,* 1276-1283.

Smith, T. W., & Rhodewalt, F. T. (1991). Methodological challenges at the social/clinical interface. In C. R. Snyder & D. R. Forsyth (Eds.), *Handbook of social and clinical psychology* (pp. 739-756). New York: Pergamon.

Teasdale, J. D. (1983). Negative thinking in depression: Cause, effect, or reciprocal relationship? *Advances in Behaviour Research and Therapy, 5,* 3-25.

Teasdale, J. D. (1988). Cognitive vulnerability to persistent depression. *Cognition and Emotion, 2,* 247-274.

Tellegen, A. (1982). *Brief manual for the Differential Personality Questionnaire.* Unpublished manuscript, University of Minnesota, Minneapolis.

Vredenburg, K., & Krames, L. (1983, August). *Memory scanning in depression: The disruptive effects of cognitive schemas.* Paper presented at the meeting of the American Psychological Association, Anaheim, CA.

Watson, D., & Clark, L. A. (1984). Negative affectivity: The disposition to experience aversive emotional states. *Psychological Bulletin, 96,* 465-490.

Watson, D., & Kendall, P. C. (1989). Common and differentiating features of anxiety and depression: Current findings and future directions. In P. C. Kendall & D. Watson (Eds.), *Anxiety and depression: Distinctive and overlapping features* (pp. 493-508). New York: Academic Press.

Williams, J. M. G., & Oaksford, M. R. (1992). Cognitive science, anxiety, and depression: From experiments to connectionism. In D. J. Stein & J. E. Young (Eds.), *Cognitive science and clinical disorders* (pp. 129-150). San Diego: Academic Press.

Zuroff, D. C., Colussy, S. A., & Wielgus, M. S. (1983). Selective memory and depression: A cautionary note concerning response bias. *Cognitive Therapy and Research, 7,* 223-232.

NOTE

1. It is important to note that the ANOVA metaphor should not be taken too literally. That is, the ANOVA model is simply a useful analogy for thinking about how psychopathological variance can be broken down into specific and nonspecific aspects. Any other statistical procedure partitioning sources of variance (e.g., multiple regression, factor analysis) would serve just as well as a model for separating elements of psychopathology into conceptually interesting segments.

3

An Interpersonal Comparison of Depression and Social Anxiety

LYNN E. ALDEN

PETER J. BIELING

KEN G. A. MELESHKO

A significant number of patients who seek treatment for depression and for anxiety-related conditions also report interpersonal problems. Whether these problems are the cause or the result of emotional distress is often unclear. However, interpersonal problems are often the focus of treatment (Horowitz & Vitkus, 1986). Although the interpersonal problems of each patient are to some extent unique, it is generally believed that some common cognitive and behavioral features underlie individual variations in the interpersonal responses of depressed individuals and of anxious individuals. In this chapter, we will examine depression and anxiety from an interpersonal perspective in an attempt to delineate the interpersonal features specific to each condition.

We will focus more on social anxiety and clinical disorders characterized by social anxiety than on general anxiety. In part this is necessary because the majority of published studies of interpersonal aspects of anxiety examine socially anxious individuals. Surprisingly little research has addressed the interpersonal difficulties associated with general anxiety or with anxiety-related disorders other than social phobia. However, research suggests that measures of general anxiety display at least moderate correlations with measures of social anxiety (Watson & Clark, 1984). Social anxiety of moderate intensity is also reported by many patients diagnosed with anxiety-related conditions other than social phobia, particularly patients with generalized anxiety disorder or agoraphobia (Rapee, Sanderson, & Barlow, 1988). Thus subjects who are high in general anxiety are likely to be socially anxious as well, and studies of interpersonal behavior are likely to reflect the effects of social anxiety in addition to whatever interpersonal features are attributable to general anxiety. However, we will include studies of people with high levels of general anxiety or other anxiety-related conditions wherever such studies are available.

Elsewhere in this volume, a number of writers have demonstrated that depression and anxiety are correlated, or overlapping, conditions. This is true of depression and social anxiety as well. Approximately 34% of depressed patients also meet diagnostic criteria for avoidant personality disorder, a condition which is marked by a longstanding pattern of social fear and avoidance (Shea, Glass, Pilkonis, Watkins, & Docherty, 1987). Approximately 50% of socially phobic outpatients have significant depressive symptoms (Aimes, Gelder, & Shaw, 1983). Thus a substantial number of patients diagnosed either as depressed or with a disorder marked by social anxiety are likely to have features of both conditions. In the general population, measures of depressive symptoms display moderate-level correlations ($r = .40$) with measures of social anxiety (e.g., Bruch, Mattia, Heimberg, & Holt, 1993; Ingram, 1989a, 1989b). Studies that have examined either depression or social anxiety alone undoubtedly include a significant number of subjects who have symptoms of both. This raises the possibility that interpersonal features attributed to depression may be due to social anxiety and vice versa. In particular, some of the inconsistencies in results between different studies may reflect differences in the composition of the particular sample of subjects studied. Many of the issues discussed elsewhere in this volume concerning the need to consider depression and anxiety simultaneously also apply to the study of interpersonal behavior.

In this chapter, we will examine various cognitive and behavioral theories that address interpersonal aspects of depression and social anxiety and survey the empirical literature that addresses this issue. In keeping with the cognitive-behavioral emphasis of this volume, we will focus primarily on the depressed and anxious person's cognitive and behavioral reactions to social situations: that is, how depressed and anxious people process social information and what they do in social situations. Our central focus will be to examine the extent to which depression and anxiety are associated with distinct cognitive-behavioral patterns in interpersonal situations.

CONCEPTUAL MODELS OF INTERPERSONAL BEHAVIOR

Social transactions are a complex sequence of events in which the beliefs and behaviors of two individuals interact to influence each other. The most detailed theories of interpersonal behavior come from writers within the Interpersonal school (Carson, 1969; Kiesler, 1983). Two central elements of their theories are that (a) interpersonal behavior is reciprocal in that one person's behaviors pull for reciprocal and complementary responses from others, and (b) people with interpersonal problems are locked into self-defeating cycles of interpersonal behavior in which their cognitive-emotional reactions to social situations lead them to engage in interpersonal actions that evoke negative responses from others (Strupp & Binder, 1984).

Cognitive-behavioral writers have focused more on delineating the inter-personal features specific to various disorders than on general theories of interpersonal behavior. These writers have typically placed less emphasis on background factors and personality dynamics than have writers from the Interpersonal school. However, current cognitive and behavioral theories of interpersonal behavior reflect the interactive nature of social transactions (i.e., that each person's behavior influences the responses of his or her partner) and explicitly include some aspects of Interpersonal theory, in particular the idea that the social beliefs and behaviors of depressed and anxious people lead to negative outcomes (real or imagined), which in turn exacerbate emotional distress and negative self-image. Some writers place greater emphasis on deficiencies in social behavior that result in negative social outcomes. These writers propose that the negative self-evaluations of depressed and anxious people are accurate reflections of their deficient social behavior. Other writers propose that biased social perceptions and negative beliefs lead depressed and anxious people to overestimate the negativity of others' reactions. However, the idea that underlies each of these positions is similar—for depressed and socially anxious people, interpersonal interactions exacerbate rather than alleviate emotional problems.

The majority of writers who address the role of interpersonal factors in depression emphasize behavioral deficiencies. Lewinsohn, for example, proposed that depressed people lack the complex behavioral skills necessary to obtain reinforcement from others. This lack of social reinforcement leads to a decrease in social behavior that ultimately produces an increase in depression (Libet & Lewinsohn, 1973). Coyne (1976) suggested that depressed persons and members of their environment become "enmeshed in an emergent system" in which expressions of depressive complaints and others' responses to those complaints interact to perpetuate depressed mood. According to Coyne, the depressed person's tendency to complain evokes nongenuine displays of reassurance from others and a tendency to avoid the depressed person. The depressed person accurately perceives the lack of acceptance, displays more symptoms, evokes still more negative responses, and so on, in a cyclical process. Hammen (1991) proposed that depressed persons behave in such a way as to generate stressful conditions and events, particularly interpersonal events, which in turn cause additional symptoms. Furthermore, this pattern is passed from one generation to the next, as from mother to daughter, in part through dysfunctional behavior during parent-child interactions. Swann, writing from a social psychological perspective, concluded that depressed people actively create a negative social environment through their selection of partners who are also depressed and their search for negative information about themselves (Swann, Wenzlaff, Krull, & Pelham, 1992). According to Swann, the depressed person acts to confirm his or her negative self-image and depressed mood in order to bolster his or her sense of existential security and control. In contrast to these "behavioral" views, Beck (1976) emphasized the role of cognitive factors. According to Beck, the depressed person processes social information in light of a negative self-schema, and this results in an overestimation of negative outcomes and personal shortcomings.

Some theories of social anxiety also center on notions of deficiencies in social behavior. Curran, for example, proposed that social anxiety is a reaction to an inadequate behavioral repertoire. According to Curran, skill deficits lead to inappropriate responses to social situations that elicit aversive social consequences, which in turn produce anxiety (e.g., Curran & Gilbert, 1975). Trower presented similar ideas concerning social phobia (e.g., Trower & Turland, 1984), and Turner has emphasized the role of skill deficits in avoidant personality disorder (e.g., Turner, Beidel, Dancu, & Keys, 1986). Other theorists have placed greater emphasis on cognitive factors. Goldfried suggested that social anxiety may be associated with biased processing of social information due to underlying schemata that direct attention to social evaluation and negative social outcomes (e.g., Goldfried, Padawer, & Robins, 1984). Beck and Emery's (1985) model of evaluation anxiety is similar: In social situations, those prone to evaluation anxiety engage in schematic processing of life events that make them hypersensitive to cues of impending danger (threat). For socially anxious individuals, the impending threat is social disapproval related to the person's perceived social inadequacies. Heimberg (1991) proposed that social phobia is the result of a cycle of automatic negative thoughts, physiological arousal, and behavioral avoidance.

Writing from a social psychological perspective, Schlenker and Leary (1982) developed a theory that emphasized motivational factors and strategies for presenting oneself to others. These writers suggested that most people are motivated to make a specific (usually positive) impression on others during interactions. It is when people doubt their ability to make a good impression that they experience social anxiety and adopt protective strategies for presenting themselves. Arkin extended this motivational explanation to chronically anxious or shy individuals. According to Arkin, the shy person consistently doubts his or her ability to make a favorable impression and is therefore motivated by the desire to avoid negative outcomes (e.g., disapproval) rather than the desire to gain positive outcomes (e.g., attention, recognition). Whereas nonshy people engage in behavior designed to acquire positive outcomes, the shy person adopts self-protective strategies to deflect attention and possible criticism (Arkin, Lake, & Baumgardner, 1986). Millon's (1981) formulation of avoidant personality disorder contains similar ideas, although these are expressed in terms of personality traits. According to Millon, a combination of innate autonomic hyperactivity and parental derogation results in a hypersensitivity to aversive events among some individuals. These people use a general pattern of avoidance to protect themselves from aversive social outcomes, which they consider to be inevitable. However, this pursuit of self-protection leads to social isolation, depression, and the perpetuation of a negative self-image.

Although different theories of social anxiety underscore either cognitive, behavioral, or motivational factors, there is general agreement among these writers that all three elements play a role. Accordingly, theories of social anxiety are more likely to explicitly integrate cognitive and behavioral elements than are theories of interpersonal behavior in depression. Despite this, there are obvious parallels in the theories developed to describe the interpersonal behavior of depressed and anxious people.

EMPIRICAL STUDIES

Although a number of studies have examined cognitive and behavioral factors associated with depression and anxiety, only a portion of these have addressed interpersonal issues. Studies have been conducted with both patient (depressed, social phobic) and student (dysphoric, socially anxious) populations. The majority of these interpersonal studies have examined depression and social anxiety alone and have compared depressed (or anxious) individuals to "normal" (i.e., nondepressed or nonanxious) controls. However, some studies have compared each condition to clinical control groups, and a handful of studies have directly compared the interpersonal features associated with depression to those associated with anxiety. Each body of studies will be examined below.

Comparisons to "Normal" Controls

As noted above, the majority of published studies have examined either depression or social anxiety in isolation and have compared depressed and socially anxious people to nonsymptomatic control groups. With each condition, studies have tended to focus on either cognitive or behavioral aspects, though some studies have examined both types of variables. The results of cognitive and behavioral studies will be examined in turn.

Cognitive Factors. What is particularly notable about studies of interpersonal cognitions is the similarity in the types of variables identified by researchers as relevant to depression and social anxiety. In many cases, the results obtained with depressed populations are similar to results obtained with socially anxious populations. For example, both depressed and socially anxious patients expect to handle social situations poorly (e.g., Ducharme & Bachelor, 1993; Edelmann, 1985). Both dysphoric students and socially anxious students have a negative sense of social self-efficacy. Although neither group was found to establish higher standards for their social behavior than control subjects, both groups displayed greater discrepancies between their perceptions of their social abilities and various standards of evaluation than did control subjects (Ahrens, Zeiss, & Kanfer, 1988; Kanfer & Zeiss, 1983; Wallace & Alden, 1991). Socially anxious students and social phobic outpatients report more negative and fewer positive thoughts prior to and during social interactions than do control groups (e.g., Cacioppo, Glass, & Merluzzi, 1979; Dodge, Hope, Heimberg, & Becker, 1988; Glass, Merluzzi, Biever, & Larsen, 1982; Turner, Beidel, & Larkin, 1986). Dysphoric students also report a higher frequency of negative self-referent thoughts than nondysphoric controls (e.g., Hollon & Kendall, 1980).

Both groups are also characterized by self-critical cognitions following social interactions. For example, both socially anxious and dysphoric students have been shown to attribute negative social outcomes to personal failings (e.g., Alden, 1987; Anderson, Horowitz, & French, 1983; Girodo, Dotzenroth, & Stein, 1981; Teglasi & Fagin, 1984). Some (but not all) studies found that both groups (accurately or inaccurately) perceive their social behavior during interactions as inadequate. In some studies, dysphoric and anxious subjects have been observed to underestimate their social ability relative to the ratings of objective observers (who may also rate subjects' abilities negatively, but to a lesser extent) (e.g., Clark & Arkowitz, 1975; Glasgow & Arkowitz, 1975; Gotlib & Meltzer, 1987; Heimberg, Hope, Dodge, & Becker, 1990; Lucock & Salkovskis, 1988). (Note, however, that not all studies have found that dysphoric or anxious individuals rate their social performance negatively, e.g., Ducharme & Bachelor, 1993.)

The negative cognitive style of dysphoric and socially anxious individuals may also extend to their perceptions of others' reactions to them. For example, Jones and Briggs (1984) found that shy students expected to be rated negatively and believed they were rated negatively by fellow group members. Socially anxious students and depressed patients appear to perceive and recall interpersonal feedback as more negative than do control groups (e.g., O'Banion & Arkowitz, 1977). Borden and Baum (1987) found that dysphoric students believed that their partner would be less willing to interact with them in the future than did control subjects. Pietromonaco, Rook, and Lewis (1992) concluded that dysphoric students believed strangers had been unsympathetic to their disclosures.

The picture that emerges from these studies is one of self-critical, self-blaming perceptions of the self as a social being and negative expectations regarding others' responses. The similarities between the cognitive patterns

found in socially anxious populations and those found in depressed populations are striking. On the other hand, some differences do emerge. For
example, studies of automatic thoughts and causal attributions suggest that
depressives display negative cognitions in response to both interpersonal and
noninterpersonal situations, whereas the negative attributions and thoughts
of socially anxious individuals are more specific to interpersonal events.
Furthermore, socially anxious people display discrepancies between their
perception of their ability and what they think others expect of them, for example, they doubt their ability to meet others' expectations (Wallace & Alden,
1991), whereas dysphoric people display discrepancies between perceived
ability and their own standards for social behavior, i.e., they feel unable to
meet their own standards of conduct (e.g., Kanfer & Zeiss, 1983). However,
studies that include both depressed and social anxious people would be
necessary to establish these as distinguishing factors.

Behavioral Factors. Studies of the interpersonal behaviors associated with
social anxiety have focused primarily on ratings of global social skill and
on specific "micro" behaviors, such as eye contact, pauses, and voice
volume. The results concerning both types of variables are mixed. Some
researchers found that socially anxious people were rated by their partners
or observers as low relative to nonanxious people on global measures of
skill (e.g., Arkowitz, Lichtenstein, McGovern, & Hines, 1975; Borkovec,
Stone, O'Brien, & Kaloupek, 1974; Pilkonis, 1977). However, other studies
found no differences on global skill ratings (e.g., Clark & Arkowitz, 1975;
Rapee & Lim, 1992). Likewise, some studies found that socially anxious
(shy, or socially phobic) individuals display deficiencies in specific social
behaviors (e.g., Bruch, Gorsky, Collins, & Berger, 1989; Pilkonis, 1977;
Rapee & Lim, 1992), but other studies found no differences between
socially anxious and control groups (e.g., Arkowitz et al., 1975; Borkovec
et al., 1974). A number of writers have proposed that there are behaviorally
skilled and unskilled groups among socially anxious (Curran, Wallander,
& Fischetti, 1980), shy (Pilkonis, 1977), and social phobic individuals
(Emmelkamp, Mersch, Vissia, & van der Helm, 1985). Other writers have
suggested that these behavioral deficiencies are mediated by situational
factors and occur only in situations that are ambiguous and unstructured,
or that involve evaluation or scrutiny by others (e.g., Pilkonis, 1977).
    A few studies have examined other types of interpersonal behaviors.
Kupke, Hobbs, and Cheney (1979) found that shy men emitted more com-

ments that reflected self-focused attention than nonshy men. Two studies suggested that socially anxious people engage in behaviors designed to make an innocuous (self-protective or attention-deflecting) impression (DePaulo, Epstein, & LeMay, 1990; Leary, Knight, & Johnson, 1987), but one study found no support for this self-protective pattern (Bruch et al., 1989). Finally, Meleshko and Alden (1993) compared the self-disclosures of socially anxious and nonanxious students in response to confederates who had disclosed intimate or nonintimate information. Socially anxious subjects disclosed at a moderate level of intimacy regardless of their partner's behavior. They were also less likely to reciprocate their partners' disclosures than were nonanxious subjects, and, perhaps as a result, elicited more negative reactions from their partners.

Studies that have compared the interpersonal behavior of dysphoric and nondysphoric students have produced mixed results. Some studies found that dysphoric students displayed different, and less functional, social behaviors than nondysphoric controls (e.g., Blumberg & Hokanson, 1983; Gotlib & Robinson, 1982; Strack & Coyne, 1983), but others failed to find differences (e.g., Borden & Baum, 1987; Gotlib & Meltzer, 1987; Pietromonaco et al., 1992). Studies of depressed patients interacting with nonfamily members have likewise produced mixed results, with some finding behavioral differences (e.g., Libet & Lewinsohn, 1973) and some not (e.g., Ducharme & Bachelor, 1993). The most consistent evidence of a distinct pattern of behavior among depressives is found in the small group of studies that examined behaviors of depressed people interacting with their spouses. Here the majority of studies find differences between the interactions of couples with a depressed partner and those without (e.g., Biglan et al., 1985; Hinchliffe, Hooper, Roberts, & Vaughan, 1975; Kahn, Coyne, & Margolin, 1985).

In those studies that find clear evidence of dysfunctional behavior, three general categories of behavior have been associated with depression/ dysphoria. The first is the type of unskilled, inhibited behavior that also characterizes socially anxious populations. For example, some researchers found that observers rated depressed patients low on global measures of skill and high on specific measures of behavioral inhibition (e.g., poor eye contact, speaking less) (e.g., Libet & Lewinsohn, 1973). The second and most consistent pattern to emerge is the presence of negative verbal behavior. Depressed patients and dysphoric students express more negative emotions, engage in more self-criticism, and emit a lower proportion of positive comments than do control subjects (e.g., Biglan et al., 1985; Blumberg &

Hokanson, 1983; Gotlib & Robinson, 1982). Finally, several studies indicated that depressed individuals may express more anger or blaming of others than nondepressed people (e.g., Blumberg & Hokanson, 1983; Kahn et al., 1985). These last two categories of behavior are quite distinct from the behaviors typically implicated in social anxiety. Thus whereas the cognitions of depressed and socially anxious individuals have many shared features, studies that have compared either depressed or socially anxious groups to normal controls indicate that distinct patterns of social behavior are associated with each condition.

Studies With Pathology Control Groups

Relatively few studies of the interpersonal aspects of either condition have included controls for psychopathology. For example, a recent review indicated that fewer than 30% of studies examining interpersonal behavior and depression contained clinical comparison groups (Alden, Bieling, & Meleshko, in preparation). Similarly, only a handful of clinical studies of social phobia involved a comparison with another clinical condition.

Social phobic patients have been compared to outpatients with other anxiety-disorder diagnoses. Two studies compared social phobic to panic-disordered patients and found evidence that the two groups were cognitively distinct. Social phobics displayed schematic processing of information related to social threat (Hope, Rapee, Heimberg, & Dombeck, 1990) and endorsed the belief that events were controlled by "powerful others" (Cloitre, Heimberg, Liebowitz, & Gitow, 1992). Comparisons with agoraphobic outpatients have yielded mixed results. Persson and Nordlund (1985) found that social phobics perceived their therapists more negatively and preferred more directive therapists than did agoraphobic outpatients (Persson & Nordlund, 1985). However, Capreol and Alden (1993) found that social phobic and agoraphobic outpatients displayed many similarities in the content of their dysfunctional interpersonal beliefs. The one study that examined interpersonal behavior found that social phobics displayed less skillful social behavior than a mixed group of outpatients with other anxiety disorders and, in addition, underestimated their abilities relative to observers' ratings (Stopa & Clark, 1993). Unfortunately, none of these studies took depression into consideration.

Studies of depressed patients and dysphoric students generally use clinical comparison groups whose members are heterogeneous in symptomatology.

For example, studies of depressed patients typically compare depressives to a cross section of other patients seeking treatment. Studies that compared depressed or dysphoric people to mixed clinical controls have found that depressives have more negative expectations for social interactions (Hokanson & Meyer, 1984), display less effective interpersonal problem-solving skills (Gotlib & Asarnow, 1979), show less accurate social perceptions (Hollander & Hokanson, 1988), and prefer more subordinate roles (Hokanson & Meyer, 1984) than the clinical comparison or the "normal" control group. Depressed patients were also found to evaluate feedback more negatively than a mixed group of patients (Gotlib, 1983). However, not all studies find differences. Anderson et al. (1983) found that depression and loneliness displayed similar patterns of correlations with self-blaming causal attributions.

Several behavioral studies found that depressed patients and dysphoric students differed from mixed-symptom comparison groups in terms of lower ratings on global skill (Lewinsohn, Mischel, Chaplin, & Barton, 1980; Youngren & Lewinsohn, 1980) and the presence of more self-evaluative, sad, and blaming communications (Hokanson, Sacco, Blumberg, & Landrum, 1980). However, depressed groups were no different than pathology comparison groups on specific behavioral ratings (Youngren & Lewinsohn, 1980) or assertiveness in a lab social task (Hollander & Hokanson, 1988). Two studies that compared the marital interactions of depressed patients to those of mixed controls found that depressed spouses expressed more negative content in their verbalizations (Hautzinger, Linden, & Hoffman, 1982; Nelson & Beach, 1990), but one study did not (Kowalik & Gotlib, 1987).

Thus comparisons to mixed-pathology control groups clearly indicate that depressed groups display negative social cognitions. The evidence for behavioral differences is once again less than consistent. However, the differences that emerge are similar to those found in comparisons to nondepressed "normals." From an interpersonal perspective, however, there are problems with the types of pathology comparison groups that have been used. First, not all patients' difficulties center on interpersonal problems. When studying interpersonal behavior, it may be more meaningful to compare depressed groups to patients who are known to have interpersonal difficulties. Second, although mixed groups control for the presence of pathology per se, the interpersonal behaviors of the subjects in these groups are likely to be heterogeneous and may "average" out. This may result in depressed subjects looking more distinct than if they had been compared to a group with a homogeneous interpersonal profile. Finally, mixed clinical controls do not discriminate the effects of depression from those of anxiety.

Comparative Studies

A number of researchers have systematically compared the interpersonal features associated with anxiety and with depression. Because these studies are particularly valuable in delineating the interpersonal features of each condition, they will be examined in more detail. The majority of these comparative studies examined cognitive factors; however, four studies measured overt behavior. Cognitive and behavioral factors will be examined separately.

Cognitive Factors: General Questionnaires. Most cognitive studies have examined subjects' responses to written descriptions of social situations or to questionnaires that ask for global assessments of thought processes as opposed to studying the beliefs and thoughts activated during actual interactions. Automatic thoughts have received the most empirical attention. Beck, Brown, Steer, Eidelson, and Riskind (1987) compared the types of automatic thoughts reported by depressed and by anxiety-disordered patients in cognitive therapy. Although a number of the thoughts generated by patients were interpersonal in nature, only seven of them were among those items found to clearly differentiate the two groups of patients. Interestingly, most of these items loaded on the depression scale and reflected themes of being unworthy of others' attention, the loss of friends, and the loss of respect and caring from others. This study indicated that depressed patients do experience automatic thoughts related to interpersonal events and that anxiety-disordered patients as a group are not characterized by a distinctive pattern of thoughts related to social events.

Ingram (1989a, 1989b) compared four groups of students, who represented all combinations of social anxiety and dysphoria, on the Automatic Thoughts Questionnaire (ATQ; Hollon & Kendall, 1980), a scale developed to assess depression-relevant negative thoughts, and on a companion measure of positive self-referent thoughts (the ATQ-P; Ingram & Wisnicki, 1988). A higher frequency of negative automatic thoughts was found among dysphoric subjects. Deficits in positive thoughts were found only for the combined socially anxious and dysphoric group. Ingram concluded that the negative cognitions reported by socially anxious subjects were primarily due to dysphoria. He also suggested that the effects of anxiety and depression might be synergistic—that is, might produce greater cognitive dysfunction than either condition alone.

Bruch et al. (1993, Study 1) replicated the Ingram study but included a measure of positive and negative thoughts related to *social* situations (the Social Interaction Self-Statement Test; SISST; Glass et al., 1982). The results with the ATQ largely replicated Ingram's earlier study, although in contrast to Ingram, the two "pure" (dysphoric only and socially anxious only) groups reported fewer positive thoughts on the ATQ-P than control subjects. In terms of socially related automatic thoughts, the combined group reported significantly more negative thoughts and fewer positive thoughts than the other three groups. The two pure groups reported more negative thoughts than control subjects but did not differ from each other. The socially-anxious-only group reported fewer positive thoughts than either the dysphoric or the control groups who did not differ from each other. Thus this study supported Ingram's suggestion that social anxiety and dysphoria are synergistic in that the combined group in this study displayed more extreme scores on three of four measures (all except the ATQ-N, on which both dysphoric groups obtained equally high scores). In contrast to Ingram, however, the authors concluded that social anxiety was associated with negative thoughts but that those negative thoughts tended to be specific to social events. Finally, the results indicated that dysphoric subjects had negative thoughts related to interpersonal situations as well as thoughts of more general self-criticism.

Bruch et al. (1993, Study 2) assessed positive and negative thoughts on the SISST in three groups of social phobic outpatients who differed in severity of dysphoria. Social phobics with higher levels of dysphoria reported more negative thoughts than patients with lower levels of dysphoria. The three groups reported similar levels of positive thoughts. It was not clear, however, if the three groups differed on factors in addition to dysphoria, such as severity of impairment or type of social phobia.

Several studies have compared depressed and socially anxious groups in terms of discrepancy in self-beliefs. Strauman and Higgins (1988, Study 2) examined two types of self-discrepancies: Actual:Ideal, or the difference between subjects' ratings of themselves as they actually are (Actual self) and what they would like to be (Ideal self), and Actual:Ought/other, or the difference between subjects' ratings of their actual self and what they believe others would like them to be (Ought/other). Using structural equation modeling, the authors concluded that Actual:Ideal discrepancies were more strongly associated with dysphoria than social anxiety and that Actual: Ought/other discrepancies were more strongly associated with social anxiety than dysphoria. Strauman (1989) examined this same issue in a clinical sample. Consistent with the earlier study, depressed patients had larger Actual:Ideal discrepancies than either the social phobic patients or a control group of nondepressed, nonanxious students, and social phobic patients displayed greater Actual: Ought/other discrepancies than depressed patients or the control group. In addition, the social phobic and depressed patients displayed different patterns of self-reported mood and skin conductance in response to a procedure that primed either Actual:Ideal or Actual: Ought/Other discrepancies. It is notable that the depressed patients also displayed arousal to priming of the Ought/other structure, which indicated that others' expectations were of as much concern for them as for the social phobic patients. The author concluded that different types of self-discrepancies function as cognitive vulnerability factors for depression and for social phobia.

Anxious and depressed groups have been compared on three other questionnaire measures. Anderson and Arnoult (1985) found that both dysphoria and shyness among college students were associated with a reversal of the self-serving attribution pattern typically found in nonsymptomatic students. However, there were some indications that dysphoric individuals applied this pattern to a broader range of situations—that is, both social and nonsocial situations—than did shy subjects. Alden and Phillips (1990) found that both dysphoric and nondysphoric socially anxious subjects perceived themselves to have more interpersonal problems than control subjects on the Inventory of Interpersonal Problems Circumplex Scales. The dysphoric-only group did not differ from controls. Finally, Marx, Claridge, and Williams (1992) compared a group of depressed patients, a mixed group of anxiety-disordered patients, and normal control subjects on the Means-Ends Problem-Solving Test. Both groups of patients displayed deficits relative to normal controls in terms of generating relevant means for solving social problem situations, identifying obstacles to overcoming problems, and number of alternative strategies produced. The depressed patients differed from the anxiety-disordered patients on only one variable—they generated less effective strategies for handling problem situations than did the anxiety-disordered patients, who did not differ from controls on this variable.

Cognitive Factors: Reactions to Actual Interactions. Four studies investigated cognitive reactions to actual social interactions. In two of these studies, dysphoric individuals were compared to subjects who received high scores on measures of general (trait) anxiety. Dow and Craighead (1987) compared a group of students in treatment for depression (referred to as the *client group*) to three other groups of students: a group that was both dysphoric and high on trait anxiety; an anxious, nondysphoric group; and a nonanxious, nondysphoric (control) group. Prior to a lab interaction, the dysphoric anxious students, and to a lesser extent the depressed clients, reported more negative expectations about how they would appear to their partners than did the other groups. The dysphoric anxious students, and to a lesser extent the depressed clients, also evaluated themselves more negatively following the interaction than did the nondysphoric anxious and control groups. The anxious subjects reported more negative expectations and self-evaluations than did controls, but to a lesser extent than the dysphoric groups.

Dobson (1989) compared groups of students who were (a) both dysphoric and generally anxious, (b) anxious but nondysphoric, and (c) nonanxious and nondysphoric in terms of their perceptions of their partner's reactions and their partner's actual reactions during a brief unstructured interaction with another undergraduate subject. There were no differences in how the three groups perceived their partner's behavior toward them and in their partner's actual responses. However, both the dysphoric anxious and the anxious nondysphoric groups believed that their partner would be unwilling to interact with them in the future. Dobson concluded that the tendency to overestimate rejection may be more strongly associated with anxiety than dysphoria.

Two studies examined dysphoria and *social* anxiety. One of these studies assessed the effects of dysphoric mood on the thoughts of social phobics and found that social phobics who reported dysphoric mood reported fewer positive thoughts prior to individualized behavioral simulations of anxiety-provoking situations than did nondysphoric social phobics (Bruch et al., 1993, Study 2). The other study compared dysphoric and socially anxious students in terms of self-regulatory processes in social situations (Alden, Bieling, & Wallace, 1994). Subjects rated their personal standard for evaluating an upcoming interaction, their perception of their partner's standard for evaluating their behavior, frequency of self-appraisal, and perceptions of their own ability (social self-efficacy). Frequent self-appraisal was associated with dysphoria, whereas low social self-efficacy was associated with social anxiety. Thus subjects who were both socially anxious and dysphoric bore the burden of two negative processes: They repeatedly appraised social behavior they judged to be inadequate. The four groups did not differ in their perceptions of their partner's standard for evaluating their social behavior. However, the two socially anxious groups (dysphoric and nondysphoric) judged their social ability as falling short of others' expectations. These results are reminiscent of the discrepancy between Actual self and Ought/other self identified by Strauman (1989) in social phobic patients. However, the dysphoric students did not display a discrepancy between their perceptions of their ability and their personal standards, as Strauman's work might suggest.

It is difficult to summarize these cognitive studies in light of differences in samples (patients versus students, generally anxious versus socially anxious), dependent variables, and methodology. However, several conclusions do emerge. First, as Ingram (1989a, 1989b) proposed, people who complain of both depression and social anxiety (or general anxiety) display more negative cognitive reactions to social events than people who have either complaint alone. Five of seven studies to address this issue found evidence for synergistic or additive effects of depression and anxiety. This was true for both questionnaire studies (Bruch et al., 1993, Study 1 and 2; Ingram, 1989a, 1989b) and studies of actual interactions (Alden et al., 1994; Dow & Craighead, 1987) and included variables reflecting negative expectations prior to interactions, negative thoughts during interactions, and negative self-evaluations after interactions. The two exceptions (Alden & Phillips, 1990; Dobson, 1989) found that dysphoric and anxious subjects displayed no greater dysfunction than subjects who were anxious only. Second, it also appears that people who are depressed only or socially anxious (generally anxious) only display different cognitive reactions to social stimuli than do control subjects. Finally, in most studies, the depressed-only and anxious-only groups also differed from each other. This indicates that quite apart from synergistic effects, there are likely to be differences in the social cognitions of depressed and anxious people. However, because so few studies have examined this issue, the exact nature of the cognitive patterns that distinguish the two groups remains to be determined.

Behavioral Factors. Relatively few comparative studies of interpersonal behavior have been published. However, two studies have contrasted depressed patient samples with samples of anxious individuals. Dow and Craighead (1987) examined the interpersonal behavior of the four groups of subjects described earlier. Subjects' behaviors during two brief unstructured interactions were rated by trained observers and by confederates on six dimensions. Observers' ratings revealed no differences between the four groups. Confederates' ratings revealed only one significant difference between the dysphoric and the anxious groups: The dysphoric anxious students were rated as appearing more depressed by the confederate than were the nondysphoric anxious students. However, the depressed client group did not differ from the anxious students on any of the behavioral ratings. The authors concluded that dysphoric students and clients were more clearly different from generally anxious students in terms of negative expectancies prior to the interaction and negative self-evaluations following the interaction than in behavioral skill during the interaction.

Belsher and Costello (1991) compared depressed outpatients to a clinical comparison group composed primarily of anxiety-disordered patients and to nonpsychiatric controls. Observers rated the positivity or negativity of subjects' speech during a telephone conversation with a confidant (selected by the subject). A greater proportion of the speech of the depressed patients was judged to be depressotypic (i.e., to contain negative comments that were focused on themselves and their situations in life) than for either the psychiatric or the normal control group, who did not differ. No between-group differences emerged on nontopical, neutral, or antidepressotypic speech. Interestingly, the confidants echoed the speech of the subjects (i.e., the confidants of depressed patients were more likely to engage in depressotypic speech).

Two studies compared groups of students representing all combinations of dysphoria and *social* anxiety. Both of these studies examined patterns of self-disclosure displayed by the four groups. Jacobson and Anderson (1982) examined the conversations of subjects interacting with a confederate (believed to be another student) while the two were ostensibly waiting for a laboratory task to begin. Subjects' verbalizations were coded into eight categories. The only difference in verbal behavior was that dysphoric students emitted more negative (self-critical) self-statements than the nondysphoric groups. An examination of sequencing of responses revealed that the dysphoric students were significantly more likely to reciprocate confederate self-disclosure and to emit unsolicited self-disclosures than their nondysphoric counterparts. The socially anxious subjects did not differ from the control group.

Meleshko and Alden (in preparation) used the classic self-disclosure reciprocity paradigm in which subjects responded to intimate or nonintimate confederate disclosures. The disclosures of both dysphoric groups (socially anxious and nonanxious) were more intimate and more negative in valence than those of control subjects in response to both the intimate and the nonintimate confederate. The socially anxious nondysphoric subjects, however, disclosed at a moderate level of intimacy regardless of the intimacy of their partner's disclosure, a pattern that replicated the earlier Meleshko and Alden (1993) finding. These results indicated that both dysphoric and socially anxious people self-disclose in a dysfunctional manner, but that the pattern of dysfunction is different. Interestingly, the different patterns of disclosure elicited different partner reactions. Partners displayed an ambivalent response to the disclosures of dysphoric subjects (i.e., they reported increases in both positive and negative affect). Partners of socially anxious subjects were more consistently negative: They reported increases in negative affect only and were less willing to interact with the socially anxious subjects in the future. Finally, this study found some support for synergistic effects of dysphoria and social anxiety. Subjects who were both dysphoric and socially anxious shared with dysphoric subjects the tendency to disclosure in an overly intimate, negative manner and shared with socially anxious subjects the tendency to experience high levels of physiological arousal during the interaction.

All four of these behavioral studies indicated that depressed people are characterized by negative, or "depressotypic," verbal behavior in contrast to either anxious or nonsymptomatic people. The weakest support came from the Dow and Craighead (1987) study, but even in this study the depressed groups were perceived as more depressed by their conversational partners than were anxious subjects. Evidence of dysfunctional social behavior in anxious people was mixed. Two studies found no differences between generally anxious (Belsher & Costello, 1991) or socially anxious (Jacobson & Anderson, 1982) people and control subjects. However, the focus in these two studies was primarily on depression, and the dependent measures may not have been sensitive to the subtle behavioral patterns found in socially anxious individuals. One study found that generally anxious students were rated by their conversational partners as less skilled than control subjects. On the other hand, these anxious subjects did not differ from controls on five other ratings (Dow & Craighead, 1987). Finally, one study found clear evidence for a distinct pattern of interpersonal behavior in socially anxious students (Meleshko & Alden, in preparation). It is clear that more comparative analyses are necessary to identify aspects of interpersonal behavior unique to socially anxious populations.

CONCLUSIONS

Our objective in this chapter was to examine depression and anxiety from an interpersonal perspective to determine whether these conditions are associated with distinctive cognitive and behavioral reactions to interpersonal situations. Overall, empirical studies paint a somewhat different picture for cognitive variables than for behavioral ones. The overwhelming majority of studies of cognitive factors find that both depressed and socially anxious groups are characterized by negative cognitions before, during, and after social situations, are less adept at solving social problems, and generally process social information in a way that accentuates negative views of self and others' response to self. In addition, the comparative literature clearly indicates that different combinations of depression and social anxiety are associated with cognitive patterns that differ in severity or in content. In particular, people who complain of both depression and social anxiety display more negative and perhaps more dysfunctional cognitive reactions to social stimuli than people with either complaint alone (Ingram, 1989a, 1989b). Future work has to consider the synergistic effects of depression and anxiety.

Studies of overt interpersonal behavior are less consistent in that some studies find distinct behavioral patterns associated with depression or social anxiety and others do not. However, if one examines studies in which behavioral differences are found to be associated with either condition, the picture that emerges is of two distinct behavioral patterns with some overlapping features. Both groups appear to impress others as low on social skill, and some work suggests that both groups display signs of behavioral inhibition, particularly in unfamiliar or ambiguous situations. However, depressed individuals are most consistently found to engage in negative verbal behavior. They derogate themselves, express their unhappy emotions, and, in general, appear to engage in self-preoccupied complaining. Some studies suggest that they are also more likely than control subjects to display anger toward others. Socially anxious and social phobic individuals, on the other hand, display a more consistent pattern of behavioral inhibition and, when forced to interact, behave in ways designed to protect themselves from attention and potential criticism (e.g., agreeing, disclosing at moderate levels of intimacy, avoiding strong positions). Few comparative studies have focused on the behavioral patterns associated with social anxiety. Virtually no empirical

work has examined the possibility of synergistic effects of depression and
social anxiety on interpersonal behavior. However, one recent study suggests
this may be an avenue for future work (Meleshko & Alden, in preparation).

One issue that will require consideration in future studies is the existence
of interpersonal subtypes within each of these conditions. A number of
writers suggest that a distinction can be made between depressive states that
are related to interpersonal dependency and those related to self-criticism.
Furthermore, recent work indicates that dependent and self-critical depressives may display distinct interpersonal patterns (e.g., Blatt & Zuroff, 1992;
Robins & Luten, 1991). Similarly, the literature on social anxiety contains
frequent distinctions between skilled and unskilled shy, anxious, or social
phobic individuals. The unskilled variant is marked by overt signs of behavioral awkwardness and inhibition, whereas the skilled variant is marked
primarily by negative cognitions. One difficulty facing researchers is how to
consider these and other subtypes of depression and anxiety in the same
empirical studies without resorting to multiple, probably overlapping, groups.
We suggest that conceptual models from the Interpersonal school may
provide the type of overarching framework necessary to identify the cognitive-behavioral patterns associated with depression and with social anxiety
(see Alden et al., in preparation).

REFERENCES

Ahrens, A. H., Zeiss, A. M., & Kanfer, R. (1988). Dysphoric deficits in interpersonal
    standards, self-efficacy, and social comparison. *Cognitive Therapy and Research, 12,*
    53-67.
Aimes, P. L., Gelder, M. C., & Shaw, P. M. (1983). Social phobia: A comparative clinical
    study. *British Journal of Psychiatry, 142,* 174-179.
Alden, L. E. (1987). Attributional responses of anxious individuals to different patterns of
    social feedback: Nothing succeeds like improvement. *Journal of Personality and
    Social Psychology, 52,* 100-106.
Alden, L. E., Bieling, P. J., & Meleshko, K. G. A. (in preparation). *A comparison of the
    interpersonal beliefs and behaviors of depressed and socially anxious people as
    viewed from the perspective of Interpersonal theory.* University of British Columbia,
    Vancouver.
Alden, L. E., Bieling, P. J., & Wallace, S. T. (1994). Perfectionism in an interpersonal context:
    A self-regulation analysis of social anxiety and dysphoria. *Cognitive Therapy and
    Research, 18,* 297-316.
Alden, L. E., & Phillips, N. (1990). An interpersonal analysis of social anxiety and depres-
    sion. *Cognitive Therapy and Research, 14,* 499-513.

Anderson, C. A., & Arnoult, L. H. (1985). Attributional style and everyday problems in living: Depression, loneliness and shyness. *Social Cognition, 3,* 16-35.

Anderson, C. A., Horowitz, L. M., & French, R. D. (1983). Attributional style of lonely and depressed people. *Journal of Personality and Social Psychology, 45,* 127-136.

Arkin, R. M., Lake, E. A., & Baumgardner, A. H. (1986). Shyness and self-presentation. In W. H. Jones, J. M. Cheek, & S. R. Briggs (Eds.), *Shyness: Perspectives on research and treatment* (pp. 189-203). New York: Plenum.

Arkowitz, H., Lichtenstein, E., McGovern, K., & Hines, P. (1975). The behavioral assessment of social competence in males. *Behavior Therapy, 5,* 3-13.

Beck, A. T. (1976). *Cognitive therapy for the emotional disorders.* New York: International Universities Press.

Beck, A. T., Brown, G., Steer, R. A., Eidelson, J. I., & Riskind, J. H. (1987). Differentiating anxiety and depression: A test of the cognitive content-specificity hypothesis. *Journal of Abnormal Psychology, 96,* 179-183.

Beck, A. T., & Emery, G. (1985). *Anxiety disorders and phobias: A cognitive perspective.* New York: Basic Books.

Belsher, G., & Costello, C. G. (1991). Do confidants of depressed women provide less social support than confidants of non-depressed women? *Journal of Abnormal Psychology, 199,* 516-525.

Biglan, A., Hops, H., Sherman, L., Friedman, L. S., Arthur, J., & Osteen, V. (1985). Problem-solving interactions of depressed women and their husbands. *Behavior Therapy, 16,* 431-451.

Blatt, S. J., & Zuroff, D. C. (1992). Interpersonal relatedness and self-definition: Two prototypes for depression. *Clinical Psychology Review, 12,* 527-562.

Blumberg, S. R., & Hokanson, J. E. (1983). The effects of another person's response style on interpersonal behavior in depression. *Journal of Abnormal Psychology, 92,* 196-209.

Borden, J. W., & Baum, C. G. (1987). Investigation of a social-interactional model of depression with mildly depressed males and females. *Sex Roles, 17,* 449-465.

Borkovec, T. D., Stone, N. M., O'Brien, G. T., & Kaloupek, D. G. (1974). Evaluation of a clinically relevant target behavior for analog outcome research. *Behavior Therapy, 5,* 503-513.

Bruch, M. A., Gorsky, J. M., Collins, T. M., & Berger, P. A. (1989). Shyness and sociability reexamined: A multicomponent analysis. *Journal of Personality and Social Psychology, 57,* 904-915.

Bruch, M. A., Mattia, J. I., Heimberg, R. G., & Holt, C. S. (1993). Cognitive specificity in social anxiety and depression: Supporting evidence and qualifications due to affective confounding. *Cognitive Therapy and Research, 17,* 1-21.

Cacioppo, J. T., Glass, C. R., & Merluzzi, T. V. (1979). Self-statements and self-evaluations: A cognitive-response analysis of heterosocial anxiety. *Cognitive and Research, 3,* 249-262.

Capreol, M. J., & Alden, L. E. (1993). *Anxiety sensitivity and dysfunctional interpersonal beliefs in agoraphobic and social phobic outpatients.* Manuscript submitted for publication.

Carson, R. C. (1969). *Interaction concepts of personality.* Chicago: Aldine.

Clark, J. V., & Arkowitz, H. (1975). Social anxiety and self-evaluation of interpersonal performance. *Psychological Reports, 36,* 211-221.

Cloitre, M., Heimberg, R. G., Liebowitz, M. R., & Gitow, A. (1992). Perceptions of control in panic disorder and social phobia. *Cognitive Therapy and Research, 16,* 569-577.

Coyne, J. C. (1976). Toward an interactional description of depression. *Psychiatry, 39,* 28-40.

Curran, J. P., & Gilbert, F. S. (1975). A test of the relative effectiveness of a systematic desensitization program and an interpersonal skills training program with date anxious subjects. *Behavior Therapy, 6,* 510-521.

Curran, J. P., Wallander, J. L., & Fischetti, M. (1980). The importance of behavioral and cognitive factors in heterosexual-social anxiety. *Journal of Personality, 48,* 285-292.

DePaulo, B. M., Epstein, J. A., & LeMay, C. S. (1990). Responses of the socially anxious to the prospect of interpersonal evaluation. *Journal of Personality, 58,* 623-640.

Dobson, K. S. (1989). Real and perceived interpersonal response to subclinically anxious and depressed targets. *Cognitive Therapy and Research, 13,* 37-47.

Dodge, C. S., Hope, D. A., Heimberg, R. G., & Becker, R. E. (1988). Evaluation of the social interaction self-statement test with a social phobic population. *Cognitive Therapy and Research, 12,* 211-222.

Dow, M. G., & Craighead, W. E. (1987). Social inadequacy and depression: Overt behavior and self-evaluation processes. *Journal of Social and Clinical Psychology, 5,* 99-113.

Ducharme, J., & Bachelor, A. (1993). Perception of social functioning in dysphoria. *Cognitive Therapy and Research, 17,* 53-70.

Edelmann, R. J. (1985). Dealing with embarrassing events: Socially anxious and non-socially anxious groups compared. *British Journal of Clinical Psychology, 24,* 281-288.

Emmelkamp, P. M. G., Mersch, P. P., Vissia, E., & van der Helm, M. (1985). Social phobia: A comparative evaluation of cognitive and behavioral interventions. *Behaviour Research and Therapy, 23,* 365-369.

Girodo, M., Dotzenroth, S. E., & Stein, S. J. (1981). Causal attribution bias in shy males: Implications for self-esteem and self-confidence. *Cognitive Therapy and Research, 5,* 325-338.

Glasgow, R. E., & Arkowitz, H. (1975). The behavioral assessment of male and female social competence in dyadic heterosexual interactions. *Behavior Therapy, 6,* 488-498.

Glass, C. R., Merluzzi, T. V., Biever, J. I., & Larsen, K. H. (1982). Cognitive assessment of social anxiety: Development and validation of a self-statement questionnaire. *Cognitive Therapy and Research, 6,* 37-55.

Goldfried, M. R., Padawer, W., & Robins, C. (1984). Social anxiety and the semantic structure of heterosocial interactions. *Journal of Abnormal Psychology, 93,* 87-97.

Gotlib, I. H. (1983). Perception and recall of interpersonal feedback: Negative bias in depression. *Cognitive Therapy and Research, 7,* 399-412.

Gotlib, I. H., & Asarnow, R. F. (1979). Interpersonal and impersonal problem-solving skills in mildly and clinically depressed university students. *Journal of Consulting and Clinical Psychology, 47,* 86-95.

Gotlib, I. H., & Meltzer, S. J. (1987). Depression and the perception of social skill in dyadic interaction. *Cognitive Therapy and Research, 11,* 41-54.

Gotlib, I. H., & Robinson, L. A. (1982). Responses to depressed individuals: Discrepancies between self-report and observer rated behavior. *Journal of Abnormal Psychology, 9,* 231-240.

Hammen, C. (1991). Generation of stress in the course of unipolar depression. *Journal of Abnormal Psychology, 100,* 555-561.

Hautzinger, M., Linden, M., & Hoffman, N. (1982). Distressed couples with and without a depressed partner: An analysis of their verbal interaction. *Journal of Behaviour Therapy and Experimental Psychiatry, 13,* 307-314.

Heimberg, R. (1991). *Cognitive behavioral treatment of social phobia in a group setting: A treatment manual.* Albany, NY: Center for Stress and Anxiety Disorders.

Heimberg, R. G., Hope, D. A., Dodge, C. S., & Becker, R. E. (1990). DSM-III-R subtypes of social phobia: Comparison of generalized social phobics and public speaking phobics. *Journal of Nervous and Mental Disease, 178,* 172-179.

Hinchliffe, M., Hooper, D., Roberts, F. J., & Vaughan, P. W. (1975). A study of the interaction between depressed patients and their spouses. *British Journal of Psychiatry, 126,* 164-172.

Hokanson, J. E., & Meyer, B. E. (1984). Interpersonal expectancies and preferences for various types of social behaviours of depressed outpatients. *Journal of Personal and Social Relationships, 1,* 279-292.

Hokanson, J. E., Sacco, W. P., Blumberg, S. R., & Landrum, G. C. (1980). Interpersonal behavior of depressive individuals in a mixed-motive game. *Journal of Abnormal Psychology, 89,* 320-332.

Hollander, G. R., & Hokanson, J. E. (1988). Dysphoria and the perception of incongruent communications. *Cognitive Therapy and Research, 12,* 577-589.

Hollon, S. D., & Kendall, P. C. (1980). Cognitive self-statements in depression: Development of an automatic thoughts questionnaire. *Cognitive Therapy and Research, 4,* 383-395.

Hope, D. A., Rapee, R. M., Heimberg, R. G., & Dombeck, M. J. (1990). Representations of the self in social phobia: Vulnerability to social threat. *Cognitive Therapy and Research, 14,* 177-189.

Horowitz, L. M., & Vitkus, J. (1986). The interpersonal basis of psychiatric symptoms. *Clinical Psychology Review, 6,* 443-469.

Ingram, R. E. (1989a). Affective confounds in social-cognitive research. *Journal of Personality and Social Psychology, 57,* 715-722.

Ingram, R. E. (1989b). Unique and shared cognitive factors in social anxiety and depression: Automatic thinking and self-appraisal. *Journal of Social and Clinical Psychology, 8,* 198-208.

Ingram, R. E., & Wisnicki, R. (1988). Assessment of positive automatic cognition. *Journal of Consulting and Clinical Psychology, 56,* 898-902.

Jacobson, N. S., & Anderson, E. A. (1982). Interpersonal skill and depression in college students: An analysis of the timing of self-disclosures. *Behavior Therapy, 13,* 271-282.

Jones, W. H., & Briggs, S. R. (1984). The self-other discrepancy in social shyness. In R. Schwarzer (Ed.), *The self in anxiety, stress, and depression* (pp. 93-107). Amsterdam: North Holland.

Kahn, J., Coyne, J. C., & Margolin, G. (1985). Depression and marital disagreement: The social construction of despair. *Journal of Social and Personal Relationships, 2,* 447-461.

Kanfer, R., & Zeiss, A. M. (1983). Standards and self-efficacy in depression. *Journal of Abnormal Psychology, 92,* 319-329.

Kiesler, D. J. (1983). The 1982 Interpersonal Circle: A taxonomy for complementarity in human transactions. *Psychological Review, 90,* 185-214.

Kowalik, D. L., & Gotlib, I. H. (1987). Depression and marital interaction: Concordance between intent and perception of communication. *Journal of Abnormal Psychology, 96,* 127-134.

Kupke, T. E., Hobbs, S. A., & Cheney, T. H. (1979). Selection of heterosocial skills: I. Criterion-related validity. *Behavior Therapy, 10,* 327-335.

Leary, M. R., Knight, P. D., & Johnson, K. A. (1987). Social anxiety and dyadic conversation: A verbal response analysis. *Journal of Social and Clinical Psychology, 5,* 34-50.

Lewinsohn, P. M., Mischel, W., Chaplin, W., & Barton, R. (1980). Social competence and depression: The role of illusory self-perceptions. *Journal of Abnormal Psychology, 89,* 203-212.

Libet, J. M., & Lewinsohn, P. M. (1973). Concept of social skill with special reference to the behavior of depressed persons. *Journal of Consulting and Clinical Psychology, 40,* 304-312.

Lucock, M. P., & Salkovskis, P. M. (1988). Cognitive factors in social anxiety and its treatment. *Behaviour Research and Therapy, 4,* 297-302.

Marx, E. M., Claridge, G. C., & Williams, J. M. (1992). Depression and social problem solving. *Journal of Abnormal Psychology, 10,* 78-86.

Meleshko, K. G., & Alden, L. E. (1993). Anxiety and self-disclosure: Toward a motivational model. *Journal of Personality and Social Psychology, 64,* 1000-1009.

Meleshko, K. G., & Alden, L. E. (in preparation). *Self-disclosure in dysphoric and anxious individuals: Evidence for specificity of dysfunctional interpersonal patterns.*

Millon, T. M. (1981). *Disorders of personality: DSM III: Axis II.* New York: John Wiley.

Nelson, G. M., & Beach, S. R. H. (1990). Sequential interaction in depression: Effects of depressive behavior on spousal aggression. *Behavior Therapy, 21,* 167-182.

O'Banion, K., & Arkowitz, H. (1977). Social anxiety and selective memory for affective information about the self. *Social Behavior and Personality, 5,* 321-328.

Persson, G., & Nordlund, C. L. (1985). Agoraphobics and social phobics: Differences in background factors, syndrome profiles, and therapeutic response. *Acta Psychiatrica Scandinavica, 71,* 148-159.

Pietromonaco, P. R., Rook, K. S., & Lewis, M. A. (1992). Accuracy in perceptions of interpersonal interactions: Effects of dysphoria, friendship, and similarity. *Journal of Personality and Social Psychology, 63,* 247-259.

Pilkonis, P. A. (1977). The behavioral consequences of shyness. *Journal of Personality, 45,* 596-611.

Rapee, R. M., & Lim, L. (1992). Discrepancy between self- and observer ratings of performance in social phobics. *Journal of Abnormal Psychology, 101,* 728-731.

Rapee, R. M., Sanderson, W. C., & Barlow, D. H. (1988). Social phobia features across the DSM-III-R anxiety disorders. *Journal of Psychopathology and Behavioral Assessment, 10,* 287-299.

Robins, C. J., & Luten, A. G. (1991). Sociotropy and autonomy: Differential patterns of clinical presentation in unipolar depression. *Journal of Abnormal Psychology, 100,* 74-77.

Schlenker, B. R., & Leary, M. R. (1982). Social anxiety and self-presentation: A conceptualization and model. *Psychological Bulletin, 92,* 641-669.

Shea, M. T., Glass, D. R., Pilkonis, P. A., Watkins, J., & Docherty, J. P. (1987). Frequency and implications of personality disorders in a sample of depressed outpatients. *Journal of Personality Disorders, 1,* 27-42.

Stopa, L., & Clark, D. M. (1993). Cognitive processes in social phobia. *Behaviour Research and Therapy, 31,* 255-267.

Strack, S., & Coyne, J. C. (1983). Social confirmation of dysphoria: Shared and private reactions of depression. *Journal of Personality and Social Psychology, 44,* 798-806.

Strauman, T. J. (1989). Self-discrepancies in clinical depression and social phobia: Cognitive structures that underlie emotional disorders? *Journal of Abnormal Psychology, 98,* 14-22.

Strauman, T. J., & Higgins, E. T. (1988). Self-discrepancies as predictors of vulnerability to distinct syndromes of chronic emotional distress. *Journal of Personality, 56,* 685-707.

Strupp, H. H., & Binder, J. L. (1984). *Psychotherapy in a new key.* New York: Basic Books.

Swann, W. B., Wenzlaff, R. M., Krull, D. S., & Pelham, B. W. (1992). Allure of negative feedback: Self-verification strivings among depressed persons. *Journal of Abnormal Psychology, 101,* 293-306.

Teglasi, H., & Fagin, S. S. (1984). Social anxiety and the self-other biases in causal attribution. *Journal of Research in Personality, 18,* 64-80.

Trower, P., & Turland, O. (1984). Social phobia. In S. Turner (Ed.), *Behavioral theories and treatment of anxiety* (pp. 141-157). New York: Plenum.

Turner, S. M., Beidel, D. C., Dancu, D. V., & Keys, D. J. (1986). Psychopathology of social phobia and comparison to avoidant personality disorder. *Journal of Abnormal Psychology, 95,* 389-394.

Turner, S. M., Beidel, D. C., & Larkin, K. T. (1986). Situational determinants of social anxiety in clinic and non-clinic samples: Physiological and cognitive correlates. *Journal of Consulting and Clinical Psychology, 54,* 523-527.

Wallace, S. T., & Alden, L. E. (1991). A comparison of social standards and perceived ability in anxious and nonanxious men. *Cognitive Therapy and Research, 15,* 237-254.

Watson, D., & Clark, L. A. (1984). Negative affectivity: The disposition to experience aversive emotional states. *Psychological Bulletin, 96,* 465-490.

Youngren, M. A., & Lewinsohn, P. M. (1980). The functional relation between depression and problematic interpersonal behavior. *Journal of Abnormal Psychology, 89,* 333-341.

4

The Social Context of Risk for Depression

CONSTANCE HAMMEN

R esearch in depression has progressed enormously in the past 25 years since this conference series began. There have been significant developments in treatment, including the introduction and empirical validation of brief psychotherapies for patients who were formerly considered too difficult or unrewarding, as well as proliferation of antidepressant medications. There have also been important diagnostic refinements and decisions that have shaped our field, including the unipolar-bipolar distinction, the recognition of clinical depression in children and adolescents, and the recognition that despite heterogeneity, use of clear criteria for major depression has greatly improved our research methods (topics reviewed in Gotlib & Hammen, 1992).

These achievements in diagnosis and treatment are equaled by what we have discovered about the phenomenology and correlates of depression—and this information in turn requires us to alter our theories to be consistent with the facts about this disorder. Some of the key attributes of depression that must be considered by theories are the following.

1. *Depression affects lives.* Not only does the afflicted person experience the subjective and biological symptoms of depression, but his or her ability to function in important roles is greatly impaired. Ample evidence documents the disruption of parental and marital roles (e.g., reviewed in Barnett &

Gotlib, 1988; Downey & Coyne, 1990; Gotlib & Hammen, 1992). Occupational functioning is commonly disrupted as well. Overall, depressed people—even those whose symptoms are relatively mild rather than severe—report subjective distress, impaired functioning, and days spent in bed at levels that are greater than those of individuals with major forms of chronic medical illness (Wells et al., 1989). Disrupted lives that result from depression doubtless contribute to further depression and demoralization.

2. *Depression is recurrent.* It is increasingly recognized that most people who experience a major depressive episode will have multiple episodes. It has been estimated that at least 85% of depressed individuals have more than one major depression (Keller, 1985) and that the average treatment-seeking depressed person will have five or six. In addition, a substantial proportion of depressed people—about 25 to 30%—have chronic symptoms (Depue & Monroe, 1986; Keller, Lavori, Rice, Coryell, & Hirschfeld, 1986). The extent of symptomatology, of course, is likely to be strongly associated with the extent of impairment and disruption in the patients' lives.

A corollary of the extent of recurrence and chronicity is that most studies of depression are about relapse, rather than about initial onset. Indeed, new onsets of depression are relatively rare compared to depression in those who have already been depressed.

3. *Depression is heterogeneous.* It is assumed that there are different subtypes of depression—both in symptom profile and in etiology. On the other hand, distinctions such as endogenous-reactive, melancholic-nonmelancholic, and others have met with relatively little success in terms of causal factors, phenomenology, or treatment outcomes (reviewed in Gotlib & Hammen, 1992). Although we accept on faith the assumption of different subtypes, relatively little productive research has illuminated this topic. Meanwhile, many theories of depression seem to intend application to all types.

4. *Comorbidity is typical in depression,* as it is in many disorders. For instance, anxiety disorders, alcoholism, and personality disorders are extremely common among those with diagnosed depression. Nevertheless, the meaning of such covariation is rarely considered by depression models. Moreover, many if not most research studies fail to consider the implications of coexisting disorders for the hypotheses or phenomena under study and may not even report their existence.

A related topic is the relative neglect of the question of specificity of depression models. Are they really only about depression, or might they apply more generally, or jointly, to depression and anxiety? Questions like these are increasingly appropriate to the stage of development of our knowledge of depression and need to be vigorously pursued.

5. *Depression primarily affects women and youth.* The extent to which more women than men experience and seek help for depression has been well documented (e.g., Nolen-Hoeksema, 1990). Obviously, theoretical models must be able to account for the differences. In addition, models need to explain the apparent gender divergence in early adolescence, after a period in which boys and girls generally have similar rates of depression.

In addition to the sex differences, age-related patterns are increasingly demanding attention. It seems that rates of depression are increasing in young people and that many depressions have an onset in adolescence (Burke, Burke, Regier, & Rae, 1990; Klerman & Weissman, 1989). Important demographic patterns such as sex and age require models of depression that can take broad contextual factors into account, rather than relying on simple intraindividual factors, whether they be neuroendocrinological or cognitive.

Elsewhere I have argued that when we develop models of depression, they need to be limited to specific types of depression because of its heterogeneity, and focused on different aspects of the course of depression because the predictors of first onset may be somewhat different from those concerning relapse (Gotlib & Hammen, 1992). Consequently it is fair to say that most of the focus of my work is on recurrent depression and on those who suffer from chronic and relapsing courses. Our program of research is oriented toward questions of how the depressed person's life is affected by depression and how in turn such disruptions contribute to further depression. In addition, our work is currently focused on questions relevant to why young people— and especially women—are at risk.

TOWARD A COGNITIVE-INTERPERSONAL
MODEL OF DEPRESSION

This is really a shorthand title for a model that is more accurately termed a multifactorial, transactional, transgenerational, cognitive/life stress/interpersonal model of depression. In order to be congruent with realities about recurrent affective disorder, psychological models have had to become increasingly complex. Also, they have had to become increasingly *interpersonal,* in my view. My own work has evolved to focus increasingly on the social context of depression and the cognitions and skills that affect interpersonal functioning. I draw most of my conclusions and hypotheses about depression risk from a variety of studies we have conducted over the past 15 years and currently. All are longitudinal studies that included extensive "contextual threat" interviewing (Brown & Harris, 1978) to determine episodic and chronic life events so that we got to know the context of people's lives quite intimately. These included studies of unipolar outpatients, children of mothers with affective disorders, and young women (late adolescents) at potential risk for depression.

Why focus on interpersonal features of depression? When we ask nondepressed people what would be the most depressing event that could happen to them, or when we study the lives of depressed people and the events that appear to trigger episodes, by far the most common theme is interpersonal. There is a particular, nearly universal, vulnerability to the loss of close relationships. This pattern has been noticed for 2,500 years—and I think we need to take it more seriously. I am going to argue that although most people would have at least mild and brief depressive responses to an important loss, some people are highly sensitized to such experiences as a result of dysfunctions in their ability to elicit and maintain stable, secure connections with others, they experience increased vulnerability to depression.

The focus on interpersonal aspects of depression is instigated and supported by numerous observations of other investigators (e.g., reviewed in Barnett & Gotlib, 1988). It also emerges from much of the work that our group has conducted over the past 15 years. In the sections that follows, some of this work is reviewed and discussed in the form of three propositions that, in my view, capture key elements of a model of depression.

DEPRESSION RUNS IN FAMILIES

There are several themes to emphasize about depression risk. The first proposition is: *For most people, recurring depression arises in a family context; for many depressed people the origins of their depression vulnerability are in childhood experiences.*

Depression runs in families. This was the title of one of my recent books, based on a study of children of depressed women compared with children of bipolar, medically ill, and normal women (Hammen, 1991a). Our study found that children of women with affective disorders were at enormous risk for developing significant disorders—especially the children of women with recurrent unipolar depression. Nearly 70% of these 8- to 16-year-old off-spring developed a major depressive episode at some point, and many also had significant behavioral problems such as conduct disorder, substance abuse problems, and anxiety disorders (Hammen et al., 1987; Hammen, Burge, Burney, & Adrian, 1990). Our research is certainly consistent with that of other investigators indicating substantial risk if a parent is depressed (see reviews by Downey & Coyne, 1990; Weissman, 1988).

In our study the depressed mothers themselves had high rates of parental depression, especially in their mothers. Forty percent had mothers treated for depression—but they also had high rates of psychopathology in general in their parents; fully 88% of the depressed mothers in our sample had at least one diagnosable parent (Hammen, 1991a).

In our current study of late adolescent women, we have found quite incidentally (because they were not selected for parental disorder) that the depressed young women in our sample were significantly more likely to have depressed mothers than were the nondepressed women. In addition to in-creased past depression compared to daughters of nondepressed mothers, daughters of depressed mothers were also significantly more depressed during a 6-month follow-up.

In yet a different study—the longitudinal follow-up of unipolar depressed outpatients—we also found that parental psychopathology (both affective and nonaffective disorders) played an important role in the severity of patients' episodes (Hammen, Davila, Brown, Ellicott, & Gitlin, 1992). The effect appeared to occur because it caused early onset of patients' disorders that in turn diminished patients' abilities to avoid or to resolve stressful circumstances appropriately.

Thus depression runs in families. This is likely to be more true for those with recurrent depression. Hence family history of depression must be considered a substantial risk factor. Although genetic contribution may play a role in trans-mission of depression risk, we emphasize that people inherit not only genes but also environments. Our offspring study focused extensively on the environments that may contribute to intergenerational transmission. Two specific elements, stress and mother-child interactions, were particular ob-jects of investigation. Both unipolar mothers and their children experienced highly stressful environments, both in episodic and chronic stressors, com-pared to the other groups (Adrian & Hammen, 1993; Hammen, 1991b). In terms of mother-child interactions, the following findings emerged.

1. On the basis of observations of a brief conflict discussion task, unipolar depressed mothers were significantly more negative (critical and disconfirming) toward their children, less positive, and less involved in the task than mothers in the other groups (Gordon et al., 1989).

2. The mothers' negativity toward their children was significantly related to their current and past contexts. Specifically, current chronic stress and dysphoric mood, as well as the children's own interaction styles, contributed to maternal behavior (Hammen, Burge, & Stansbury, 1990). Negativity was especially predicted by chronic stress, and current depressed mood predicted less involvement in the task (Burge & Hammen, 1991). Also, there were significant correlations between the mother's own family loading for psychopathology and maternal negativity and low task productivity (Hammen, 1991b). This suggests a possible association between quality of the current parent-child relationship and the likely quality of the mother's past relationship with her own parents.

3. The patterns of mother-child relationship quality suggest not just maternal dysfunction in parenting skills but rather a reciprocal relationship between mother and child behaviors. For example, negativity in the mothers typically correlated with negativity in the child. Many of the youngsters were very disturbed and difficult and probably overwhelmed their mothers' capabilities to deal with them. Also, there was no evidence that depressed women were uniformly negative and intolerant toward their children, as simplistic cognitive distortion models might predict. If anything, the distortions occurred in the nondepressed mothers, in that the latter were inaccurate in their perceptions of their children's problems when the children actually had problems. In contrast, depressed mothers accurately discriminated between well and dysfunctional children (Conrad & Hammen, 1989). Moreover, women interacted with their children consistently with their reports of children's problems. Those who saw their child as normal and healthy interacted with him or her in significantly more positive ways than if they saw the child as dysfunctional. Thus depressed women were not indiscriminately ineffective in interacting with their children but had much greater difficulty with their difficult children.

4. Negativity in the mother-child relationship, both as observed and as reported by the children, was associated with negative self-concept in the children (Jaenicke et al., 1987). Thus negative relations with the mother take a toll on the child's self-esteem. There was a significant direct relationship between the child's self-critical communications and the mother's negative, critical comments toward the child.

In addition to its effects on self-esteem, poor quality of mother-child interactions was associated with greater symptomatology in the child and greater psychosocial impairment in school and academic performance (Burge & Hammen, 1991; Hammen, Burge, & Stansbury, 1990). Not only were there concurrent associations, but also maternal quality of interacting predicted child dysfunction at a later follow-up.

5. We characterize the mothers and children as having considerable impact on each other's well-being. Not only did we see reciprocation of negativity in the interaction task and an influence of maternal communication style on children's adjustment, but we determined that there was a significant temporal association between maternal and child episodes over the longitudinal course of our study (up to 3 years) (Hammen, Burge, & Adrian, 1991). That is, when one would have an increase in symptomatology (typically depression), it would be followed by an increase in symptoms in the other. Although the exact mechanisms of such temporally linked patterns are unknown, the patterns clearly reflect the impact each party has on the other.

What conclusions may be drawn overall? Families with depressed parents contribute dysfunctional climates for children to grow in. We think there are two main psychosocial attributes or consequences of this process: development of dysfunctional cognitions and skills that in turn create or contribute to stressful environments. This leads to a second proposition about depression risk.

DYSFUNCTIONAL COGNITIONS
AND RISK FOR DEPRESSION

The second proposition is that *depression risk is mediated by dysfunctional schemata about the self and others, and by maladaptive interpersonal skills, especially those related to social problem solving.*

Dysfunctional Schemata

Dysfunctional cognitions have been implicated in depression risk by a substantial body of evidence (e.g., see reviews in Barnett & Gotlib, 1988; Gotlib & Hammen, 1992; Haaga, Dyck, & Ernst, 1991). There are several ways in which cognitions are important in depression vulnerability. These include the link between interpretations of events and emotions, the acquisition of negativistic schemata and beliefs about the self and others, and the development of specific beliefs and attitudes about the importance of certain sources of self-worth.

With respect to the development of vulnerability schemata, in general, our work and that of others point to two conclusions. The first is that individuals may develop domains of particular centrality of self-worth, such that they are vulnerable to depression if negative events that are interpreted as depletions of important sources of esteem occur in that domain. Both psychodynamically and cognitively oriented theorists have identified the two major domains, sociotropy/dependency and achievement/autonomy (Arieti & Bemporad, 1980; Beck, 1983; Blatt, Quinlan, Chevron, McDonald, & Zuroff, 1982). Various studies, using different measures of the vulnerability constructs and assessments of stressors, have generally supported specific life event vulnerability (Hammen, Ellicott, Gitlin, & Jamison, 1989; Hammen, Marks, Mayol, & DeMayo, 1985; Robins, 1990; Robins & Block, 1988; Segal, Shaw, Vella, & Katz, 1992; Zuroff & Mongrain, 1987). Individuals appear to experience depression, or more severe depression, following events that match their vulnerability. It is presumed that such events are interpreted as losses of important sources of gratification and self-esteem, whereas other events—even if relatively negative—are construed as less threatening and therefore have less emotional consequence. The actual mechanisms, such as interpretations, have not been studied directly. Nevertheless, these studies indicate an important refinement in the simple life event-depression equation that predicted that depression occurs when negative events occur (see also Brown, Bifulco, & Harris, 1987, for a somewhat different approach to individual vulnerability to stressors).

The other finding, emerging from both life event-cognition matching studies and investigations of personality and attitudes in depressed people, is the apparent centrality of *dependency* or *sociotropic* attitudes. Many of the specific vulnerability studies noted above have reported stronger confirmation of hypotheses for sociotropic or dependent schemata. In addition, studies of personality characteristics of depressed people have consistently identified dependency as a stable trait in many unipolar patients (reviewed in Barnett & Gotlib, 1988). Although certainly not true of all depressives, it appears that a good many hold beliefs about the necessity of approval and nurturance from other people.

This raises an issue that has become a focus of some of our current research: Cognitions about the self and others, arising in the context of early parent-child relationships, may be vitally important aspects of depression vulnerability. Bowlby (1969, 1981) has termed such representations of early relationships "working models." A great deal of interest among developmental psychologists and developmental psychopathologists has arisen concerning the behavioral manifestations of "attachment" in young children, as well as its potential relevance to depression (reviewed in Cicchetti & Schneider-Rosen, 1986; Cummings & Cicchetti, 1990). However, cognitively oriented depression researchers would do well to seize a golden opportunity to measure and study such constructs from a cognitive perspective.

Although there has been some work on self-schemata, there has been very little work on cognitive representations of others that arise from the parent-child relationship. One of my UCLA students, Karen Rudolph, has attempted to devise ways of measuring such cognitions in children. She has found considerable evidence that negative representations of peers are closely related to negative representations of the child's mother and the self. In turn, negative representations of family support and peers are inversely related to teachers' ratings of prosocial behavior ($r = -.37$ and $r = -.47$, $p < .05$, respectively, for family and self ratings with teacher ratings) (Rudolph, 1992). Thus cognitive representations appear to be general across interpersonal domains and related to actual social behavior in children.

In our current work on depression risk in young women, we have also found that cognitive representations of attachment are predictive of symptomatology and are also related to quality of relationships with family and peers. That is, women who have attitudes of anxiety about abandonment or who believe that they cannot depend on other people or be close with others are showing difficulties in both symptoms and behaviors. These results are preliminary but strongly encourage us to continue studying cognitive vulnerability based on representations of others.

Maladaptive Interpersonal Problem Solving

The other part of the proposition is that dysfunctional social skills—especially interpersonal problem solving—may increase vulnerability to depression. Evidence from our research for this proposition is both indirect and direct. Indirect evidence comes from our offspring study and from our longitudinal outpatient studies indicating high levels of conflict-related events, especially in unipolar depressed patients. These findings are discussed more fully below. The occurrence of conflict events in part reflects a failure to resolve disagreements, and it may be hypothesized that failure to resolve disagreements may result from poor interpersonal negotiation skills.

Direct evidence of poor social problem solving among those vulnerable to depression comes from observations of problem-solving situations. Rudolph's study of 8- to 12-year-old children found that the relatively depressed children were significantly more dysfunctional in their interactions with a nondepressed child in a conflict discussion task. In addition, lower levels of effective problem solving were highly associated with more negative representations of the family, peers, and the self.

Also, in our study of adolescent women, my student Joanne Davila measured interpersonal negotiation strategies in hypothetical situations. She found that avoidance as a problem-solving method was more characteristic of young women who endorsed more insecure attachment cognitions on subscales of an adult attachment scale (Davila, 1993). Also, Davila found that problem-solving ability was predictive of family-related stress 6 months later and that behavioral avoidance as a problem-solving strategy was especially predictive of later interpersonal stress.

There is a great deal of work left to do to understand further both the cognitions and the skills related to interpersonal functioning that might contribute to depression vulnerability. However, this appears to be a very promising area for further investigation.

STRESS GENERATION AND RISK FOR DEPRESSION

Why are cognitions and skills associated with interpersonal behaviors relevant to depression? This leads to a third major proposition: *Vulnerability to depression in part consists of stressful environments to which the person is exposed and that the person creates.*

Considerable research supports the link between negative life events and depressive reactions. Although most people do not become clinically depressed even when dreadful events occur, most depression results from negative events. However, most research on the link between stressors and depression has tested a linear model in which negative events lead to depression. Only recently have investigators come to emphasize the reciprocal relationship between the person and the environment. Coyne and others, for example, have stressed the negative impact of depressed people on others (e.g., reviewed in Coyne, Burchill, & Stiles, 1990). Considerable research supports the association between depression and divorce or marital conflict—some of which is doubtless due to the burden of trying to help and support a depressed spouse. Also, as noted earlier, research consistently indicates that being a depressed parent is associated with disorder and dysfunction in children (e.g., Hammen, 1991a). Clearly, therefore, being depressed has a potentially negative impact on one's social world that may lead to adverse events.

Stressful circumstances in general may also accompany recurrent depression. Our offspring study has emphasized the extent to which a diagnosis of depression is often confounded with chronic stress—due both to the symptomatology and disruption created by depression and to conditions that may have contributed to the depression. Thus typical adults with recurrent unipolar depression not only have chronic marital and parental difficulties but usually also suffer problems with employment or job performance and attendant financial difficulties. Many also have chronic or intermittent medical problems. Clearly, therefore, they face real stressors that are difficult to cope with—especially if they are depressed (with negative expectations about adequacy and efficacy and low energy) and are unskilled in resolving difficulties. Thus those with chronic or recurrent depression commonly find themselves in difficult circumstances.

There is also the issue of what may be termed *stress generation*. This term refers to those negative life events that are dependent at least in part on the person's behaviors and characteristics—in contrast to independent events, sometimes called "fateful." Our longitudinal studies of patients, families, and high-risk subjects employ the contextual threat procedure for interviewing about circumstances as well as judging the significance and independence of events (based on procedures of Brown & Harris, 1978). On the basis of these methods, we have determined that a considerable proportion of stressful life events may be judged to have been caused at least in part by the depressed person's behaviors or characteristics. For instance, an analysis of events in a 1-year period among unipolar outpatients determined that 60% of stressors were contributed in part by the person.

Exploring this issue further, Hammen (1991b) compared the demographically similar women in the offspring study. Unipolar women had more dependent events than the other groups; they also experienced more interpersonal events, a subcategory of dependent events. Of particular note, conflict events were significantly higher among the unipolar women than among women in the other groups—even those with bipolar disorder. Conflict events are the largest content category among the interpersonal events and refer to conflicts with spouses, boyfriends, children, and also teachers, neighbors, bosses, and others. Interestingly, a similar pattern occurred with the children of unipolar women: They reported not only high degrees of family conflict events but also high levels of peer conflict events (Adrian & Hammen, 1993).

What does the excess of conflict events in the lives of depressed women and their children mean? We speculate that conflict events occur because of dysfunctional cognitions about other people, as well as dysfunctional problem-solving skills. This arena provides a useful topic for further study and certainly indicates a potential area of therapeutic intervention.

Another element of stress generation is, of course, poor relationships with family members—spouses and children. Even beyond that, however, we observed, as others have, that more than half of the unipolar depressed mothers in our study married men who were themselves diagnosed—usually with a behavioral disorder such as antisocial personality disorder or substance abuse. Obviously, such marriages set the stage for potential disruption and marital conflict, potentially contributing to being a depressed parent.

This intriguing pattern stimulated my interest in how young women become depressed mothers. Consequently we have embarked on an investigation of women in late adolescence making the transition from high school to adulthood. One of the specific purposes is to learn more about *mate selection* and romantic relationship development. We are currently trying to understand the predictors of relationship satisfaction, as well as correlates of early marriage and even pregnancy. We view the period of adolescent to adult transition as a critical period in which young women may be faced with, or even create, environments that provide ongoing stressors and therefore the context for depression.

CONCLUSIONS

Certainly not all depression has its origins in childhood—although we do know that the majority of those reporting major depression indicate that it began in adolescence. Depression researchers have had to abandon overly simple main-effects models of stress, cognition, or family relations. Many cognitive theorists, in my view, have been reluctant to look beyond what is going on inside the person. Moreover, we have been slow to conduct studies of the *origins* of depression vulnerability and to explore the stress context of depression. Although we have accumulated considerable knowledge about depression and how to treat it, I believe we have a long way to go to fully integrate elements of an intergenerational, contextual, transactive approach. Meanwhile, too, as the statistics mount concerning increasing incidence of depression in young people, I think we can also aim for preventive efforts as well as improvements in our therapeutic methods of dealing with recurrent depressions. Finally, we need to know a great deal more about interpersonal functioning: What is it that depressed people think and do in their relations with others, and how do disruptions of interpersonal bonds come to have such powerful effects on depression?

REFERENCES

Adrian, C., & Hammen, C. (1993). Stress exposure and stress generation in children of depressed mothers. *Journal of Consulting and Clinical Psychology, 61,* 354-359.

Arieti, S., & Bemporad, J. (1980). The psychological organization of depression. *American Journal of Psychiatry, 137,* 1360-1365.

Barnett, P. A., & Gotlib, I. H. (1988). Psychosocial functioning and depression: Distinguishing among antecedents, concomitants, and consequences. *Psychological Bulletin, 104,* 97-126.

Beck, A. T. (1983). Cognitive therapy of depression: New perspectives. In P. J. Clayton & J. E. Barrett (Eds.), *Treatment of depression: Old controversies and new approaches.* New York: Raven.

Blatt, S., Quinlan, D., Chevron, E., McDonald, C., & Zuroff, D. (1982). Dependency and self criticism: Psychological dimensions of depression. *Journal of Consulting and Clinical Psychology, 50,* 113-124.

Bowlby, J. (1969). *Attachment and loss: Vol. 1. Attachment.* New York: Basic Books.

Bowlby, J. (1981). *Attachment and loss: Vol. 3. Loss: Sadness and depression.* Harmondsworth, UK: Penguin.

Brown, G. W., Bifulco, A., & Harris, T. O. (1987). Life events, vulnerability and onset of depression: Some refinements. *British Journal of Psychiatry, 150,* 30-42.

Brown, G. W., & Harris, T. (1978). *Social origins of depression.* London: Free Press.

Burge, D., & Hammen, C. (1991). Maternal communication: Predictors of outcome at follow-up in a sample of children at high and low risk for depression. *Journal of Abnormal Psychology, 100,* 174-180.

Burke, K. C., Burke, J. D., Regier, D. A., & Rae, D. S. (1990). Age at onset of selected mental disorders in five community populations. *Archives of General Psychiatry, 47,* 511-518.

Cicchetti, D., & Schneider-Rosen, K. (1986). An organizational approach to childhood depression. In M. Rutter, C. E. Izard, & P. E. Read (Eds.), *Depression in young people* (pp. 71-134). New York: Guilford.

Conrad, M., & Hammen, C. (1989). Role of maternal depression in perceptions of child maladjustment. *Journal of Consulting and Clinical Psychology, 57,* 663-667.

Coyne, J. C., Burchill, S., & Stiles, W. (1990). An interactional perspective on depression. In C. R. Snyder & D. O. Forsyth (Eds.), *Handbook of social and clinical psychology: The health perspective* (pp. 327-349). New York: Pergamon.

Cummings, E. M., & Cicchetti, D. (1990). Attachment, depression, and the transmission of depression. In M. T. Greenberg, D. Cicchetti, & E. M. Cummings (Eds.), *Attachment during the preschool years* (pp. 339-372). Chicago: University of Chicago Press.

Davila, J. (1993). *Attachment, interpersonal problem-solving, and stress in depression: An integrated developmental approach.* Unpublished doctoral dissertation, University of California, Los Angeles.

Depue, R. A., & Monroe, S. M. (1986). Conceptualization and measurement of human disorder and life stress research: The problem of chronic disturbance. *Psychological Bulletin, 99,* 36-51.

Downey, G., & Coyne, J. C. (1990). Children of depressed parents: An integrative review. *Psychological Bulletin, 108,* 50-76.

Gordon, D., Burge, D., Hammen, C., Adrian, C., Jaenicke, C., & Hiroto, D. (1989). Observations of interactions of depressed women with their children. *American Journal of Psychiatry, 146,* 50-55.

Gotlib, I., & Hammen, C. (1992). *Psychological aspects of depression: Toward a cognitive-interpersonal integration.* Chichester, UK: John Wiley.

Haaga, D. A. F., Dyck, M. J., & Ernst, D. (1991). Empirical status of cognitive therapy of depression. *Psychological Bulletin, 110,* 215-236.

Hammen, C. (1991a). *Depression runs in families: The social context of risk and resilience in children of depressed mothers.* New York: Springer-Verlag.

Hammen, C. (1991b). The generation of stress in the course of unipolar depression. *Journal of Abnormal Psychology, 100,* 555-561.

Hammen, C., Burge, D., & Adrian, C. (1991). Timing of mother and child depression in a longitudinal study of children at risk. *Journal of Consulting and Clinical Psychology, 59,* 341-345.

Hammen, C., Burge, D., Burney, E., & Adrian, C. (1990). Longitudinal study of diagnoses in children of women with unipolar and bipolar affective disorder. *Archives of General Psychiatry, 47,* 1112-1117.

Hammen, C., Burge, D., & Stansbury, K. (1990). Relationship of mother and child variables to child outcomes in a high risk sample: A causal modeling analysis. *Developmental Psychology, 26,* 24-30.

Hammen, C., Davila, J., Brown, G., Ellicott, A., & Gitlin, M. (1992). Psychiatric history and stress: Stress as a mediator of the effects of psychiatric background on severity of unipolar depression. *Journal of Abnormal Psychology, 101,* 45-52.

Hammen, C., Ellicott, A., Gitlin, M., & Jamison, K. R. (1989). Sociotropy/autonomy and vulnerability to specific life events in unipolar and bipolar patients. *Journal of Abnormal Psychology, 98,* 154-160.

Hammen, C., Gordon, D., Burge, D., Adrian, C., Jaenicke, C., & Hiroto, D. (1987). Maternal affective disorders, illness, and stress: Risk for children's psychopathology. *American Journal of Psychiatry, 144,* 736-741.

Hammen, C., Marks, T., Mayol, A., & deMayo, R. (1985). Depressive self-schemas, life stress, and vulnerability to depression. *Journal of Abnormal Psychology, 94,* 308-319.

Jaenicke, C., Hammen, C., Zupan, B., Hiroto, D., Gordon, D., Adrian, C., & Burge, D. (1987). Cognitive vulnerability in children at risk for depression. *Journal of Abnormal Child Psychology, 15,* 559-572.

Keller, M. B. (1985). Chronic and recurrent affective disorders: Incidence, course, and influencing factors. In D. Kemali & G. Recagni (Eds.), *Chronic treatments in neuropsychiatry*. New York: Raven.

Keller, M. B., Lavori, P. W., Rice, J., Coryell, W., & Hirschfeld, R. M. A. (1986). The persistent risk of chronicity in recurrent episodes of nonbipolar major depressive disorder: A prospective follow-up. *American Journal of Psychiatry, 143,* 24-28.

Klerman, G. L., & Weissman, M. M. (1989). Increasing rates of depression. *Journal of the American Medical Association, 261,* 2229-2235.

Nolen-Hoeksema, S. (1990). Sex differences in depression. Stanford, CA: Stanford University Press.

Robins, C. J. (1990). Congruence of personality and life events in depression. *Journal of Abnormal Psychology, 99,* 393-397.

Robins, C. J., & Block, P. (1988). Personal vulnerability, life events, and depressive symptoms: A test of a specific international model. *Journal of Personality and Social Psychology, 54,* 847-852.

Rudolph, K. (1992). *Depression vulnerability in children: The role of cognitive interpersonal variables.* Unpublished doctoral dissertation, University of California, Los Angeles.

Segal, Z. V., Shaw, B. F., Vella, D. D., & Katz, R. (1992). Cognitive and life stress predictors of relapse in remitted unipolar depressed patients: A test of the congruency hypothesis. *Journal of Abnormal Psychology, 101,* 26-36.

Weissman, M. M. (1988). Psychopathology in the children of depressed parents: Direct interview studies. In D. L. Dunner & E. S. Gershon, *Relatives at risk for mental disorders* (pp. 143-159). New York: Raven.

Wells, K. B., Stewart, A., Hays, R. D., Burnam, M. A., Rogers, W., Daniels, M., Berry, S., Greenfield, S., & Ware, J. (1989). The functioning and well being of depressed patients: Results from the medical outcome study. *Journal of the American Medical Association, 262,* 914-919.

Zuroff, D. C., & Mongrain, M. (1987). Dependency and self-criticism: Vulnerability factors for depressive affective states. *Journal of Abnormal Psychology, 96,* 14-22.

PART II

Anxiety

ASSESSMENT AND MANAGEMENT

5

Assessment of Anxiety and
Phobic Disorders in Children

THOMAS H. OLLENDICK

The assessment of behavior disorders in children has a long and rich history (King, Hamilton, & Ollendick, 1988). Consistently, factor analyses have yielded two broad-band factors that describe an array of child behavior problems. The first factor, labeled originally as "personality problems" by Ackerson (1931), refers to behaviors characterized by withdrawal, isolation, and subjectively experienced depression and anxiety. Ackerson's second factor, described as "conduct problems," encompasses a set of behaviors characterized by aggression, hostility, and acting out against the environment or society. From a clinical perspective, Horney (1945) described two similar groups of children: those who "move against the world" and those who "move away from the world." The former evidenced "conduct" problems, whereas the latter evinced "personality" problems. Subsequently, Achenbach (1966) termed these dimensions *internalizing* and *externalizing,* incorporating the notion that internalizing disorders reflect behavioral problems of "overcontrol," whereas externalizing disorders consist of behavioral problems of "undercontrol." What is truly remarkable about these two broad-band factors is that they have been affirmed by a number of investigators across a variety of informants (teachers, parents, caretakers), settings (school, home, institution), and ages of children (preschool, elementary, junior high school, and senior high school). Further, they have been observed on a variety of instruments, including Achenbach's Child Behavior Checklist and Quay and Peterson's Behavior Problem Checklist, among others (Achenbach & Edelbrock, 1989; Achenbach, Howell, Quay, & Conners, 1991; Quay & Peterson, 1983).

The focus of the present chapter is on the assessment of internalizing disorders. In particular, we will examine the assessment of anxiety and phobic disorders in children from a behavioral perspective. Following this review, we shall present a case study illustrating the assessment process and discuss implications for treatment of these disorders.

CHILD BEHAVIORAL ASSESSMENT

Child behavioral assessment has embraced a conceptual approach that involves a problem-solving strategy rather than a set of specific techniques or procedures. Following the early lead of Kanfer and Saslow (1969) and the subsequent work of Mash and Terdal (1981), we have defined child behavioral assessment as "an exploratory, hypothesis-testing process in which a range of procedures is used in order to understand a given child, group, or social ecology *and* to formulate and evaluate specific intervention strategies" (Ollendick & Hersen, 1984, p. ix). As such, child behavioral assessment entails more than specification and subsequent observation of highly discrete target behaviors and their controlling variables. Recent advances in child behavioral assessment have incorporated a wide range of procedures, including behavioral interviews, self- and other-reports, self-monitoring, physiological recording, *and* behavioral observation. The approach can best be described as a multimethod one that attempts to provide as complete a "picture" of the child as possible (Ollendick & Hersen, 1993).

Two primary features characterize the selection of behavioral assessment procedures with children. First, the procedures must be empirically validated. All too frequently, professionals working with children have used assessment procedures of convenience, without adequate regard for issues related to their reliability, validity, and clinical utility. Comparison across studies is difficult, if not impossible, and the advancement of an assessment technology, let alone an understanding of child behavior disorders, is not achieved with such practices. Second, the procedures must be developmentally sensitive. Perhaps the most noteworthy characteristic of children is developmental change. Such change, whether based on hypothetical stages of cognitive and social development or empirically derived norms, has clear implications for the selection of specific assessment methods. It also has implications for the determination of response-response relationships at differing age levels and for the stability and continuity of specific behavior problems (Sroufe & Rutter, 1984).

Let us now turn our attention to specific assessment strategies for the assessment of fears and anxieties in children. It should be restated at the outset that the procedures reviewed here are representative ones. Consistent with the hypothesis-testing approach espoused, the selection of procedures and strategies depends upon the exact referral question, as well as the time, energy, and resources available to the clinician (Ollendick & Cerny, 1981). Discussion of each type of procedure will be necessarily brief. An illustration of the multimethod approach will follow.

Behavioral Interviews

The behavioral interview is an important first step in the assessment process. The purposes of the interview are threefold: (a) to establish rapport with the child and family, (b) to obtain information as to the nature of the anxious behavior as well as its antecedents and consequences, and (c) to determine the broader sociocultural context in which the anxious behavior occurs.

Interviewing an anxious child and his or her family requires an understanding that such a child may be timid, shy, and relatively unresponsive in the presence of a "strange adult." Thus it frequently is necessary to provide additional support and encouragement for responding (Bierman & Schwartz, 1986; Ollendick & Francis, 1988). Further, it is necessary to state questions in simple, direct terms that the child will understand. Generally, open-ended questions such as "How do you feel?" or "How are things going?" result in unelaborated responses such as "OK" or "I don't know." More specific questions such as "What kinds of things make you upset?" and "What do your parents do when you tell them you are afraid?" are more easily and readily responded to by the child. In addition, it is helpful to use the child's own words when discussing problem areas. For example, some children distinguish "nervous" feelings (scared, upset) from "anxious" (eager, anticipatory) ones. It is equally important to obtain information from the family regarding their view of the child's anxious behavior as well as information regarding specific antecedents and consequences. Again, it is helpful to ask specific questions such as "What is Lacy doing that makes you think she is anxious?"

In order to help the child describe the antecedents and consequences of the anxious behavior, it is often beneficial to ask the child to imagine the anxiety-provoking situation in vivid detail and to describe exactly what is happening. Prompts such as "What were you wearing?" and "Then what happened?" on the part of the interviewer are also helpful. At this time the child is observed for signs of anxiety such as crying, tremors, or flushing. This procedure has been described by Smith and Sharpe (1970) and Ollendick and Gruen (1972).

In addition to these general guidelines, we have found Blagg's (1987) recommendations for conducting interviews with school-refusing children and their parents to be particularly useful. His school refusal record form is an invaluable *aide memoire* as well as an efficient way to obtain and record relevant information. Specific areas related to the child (e.g., attendance pattern, out-of-school activities, peer relationships, and home- and school-related anxieties and fears), the family (e.g., its structure and relationships, the costs and benefits of the school refusal behavior, and the implicit and explicit patterns of influence and control), and the school itself (e.g., specific classes, conflicts with teachers and bullies) are addressed. Such a comprehensive view provides invaluable information on familial, social, and setting events that occasion and maintain school refusal behaviors. Of course, such information is obtained from the child, his or her parents, and school authorities.

With interviews, as well as other assessment procedures, important psychometric concerns are present. Children, parents, and teachers may be unreliable reporters of behavior, particularly past behavior. That is, they may find it difficult to agree on specific aspects of the problem behavior, including its occurrence and whether such a behavior is *really* a problem. It is not uncommon for children to deny that they are anxious or, for that matter, for parents to exaggerate or possibly minimize the extent of a given problem. Moreover, it is not uncommon for teachers and parents to disagree with one another. One way to maximize the reliability of reporting is to assess currently occurring behaviors and the conditions under which they are occurring (e.g., Herjanic, Herjanic, Brown, & Wheatt, 1975; Rutter & Graham, 1968). Thus the focus of the interview should be on the anxious behavior and its antecedents and consequences in the here and now.

As well as the structured, problem-focused interviews described above, other standardized interview schedules designed for research and diagnostic purposes are available: Kovacs' Interview Schedule for Children (1978b), Hodges' Child Assessment Scale (1982; see also Hodges, McKnew, Cytryn, Stern, & Kline, 1982), Herjanic and Reich's Diagnostic Interview for Children and Adolescents (1982), the Diagnostic Interview Schedule for Children designed by Costello, Edelbrock, Dulcan, Kalas, and Klaric (1984), and the Anxiety Disorders Interview Schedule for Children, recently developed by Silverman and Nelles (1988). In general, these interview schedules allow for the standard administration of questions and the observation of specific interview behaviors. For example, an examiner using the Child Assessment Scale can question the child about specific content areas (e.g., family, fears, worries, moods) and record observations about the child's behavior during the interview. Questions tap the *DSM-III-R* criteria for childhood anxiety disorders as well as conduct disorders, attention deficit disorders, pervasive developmental disorders, and depression. The interview is organized such that content areas covered become progressively more difficult or anxiety provoking as the examiner establishes rapport with the child. Examples of questions tapping childhood anxiety disorders from the Child Assessment Scale are displayed in Table 5.1.

In recent years, we have found the Anxiety Disorders Interview Schedule (ADIS; Silverman & Nelles, 1988) to be particularly useful in our work with anxious or phobic children. It is the only diagnostic interview designed specifically for such disorders and, as a result, is more extensive in coverage. There are two versions of the ADIS, a child version (ADIS-C) and a parent version (ADIS-P). The interviews, which are organized by diagnosis, permit differential diagnosis among the major *DSM-III-R* anxiety disorders (both childhood and adulthood disorders) from the perspective of both the child and the parent. Although Silverman and Nelles (1988) recommend interviewing the child first and then the parent, we have not found this practice to be essential. Whenever possible, we have one clinician interview the child while another interviews the parent. Recently, Silverman and Eisen (1992) have reported high test-retest and inter-rater reliabilities using the interview. Its clinical utility has been demonstrated in several recent studies (Beidel, 1991; Ollendick, Hagopian, & Huntzinger, 1991). Its attention to developmental issues (i.e., the wording of the questions, use of visual prompts) may be particularly important for the enhanced reliability and validity of the schedule. As we have noted elsewhere, several of the other structured

TABLE 5.1   Selections From the Child Assessment Scale (CAS) Reflecting
DSM-III Anxiety Disorders of Childhood or Adolescence

Question	Answer Indicative of Symptom	Symptom Indicative of DSM-III Diagnosis
Some kids have nervous or jumpy feelings. How much do you feel nervous?	Nervous a lot, unable to relax	Overanxious disorder
Are you the kind of person who is easily embarrassed or worries a lot about what others think of you?	Yes	Overanxious disorder
Do you worry that a family member will die or be maimed?	Yes	Separation anxiety
Do you worry about being separated from your parents?	Yes	Separation anxiety
(If child spends a lot of time alone) Do you not want to be by yourself so much, but you are shy?	Yes	Avoidant disorder
Are you afraid of strangers?	Yes	Avoidant disorder

SOURCE: Hodges, 1982.

diagnostic interviews possess questionable reliability and validity, especially for the anxiety and phobic disorders (Ollendick & Francis, 1988).

Although these structured diagnostic interviews provide a potential wealth of information, they also possess some shortcomings. Most are quite time-consuming (taking usually 1 to 2 hours to complete) and are perceived by some children (especially younger children) as threatening and/or boring. Further, although the information obtained is invaluable in arriving at a diagnosis of the child, it frequently is less useful in designing effective treatment programs. For this purpose, the problem-focused interview may be more helpful. Thus although structured interviews provide potentially rich diagnostic information, they should not be viewed as a substitute for treatment-oriented, problem-focused interviews.

Self-Report Instruments

A variety of self-report instruments are available. In general, these instruments consist of fear survey schedules that provide lists of fear-evoking stimuli, and anxiety measures that provide the child a set of responses with which to describe experiences subjectively felt in the anxiety-provoking situations.

Fear Survey Schedules. Fear survey schedules are useful both in identifying specific fear stimuli and in providing a general overall index of fearfulness. Scherer and Nakamura (1968) developed a Fear Survey Schedule for Children (FSSC) modeled after the Wolpe-Lang Fear Survey Schedule for Adults (Wolpe & Lang, 1964). On this scale, children are asked to rate their fear to each of 80 items on a 5-point scale. Factor-analytic studies show that the FSSC taps major fears—fear of death, fear of the dark, and home/school fears (Scherer & Nakamura, 1968). It was originally developed for children between 9 and 12 years of age.

Modified versions of the FSSC have been developed by Ryall and Dietikur (1979) and Ollendick (1983). The Children's Fear Survey Schedule developed by Ryall and Deitikur (1979) is a short form of the FSSC. It contains 48 specific fear items and two blanks for children to indicate additional fears not previously listed. Each item is rated on a 3-point scale ranging from *not scared or nervous or afraid* to *a little scared* to *very scared*. It was modified in order to be used with younger children and is reported to be useful with children between 5 and 12 years of age. Although no information is available as to the validity of this revised Children's Fear Survey Schedule, it does possess good test-retest reliability.

The revision of the Fear Survey Schedule for Children undertaken by Ollendick (FSSC-R; Ollendick, 1983) is another potentially useful tool for determining specific fear stimuli related to children's anxious and phobic behavior. School-aged children are asked to rate their fear of 80 fear items on a 3-point scale ranging from being frightened by the item *none, some,* or *a lot.* Normative data for children between 7 and 18 years of age are available (Ollendick, Matson, & Helsel, 1985). Further, the instrument has been used in cross-cultural studies in Australia, China, England, and the United States (Dong, Yang, & Ollendick, 1994; Ollendick, King, & Frary, 1989; Ollendick, Yule, & Ollier, 1991). Examination of this scale suggests that it is a reliable and valid revision of the FSSC. High scores on the survey are related positively to measures of anxiety and negatively to internal locus-of control and self-concept. Ollendick and Mayer (1984) reported that the FSSC-R discriminated between school phobic children whose fears were related to separation anxiety and school phobic children whose fears appeared to be related to specific aspects of the school situation itself. Further, the scale has been used to identify differences in the self-reported fears of children presenting with different anxiety disorders (Last, Francis, & Strauss, 1989).

Finally, the instrument has been found to possess a similar factor structure across age ranges and different cultures. A five-factor solution has been obtained: Fear of Failure and Criticism, Fear of the Unknown, Fear of Injury and Small Animals, Fear of Danger and Death, and Medical Fears. The Fear of Danger and Death factor is presented in Table 5.2. Interestingly, the most common fears in boys and girls can be found on this factor: "Being hit by a car or truck," "Not being able to breathe," "Fire—getting burned," "Death or dead people," and "Bombing attacks." In general, girls report a greater number of fears and a greater intensity of fears than do boys.

In brief, fear survey schedules appear particularly useful as ipsative instruments to identify specific fear sensitivities in children, as normative instruments for selecting fearful children for treatment, and as outcome measures of therapeutic efficacy. Of course, they also possess those limitations attendant to other self-report instruments (Finch & Rogers, 1984).

Anxiety Measures. In contrast to the fear survey schedules, measures of anxiety have been used primarily to determine the subjectively experienced effects associated with fearful situations. Although a variety of measures have been developed, only the most frequently used instrument will be highlighted here: the Children's Manifest Anxiety Scale.

The Children's Manifest Anxiety Scale (CMAS; Castaneda, McCandless, & Palermo, 1956) is a scaled-down version of the Manifest Anxiety Scale for Adults (Taylor, 1951). This scale consists of 37 anxiety items and 11 lie items. Reynolds and Richmond (1978) revised the CMAS and labeled it the "What I Think and Feel" test. The purpose of the 37-item revision was to clarify wording of items, decrease administration time, and lower the reading level of select items. The RCMAS is reported to be suitable for children and adolescents between 6 and 18 years of age; normative information for a variety of child groups is available (Reynolds & Paget, 1983). The scale yields three anxiety factors: Physiological, Worry/Oversensitivity, and Con-

TABLE 5.2   Items From the Fear Survey Schedule for Children-Revised
(FSSC-R; Fear of Danger and Death Factor)

NAME _____ AGE _____ DATE _____

DIRECTIONS: A number of statements which boys and girls use to describe the fears they
have are given below. Read each fear carefully, then place an X in front of the words that
best describe your fears. Remember, there are no right or wrong answers.

1. Death or dead people	☐ None ☐ Some ☐ A lot
2. Getting lost in a strange place	☐ None ☐ Some ☐ A lot
3. Being sent to the principal	☐ None ☐ Some ☐ A lot
4. Bombing attacks—being invaded	☐ None ☐ Some ☐ A lot
5. Fire—getting burned	☐ None ☐ Some ☐ A lot
6. Being hit by a car or truck	☐ None ☐ Some ☐ A lot
7. Having to go to school	☐ None ☐ Some ☐ A lot
8. Falling from high places	☐ None ☐ Some ☐ A lot
9. Getting a shock from electricity	☐ None ☐ Some ☐ A lot
10. Having to stay after school	☐ None ☐ Some ☐ A lot
11. Germs or getting a serious illness	☐ None ☐ Some ☐ A lot
12. Earthquakes	☐ None ☐ Some ☐ A lot
13. Russia	☐ None ☐ Some ☐ A lot
14. Not being able to breathe	☐ None ☐ Some ☐ A lot

SOURCE: Ollendick, 1983.

centration (Reynolds & Paget, 1981). We have found the factor scores to be
particularly useful in determining targets of intervention. Some children
report high levels of physiological arousal, whereas others report few problems with physiological arousal but extreme difficulties with concentration
or worry. Such information is helpful in determining which aspects of
anxiety to address and which treatment strategies to employ (e.g., relaxation
training versus cognitive self-instruction). Representative items from the
RCMAS are displayed in Table 5.3.

Behavior Checklists and Rating Forms

Several rating scales and checklists are available for use with children who
display fears and anxieties. Among the more frequently used are Achenbach's
Child Behavior Checklist, Quay and Peterson's Behavior Problem Checklist,

TABLE 5.3   Anxiety Items From the Children's Manifest Anxiety Scale-Revised (CMAS-R; "What I Think and Feel")

I have trouble making up my mind.

Often I have trouble getting my breath.

I worry a lot of the time.

It is hard for me to get to sleep at night.

My hands feel sweaty.

I wake up scared some of the time.

I worry when I go to bed at night.

It is hard for me to keep my mind on my schoolwork.

SOURCE: Items from *Revised Children's Manifest Anxiety Scale* copyright © 1985 by Western Psychological Service. Reprinted by permission of the publisher, Western Psychological Services, 12031 Wilshire Boulevard, Los Angeles, California 90025.

and Miller et al.'s Fear Survey for Children. Each of these rating forms has been developed and standardized for use with children between 4 and 16 years of age.

The Child Behavior Checklist (CBCL; Achenbach, 1978; Achenbach & Edelbrock, 1979) has been used extensively in factor-analytic studies by Achenbach and colleagues. Parents complete this 138-item scale, which measures both behavior problems and social competency. Social competency items address the child's participation in social organizations, activities, and school. The behavior problem items are rated on a 3-point scale as to how well they describe the child. Of particular importance, the inclusion of social competency and behavior problem items allows for a comprehensive assessment of the child's strengths and weaknesses. In addition, the scale permits the identification of children who display anxiety, social withdrawal, obsessions-compulsions, depression, noncommunicative behavior, hyperactivity, aggression, and somatic complaints. Specific anxiety items include "clings to adults," "school fears," and "shy, timid." This scale has been found to be reliable and valid and provides important normative data for boys and girls of varying ages. A similar scale is also available for teachers. Recently, Achenbach (1991) has identified a set of core problems, including an anxious/depressed syndrome that is found across different ages and informants for both boys and girls.

The Revised Behavior Problem Checklist (Quay & Peterson, 1983) consists of 89 problem behaviors that are also rated on a 3-point scale ranging

TABLE 5.4   Revised Behavior Problem Checklist: Anxiety-Withdrawal Items

---

Self-conscious; easily embarrassed

Feels inferior

Shy, bashful

Hypersensitive; feelings are easily hurt

Generally fearful, anxious

Depressed, always sad

Says nobody loves him or her

Difficulty in making choices; can't make up mind

Feels he or she can't succeed

SOURCE: © 1987 by Herbert C. Quay and Donald R. Peterson. Reprinted by permission.

from *not a problem* to *mild problem* to *severe problem.* Factor analyses of the scale yield the following six dimensions: conduct problem, socialized aggression, attention problem—immaturity, anxiety-withdrawal, psychotic behavior, and motor excess. Examples of behaviors indicative of the anxiety-withdrawal dimension are displayed in Table 5.4. Like the CBCL, the Problem Behavior Checklist is a useful tool with which to assess significant others' reports of children's anxious behavior.

Finally, the Louisville Fear Survey for Children (LFSC; Miller, Barrett, Hampe, & Noble, 1971) is an 81-item scale covering a variety of specific fears; it, too, is appropriate for use with children between 4 and 16 years of age. Although the LFSC can be administered to the child as well as significant others such as parents or teachers, very little data exist regarding its use as a self-report instrument. More generally, the rater is asked to indicate the child's level of fear on a 3-point scale ranging from *no fear* to *normal or reasonable fear* to *unrealistic or excessive fear.* Limited evidence indicates that these ratings can be used to differentiate school phobic youngsters whose fears are primarily related to school fears rather than separation anxiety fears (Miller, Barrett, & Hampe, 1974). Unfortunately, in the one study that does report both child and parent ratings, Miller, Barrett, and Hampe (1972) indicate that child and parent ratings do not correspond well. Perhaps anxious children have a number of worries that they do not share with their parents. Indeed, we have noted that parents often respond with surprise when they learn the number and types of worries/fears that their children report to us.

In sum, a variety of such measures are available for use. Although they generally possess sound test-retest and interjudge reliability, their validity in terms of how closely they correspond to other measures like self-reports and behavioral observation is less clear at this time.

Behavioral Observations

The most direct and least inferential manner in which to assess fearful and anxious behaviors is to observe them in the situations in which they occur. In behavioral observation coding systems for childhood anxiety, specific behaviors reflective of anxiety are operationally defined. Often observation is made of the antecedents and consequences of the anxious behavior as well. A number of authors have described clinical cases in which highly individualized behavioral observation systems have been used. For example, Neisworth, Madle, and Goeke (1975) detailed a set of operationally defined behaviors reflective of separation anxiety (e.g., crying, screaming) in a preschooler and observed these behaviors as well as their antecedent and consequent conditions before, during, and after treatment. Using this system, they were able to determine that the child's separation anxiety occurred in the preschool setting and was maintained by maternal attention. In addition, these observations were used to develop an intervention strategy appropriate to the particular antecedent and consequent conditions.

More general behavioral observation systems for childhood anxiety are less common than the individualized systems described above for clinical treatment studies. One exception to this is the Preschool Observation Scale of Anxiety (POSA) developed by Glennon and Weisz (1978). The POSA includes 30 specific behavioral indices of anxiety to be observed using a standard time-sampling procedure. The behavioral indices include nail biting, avoidance of eye contact, silence to questions, and rigid posture (see Table 5.5). Although more information is needed regarding its reliability and validity, this scale appears useful in a clinical setting (Ollendick, 1983). We are currently using a variant of this system to code fearful and anxious behavior of children who are called to the principal's office (being sent to the principal is one of the most common fears in children; Ollendick, 1983). In addition to the actual route and time taken to get to the principal's office, a trembling voice, lip licking, and gratuitous hand movements are being

TABLE 5.5   Sample Items From the Preschool Observation Scale of Anxiety (POSA)

---

1. Physical complaint: Child says he or she has a headache or stomachache or has to go to the bathroom.

2. Expression of fear or worry: Child complains about being afraid of or worried about something; he or she uses the word *afraid, scared, worried,* or a synonym.

3. Cry: Tears should be visible.

4. Scream.

5. Nail biting: Child actually bites his or her nails in the testing room.

6. Lip licking: Tongue should be visible.

7. Trembling lip.

8. Rigid posture: Part of body is held unusually stiff or motionless for an entire 30-second interval.

9. Avoidance of eye contact: Examiner should have clear trouble making eye contact with the child.

10. Fearful facial expression.

SOURCE: Adapted from Glennon & Weisz, 1978.

recorded and related to levels of self-reported fear about going to the principal's office.

Importantly, developmental differences in the anxiety response might also be uncovered through direct observation procedures. As one example, Katz, Kellerman, and Siegel (1980) reported important age differences in children with cancer in response to bone marrow aspirations. Children under 6 years of age were most likely to express their anxiety by crying, screaming, needing to be physically restrained, and expressing pain verbally (e.g., "That hurts," "Stop hurting me"). The intermediate age group, children between 6 and 10 years of age, required less physical restraint and were more likely to express pain verbally. In addition, muscular rigidity began to appear in this age group. The oldest children and adolescents, those between 10 and 18 years of age, evidenced only two primary modes of anxiety expression: verbal expression of pain and muscular rigidity. Thus Katz et al. observed a developmental tendency toward less diffuse vocal protest (screams, cries) and skeletal activity (motor excess) and a greater emphasis on verbal expression along with muscle tension. The general picture was that of increased body control accompanied by constriction of the musculature with age. Such findings might have important implications for treatment. In this instance, muscle relaxation procedures might be more useful for older children and adolescents, whereas operant-based procedures to help regulate motor excess behaviors might be more appropriate for younger children (Ollendick & Francis, 1988). Of course, these speculations await empirical verification.

Behavioral Avoidance Tests (BAT) represent yet another strategy for measuring anxiety (Lang & Lazovik, 1963). Typically, the BAT involves having the child enter a room containing the anxiety-provoking object and approach the feared object. As noted by Kazdin (1973), the BAT provides behavioral measures of avoidance such as amount of time spent in the presence of the anxiety-provoking object, distance from the object, and number and latency of approach responses. However, a significant number of limitations are evident: (a) The procedures and instructions are often not standardized, (b) there are little data available regarding the influence of procedural variations and demand characteristics on children's performance, and (c) there are currently no data available as to the reliability and validity of such tests with children.

Self-Monitoring Procedures

Although used less frequently, the self-monitoring of avoidance responses and the cognitions accompanying those responses is a potentially fruitful avenue of development, at least for older children (Beidel, Neal, & Lederer, 1991). With this procedure, the child is required to discriminate and record behaviors and cognitions as they occur. In this respect, they are direct measures of the anxiety or phobic response and are different from traditional self-report measures, which involve the report of behaviors or thoughts that occurred at some earlier time. Particularly promising at this time is the use of self-statement tests that are used to monitor cognitions that accompany fearful/anxious behaviors.

Self-statement tests are usually administered following participation in a simulated or real-life anxiety-provoking situation. Typically, a list of statements is provided, and the child is instructed to indicate which thoughts he or she was thinking during the task. Although this means of assessing the cognitions of children was advocated some time ago (e.g., Morris & Kratochwill, 1983), there are few examples of self-statement tests for anxious children at this time. Two notable exceptions are Zatz and Chassin's (1983, 1985) assessment of the self-statements of test-anxious children and Stefanek, Ollendick, Baldock, Francis, and Yaeger's (1987) assessment of the self-statements of socially withdrawn children. Zatz and Chassin (1983, 1985) developed the Children's Cognitive Assessment Questionnaire (CCAQ) to tap the self-statements of test-anxious children. The CCAQ contains four subscales: positive evaluation, negative evaluation, on-task thoughts, and off-task thoughts. Examples of CCAQ items are displayed in Table 5.6. The authors report that highly test-anxious children endorse more negative evaluation and off-task thoughts than do low test-anxious children.

Similarly, Stefanek et al. (1987) examined children's inhibiting and facilitating self-statements in response to a number of role-play situations in which the child was in conflict with, or was to initiate an interaction with, a peer. They reported that socially withdrawn children endorsed more inhibiting and fewer facilitating self-statements than did their well-adjusted peers.

In recent years, Francis (1986) developed a self-statement test for socially avoidant children that combines aspects of Zatz and Chassin's CCAQ and Stefanek et al.'s self-statement test. Children are instructed to pretend they are in a series of social situations involving a child whom they do not know. Following each scene, the child is asked to report his or her thoughts. The list of possible self-statements used is a slightly modified version of the CCAQ and includes positive evaluation, negative evaluation, on-task, and off-task items.

As noted above, the use of self-statement tests with anxious children is a relatively recent development. A productive area of inquiry might be to replicate studies such as those of Zatz and Chassin (1983) and Stefanek et al. (1987) in order to establish the psychometric properties of the procedure. Assessing the specific cognitions of anxious children will provide vital information in treating such children. That is, more reliable information would be available as to the content of the cognitions to be modified as well as the extent to which coping cognitions are evident in the child's repertoire.

Physiological Assessment

Principles and procedures of the physiological assessment of children are in an early stage of development. At present, no normative information is available as to children's physiological responding in general, let alone critical information about how emotional reactions differ from one another. In one of the few discussions of the physiological assessment of childhood anxiety, Barrios, Hartmann, and Shigetomi (1981) comment that little is known about the effects of laboratory or clinic settings, ambient noise, or

TABLE 5.6   Sample Items From the Children's Cognitive Assessment
Questionnaire (CCAQ)

Positive Evaluation	I usually do better than other kids.
	I am bright enough to do this.
	I am doing the best that I can.
Negative Evaluation	I have a bad memory.
	I'm doing poorly.
	I can't do this—I give up.
On-Task Thought	Pay attention.
	The harder it gets, the more I need to try.
	Take it one step at a time.
Off-Task Thought	I wish I were playing with my friends.
	I wish I were home.
	I wish this was over.

SOURCE: Adapted from Zatz & Chassin, 1983.

instructional set on physiological responding in children. Little additional progress has been made in recent years (King, 1993).

Although few studies have been reported, the most commonly used measures of physiologic responding in anxious children are those that assess cardiovascular and electrodermal responding (Beidel, 1988; Morris & Kratochwill, 1983). Cardiovascular responding can be assessed by measures of heart rate, blood pressure, and peripheral blood flow. Because it is measured easily and is least sensitive to measurement artifacts (Nietzel & Bernstein, 1981), heart rate has been used most frequently.

Unfortunately, however, it is difficult to differentiate specific heart rate patterns in children. For example, although Tal and Miklich (1976) reported increased heart rate in children who were asked to imagine a fearful situation, Johnson and Melamed (1979) reported similar increases in heart rate in response to imaginal angry experiences. Similarly, Sternbach (1962) found a low correlation between physiological responding as measured by heart rate and self-report of fear. Thus a change in heart rate in and of itself may be indicative of general emotional responding and provide little specific information as to the nature of emotional arousal. Further, it might not be related to actual self-reports of the fear. In summary, Nietzel and Bernstein (1981) caution that (a) heart rate is overly sensitive to motor and perceptual activity and may be confounded easily with stress; and (b) heart rate can be idiosyncratic in that it may increase or decrease or remain stable in response to anxiety-provoking stimuli.

Electrodermal responding has also been investigated. Typically it is assessed through measures of skin conductance and skin resistance. Two examples of such measures are Palmar Sweat Prints (PSP) and Finger Sweat Prints (FSP). Melamed and her colleagues (e.g., Melamed & Siegel, 1975) reported electrodermal responding to be correlated with both self-report and observations of dental fears and anxiety in children. Barrios et al. (1981) and King (1993) caution, however, that electrodermal responding is highly reactive and, as such, may be responsive to a large number of environmental and psychological artifacts.

In sum, although the investigation of the relationship between childhood anxiety and physiological responding holds some promise, few conclusions can be drawn at this time. Given the lack of systematic, normative data regarding physiologic responding in children and the expenses (monetarily and timewise) associated with physiological assessment, it seems premature to advocate routine use of physiological assessment in clinical practice at this time. Rather, it might prove more fruitful to explore more fully the parameters of physiological responding in children in general before encouraging excursions into the clinical world.

THE MULTIMETHOD, MULTIMODAL APPROACH

As we noted earlier, not all of these procedures will necessarily be used with each child. The selection of procedure and strategies depends on the referral question as well as the time, energy, and resources available to the practicing clinician. The case presentation that follows illustrates this process (Ollendick & Huntzinger, 1990).

Lacy, an 8-year-old, white female, was brought to our outpatient Child Anxiety Disorder Clinic by her parents. Presenting complaints centered on three problematic areas: (a) Lacy's concern that her mother might be injured and possibly die, (b) nighttime problems characterized by refusal to sleep in her own bed, and (c) repeated statements from Lacy that she was "no good," "dumb," and that she might as well die. According to her parents, these problems were reported to have begun approximately 7 months prior to the initial appointment. At that time, Lacy's mother had back surgery, with considerable pain predating and following surgery. The surgery occurred during the summer. These worries continued to mount over the summer months but did not reach a point where they kept Lacy homebound or continually at her mother's side. In fact, she was able to attend a church summer camp and spend the night with friends periodically throughout the remainder of the summer. The worries were expressed primarily through excessive questions about her mother's health, statements about Lacy's own health, and seeking reassurance from her mother (and occasionally her father) that it was okay for her to be away from home.

With the beginning of the new school year (third grade), her problems began to worsen. Although she was not school phobic at this time, she began to express continual concern about "being away from mother all day." Lacy reported that she was afraid something might happen to her mother and that no one would be there to help her. Lacy's father worked an early morning shift (6:00 a.m. to 2:00 p.m.), and her only sister (Tammy, age 19) worked a regular shift (8:00 a.m. to 3:00 p.m.). Due to travel requirements, her father left home about 5:00 a.m. and returned about 3:30 p.m. Her sister left home for work about 7:15 a.m., whereas Lacy left for school at 7:45 a.m. Lacy was the last member of her family to leave the home. Her mother, due to complications with the back surgery, remained at home temporarily unemployed. Prior to surgery, she had worked as a receptionist at a local medical clinic.

Lacy never became school avoidant, possibly because both parents insisted that she go to school each day. The parents did report, however, that she frequently complained of headaches and stomachaches on school days and that, on at least four occasions, she had been allowed to stay home from school because of reported illness. Throughout this time period, she continued to excel in school (As and Bs) and to have several friends. Teachers reported her to be well liked, a class leader, hard working, and a good student.

Around the third week of the school term, she began to express increasing concern about sleeping in her own bedroom (her bedroom was upstairs, across the hall from her sister's; her parents' bedroom was downstairs on the first floor). She complained about having nightmares and being frightened by "zombies" who came into her room. Over the course of the next 3 months, the nightmare problems increased to the point where she was sleeping either in her parents' room or outside their door. In addition, she exhibited a number of avoidant behaviors including arguing about bedtime, refusing to go to bed, getting out of bed, calling out once in bed, and making-numerous requests (e.g., drink of water, go to the bathroom). Also, she became more "clinging" to her mother, wanting to be near her after school until bedtime. She stopped spending weekend nights at her friends'; further, she didn't invite any of her friends to stay with her. She continued to go to school, however, and to do well.

About 4 weeks before her first appointment, Lacy began to make disparaging statements about herself and to seem "sad and unhappy." At this time, her father reported first hearing the statement, "Maybe I just don't belong on this earth." Although both parents felt Lacy would "outgrow" her worries about her mother's health and the nighttime fears, they were concerned by her verbal statements and sullen appearance. Referral was made at that time, upon recommendation of the family physician.

During the initial interview, conducted with her parents present, Lacy appeared more anxious than depressed. She fidgeted in her chair, clasped and unclasped her hands, swung her feet, bit her lips, and stammered as she spoke. She reported being "very afraid" that her mother "might get sick again"—even though at this time her mother had returned to work on a part-time basis. She wondered aloud, "Who will take care of her. . . . Daddy is always at work and Sissy is at work too, you know." Regarding her nighttime fears, she indicated that the zombies were real ("I really saw them! They were real!") and that they might kill her. She stated further that a boy had told her that "nightmares can cause you to be frightened to death." Presumably, linking this thought with her overarching concerns about her mother's well-being, she was convinced that she would die and "no one would be there to help Mommy." As for her depressive and suicidal-like thoughts, she stated in a rather straightforward way, "I can't be happy. . . . I used to be . . . but not now. . . . Even my friends don't like me now."

On the basis of this initial interview and the reported chronology of events, it was hypothesized that Lacy's primary problem centered on separation anxiety. She had exaggerated and unrealistic worries that harm would come to her mother and/or herself and that she would be separated from her mother. She complained of physical distress upon leaving for school, was reluctant to have friends over or to stay with friends, and refused to sleep alone. Further, social withdrawal and depression were evident. In brief, she showed signs of the nine major criteria for separation anxiety disorder (SAD; *DSM-III-R*).

During the second session, the Anxiety Disorders Inventory for Children (Silverman & Nelles, 1988) was administered. It confirmed the impression of SAD, as well as accompanying major depression. For example, she answered affirmatively to questions related to worry about being away from her parents, worry that some harm might befall them or herself, feeling sad when away from her parents, and feeling sick at the prospect of leaving them. When feeling afraid of being away from her parents, she reported experiencing headaches, nausea, dizziness, and difficulty breathing. On a 0- to 4-point scale of symptom severity, she gave herself a rating of 4 (*very severe*); further, she rated the distress caused by being away from her parents as a 3 (*severe*). Other anxiety disorders, such as avoidant disorder and overanxious disorder, were ruled out by the presence of good friendships at school and the specific focus of the separation anxiety concerns. She was not school phobic. She did have other phobias, however, most of which were related to nighttime fears and being left alone.

Results of psychometric assessment supported this picture. Lacy completed the Revised Children's Manifest Anxiety Scale (Reynolds & Richmond, 1978), the Fear Survey Schedule for Children-Revised (Ollendick, 1983), and the Children's Depression Inventory (Kovacs, 1978a). On the RCMAS, she received a score of 18, well above the mean for her age. Among her endorsements were "Often I feel sick in my stomach," "I have bad dreams," "I wake up scared some of the time," "I worry when I go to bed at night," and "It is hard for me to get to sleep at night." Similarly, she scored above age and gender norms on the FSSC-R: She obtained a total score of 168 and endorsed 26 fears ("a lot"). Among these specific fears were "ghosts or spooky things," "getting lost in a strange place," "a burglar breaking into our house," "the sight of blood," "cemeteries," "nightmares," "going to bed in the dark," "being alone," "dark places," and "having my parents argue." Similarly, on the CDI, she obtained an elevated score of 16; again, this score was well above the average for her age and gender. Items such as "I am sad many times," "I do not like myself," "I have trouble sleeping every night," and "I think about killing myself, but would not do it" were endorsed. Importantly, she also reported that "I have fun in many things," "I have fun at school many times," and "I have plenty of friends." Finally, on the Revised Behavior Problem Checklist (Quay & Peterson, 1983), both parents rated her high on the anxiety-withdrawal factor (scores of 15 and 12). Other factor scores, except the one for motor excess, were within normal limits. Clearly, these self-report and other-report instruments confirmed the overall picture of Lacy as experiencing separation anxiety to a significant degree. Physiological assessment was not attempted.

In order to obtain a behavioral measure of her nighttime problems, both Lacy and her parents were asked to monitor the number of nights she slept in her own bed and the type of avoidance behavior that she displayed (e.g., refusing to go to bed, getting out of bed, calling out, and leaving sources of light and sound on). Lacy was provided a set of forms on which to record her own behaviors. Her parents were given similar forms but also asked to record their responses to her avoidance behaviors (e.g., consoling her, getting her a drink). They were instructed to complete the evaluations independently.

Following this focused assessment, it was decided to address her night-time fears directly. This decision was based on the relationship of these fears to the reported separation problems and our previous experience that such children generally respond favorably to the available treatment procedures for nighttime fears. An integrated treatment procedure based on the work of Graziano and Mooney (1980, 1982) was used. Initially, relaxation training and self-instruction training were implemented over six 45-minute sessions. Response to these procedures was slow and only partially effective. Lacy continued to report considerable "state" anxiety about sleeping in her own bed and to average only 2 nights a week sleeping in her own room throughout this phase of treatment. Accordingly, a reinforcement component was added. Within 3 weeks, Lacy was sleeping in her own bed 7 nights a week and reporting much less anxiety. The nightmares stopped, and she started, once again, to have friends spend the night with her. An additional four weekly sessions served to maintain these effects. A total of 13 weekly treatment sessions was conducted. Follow-up sessions at 1 month and 6 months post treatment were provided to monitor these gains and to conduct post-treatment assessment. Significant reductions in anxiety (RCMAS score of 8), fear (FSSC-R score of 134), and depression (CDI score of 9) were noted. All of these scores are well within the normal limits. Further, although both mother and father continued to view Lacy as somewhat anxious (Anxiety/Withdrawal scores of 8 and 7 respectively), her scores were significantly below those at pretreatment. Finally, at follow-up, she was sleeping in her own bed 7 nights a week, reporting no nightmares, no longer expressing concern about her mother's or her own well-being, and expressing positive statements about herself. Throughout treatment, her father and sister continued to work their regular schedules; moreover, as previously noted, her mother worked on a part-time basis as well.

Overall, this case illustrates the complexity of problems associated with separation anxiety in children, as well as our proposed multimodal assessment approach. The clinical and diagnostic interviews helped us to focus our efforts and guided the selection of specific self-report, other-report, and behavioral measures. These additional measures provided us with a broader "picture" of Lacy and her presenting problems. Equally important, they provided us empirically based and developmentally sensitive measures of treatment outcome.

SUMMARY AND CONCLUSIONS

As is evident from the above brief review, a variety of procedures exist for the assessment of phobias and anxieties in children. These procedures vary from the behavioral interview and self-report of fearful and anxious states to the direct behavioral observation and physiological recording of such responses. In addition, relatively new advances in the development of assessment instruments for the measure of cognitions that accompany these states are being witnessed. Truly, we are at an exciting juncture in the history of child behavioral assessment.

Yet much remains to be achieved. From the onset, we noted that our procedures must be reliable, valid, and clinically useful and that they must be developmentally sensitive. In point of truth, we have very little data to support either of these requirements. We simply do not have all of the data on the reliability, the validity, or the appropriateness of our instruments for children of differing age levels. Is the interview equally reliable and valid for 4-year-olds and 10-year-olds? What about self-report instruments? Are they equally applicable to 6-year-olds and 12-year-olds? Although we have some initial findings that suggest that these various measures are useful, we have very little knowledge about just how useful they are for children of varying ages (Ollendick & King, 1991).

On another level, we really have very little data about the value of the multilevel, multimethod approach that we espouse. Do we really obtain additionally significant information by using all of these procedures? In psychometric terms, do we really enhance the incremental validity of our approach through such practices? Close examination of the case of "Lacy" suggests that valuable information was obtained. Yet would our treatment have differed had we observed different response covariations?

Finally, broader questions remain. Most notable among these are issues related to the long-term stability and continuity of internalizing disorders such as the phobias and anxieties (cf. Ollendick, in press). Other questions remain about the correlates of these disorders across age. Are they similar or different? Answers to questions like these will place our initial assessment efforts in richer context. In sum, although a wide array of tools exists to assist us in the multimodal hypothesis-testing approach that we espouse, much remains to be learned. Assessment of anxiety and phobias in young children is in its own state of childhood.

REFERENCES

Achenbach, T. M. (1966). The classification of children's psychiatric symptoms: A factor-analytic study. *Psychological Monographs, 80* (Whole No. 6).

Achenbach, T. M. (1978). The child behavior profile: I. Boys aged 6-11. *Journal of Consulting and Clinical Psychology, 46,* 478-488.

Achenbach, T. M. (1991). *Integrative guide for the 1991 CBCL/4-18, YSR, and TRF profiles.* Burlington: University of Vermont.

Achenbach, T. M., & Edelbrock, C. S. (1979). The child behavior profile: II. Boys aged 12-16 and girls aged 6-11 and 12-16. *Journal of Consulting and Clinical Psychology, 47,* 223-233.

Achenbach, T. M., & Edelbrock, C. R. (1989). Diagnostic and taxonomic issues. In T. H. Ollendick & M. Hersen (Eds.), *Handbook of child psychopathology* (2nd ed., pp. 53-69). New York: Plenum.

Achenbach, T. M., Howell, C. T., Quay, H. C., & Conners, C. K. (1991). National survey of competencies and problems among 4- to 16-year-olds: Parents' reports for normative and clinical samples. *Monographs of the Society for Research in Child Development, 56,* 225.

Ackerson, L. (1931). *Children's behavior problems.* Chicago: University of Chicago Press.

Barrios, B. A., Hartmann, D. P., & Shigetomi, C. (1981). Fears and anxieties in children. In E. J. Mash & L. G. Terdal (Eds.), *Behavioral assessment of childhood disorders* (pp. 259-304). New York: Guilford.

Beidel, D. (1988). Psychophysiological assessment of anxious emotional states in children. *Journal of Abnormal Psychology, 97,* 80-82.

Beidel, D. (1991). Social phobia and overanxious disorder in school age children. *Journal of the American Academy of Child and Adolescent Psychiatry, 30,* 545-552.

Beidel, D. C., Neal, A. M., & Lederer, A. S. (1991). The feasibility and validity of a daily diary for the assessment of anxiety in children. *Behavior Therapy, 22,* 505-517.

Bierman, K. L., & Schwartz, L. A. (1986). Clinical child interviews: Approaches and developmental considerations. *Journal of Child and Adolescent Psychotherapy, 3,* 267-278.

Blagg, N. (1987). *School phobia and its treatment.* London: Croom Helm.

Castaneda, A., McCandless, B. R., & Palmero, D. S. (1956). The children's form of the Manifest Anxiety Scale. *Child Development, 16,* 317-326.

Costello, A. J., Edelbrock, C. S., Dulcan, M. K., Kalas, R., & Klaric, S. H. (1984). *Report on the NIMH Diagnostic Interview Schedule for Children (DIS-C).* Washington, DC: National Institute for Mental Health.

Dong, Q., Yang, B., & Ollendick, T. H. (1994). Fears in Chinese children and adolescents. *Journal of Child Psychology and Psychiatry, 35,* 351-363.

Finch, A. J., Jr., & Rogers, T. R. (1984). Self-report instruments. In T. H. Ollendick & M. Hersen (Eds.), *Child behavioral assessment: Principles and procedures* (pp. 106-123). New York: Pergamon.

Francis, G. (1986). *The role of anxiety and depression in socially withdrawn children.* Unpublished doctoral dissertation, Virginia Polytechnic Institute and State University, Blacksburg.

Glennon, B., & Weisz, J. R. (1978). An observational approach to the assessment of anxiety in young children. *Journal of Consulting and Clinical Psychology, 46,* 1246-1257.

Graziano, A. M., & Mooney, K. C. (1980). Family self-control instruction for children's nighttime fear reduction. *Journal of Consulting and Clinical Psychology, 48,* 206-213.

Graziano, A. M., & Mooney, K. C. (1982). Behavioral treatment of "night-fears" in children: Maintenance of improvement of $2\frac{1}{2}$ to 3-year follow-up. *Journal of Consulting and Clinical Psychology, 50,* 598-599.

Herjanic, B., Herjanic, M., Brown, F., & Wheatt, T. (1975). Are children reliable reporters? *Journal of Abnormal Child Psychology, 3,* 41-48.

Herjanic, B., & Reich, W. (1982). Development of a structured psychiatric interview: Agreement between child and parent on individual symptoms. *Journal of Abnormal Child Psychology, 10,* 307-324.

Hodges, K. (1982). *The Child Assessment Schedule.* Unpublished manuscript, Duke University.

Hodges, K., McKnew, D., Cytryn, L., Stern, L., & Kline, J. (1982). The Child Assessment Schedule (CAS) Diagnostic Interview: A report on reliability and validity. *Journal of American Academy of Child Psychiatry, 21,* 468-473.

Horney, K. (1945). *Our inner conflicts.* New York: Norton.

Johnson, S. B., & Melamed, B. G. (1979). The assessment and treatment of children's fears. In B. B. Lahey & A. E. Kazdin (Eds.), *Advances in clinical child psychology* (Vol. 2, pp. 108-141). New York: Plenum.

Kanfer, F. H., & Saslow, G. (1969). Behavioral diagnosis. In C. M. Franks (Ed.), *Behavior therapy: Appraisal and status* (pp. 47-95). New York: McGraw-Hill.

Katz, E. R., Kellerman, J., & Siegel, S. E. (1980). Behavioral distress in children with cancer undergoing medical procedures: Developmental considerations. *Journal of Consulting and Clinical Psychology, 48,* 356-365.

Kazdin, A. E. (1973). The effect of suggestion and pretesting on avoidance reduction in fearful subjects. *Journal of Behavior Therapy and Experimental Psychology, 4,* 213-222.

King, N. J. (1993). Psychophysiological assessment. In T. H. Ollendick & M. Hersen (Eds.), *Handbook of child and adolescent assessment* (pp. 180-191). Boston: Allyn & Bacon.

King, N. J., Hamilton, D. I., & Ollendick, T. H. (1988). *Children's phobias: A behavioural perspective.* Chichester, UK: John Wiley.

Kovacs, M. (1978a). *Children's Depression Inventory (CDI).* Unpublished manuscript, University of Pittsburgh.

Kovacs, M. (1978b). *Interview Schedule for Children.* Unpublished manuscript, University of Pittsburgh.

Lang, P. J., & Lazovik, A. D. (1963). Experimental desensitization of a phobia. *Journal of Abnormal and Social Psychology, 66,* 519-525.

Last, C. G., Francis, G., & Strauss, C. C. (1989). Assessing fears in anxiety-disordered children with the Revised Fear Survey Schedule for Children (FSSC-R). *Journal of Clinical Child Psychology, 18,* 137-141.

Mash, E. J., & Terdal, L. G. (1981). Behavioral assessment of childhood disturbance. In E. J. Mash & L. G. Terdal (Eds.), *Behavioral assessment of childhood disorders* (pp. 3-76). New York: Guilford Press.

Melamed, B. G., & Siegel, L. J. (1975). Reduction of anxiety in children facing hospitalization and surgery by use of filmed modeling. *Journal of Consulting and Clinical Psychology, 43,* 511-521.

Miller, L. C., Barrett, C. L., & Hampe, E. (1972). Factor structure of childhood fears. *Journal of Consulting and Clinical Psychology, 39,* 261-268.

Miller, L. C., Barrett, C. L., & Hampe, E. (1974). Phobias in childhood in a prescientific era. In A. Davids (Ed.), *Child personality and psychopathology: Current topics* (Vol. 1, pp. 89-134). New York: John Wiley.

Miller, L. C., Barrett, C. L., Hampe, E., & Noble, H. (1971). Revised anxiety scales for the Louisville Behavior Checklist. *Psychological Reports, 29,* 503-511.

Morris, R. J., & Kratochwill, T. R. (1983). *Treating children's fears and phobias: A behavioral approach.* New York: Pergamon.

Neisworth, J. T., Madle, R. A., & Goeke, K. E. (1975). "Errorless" elimination of separation anxiety: A case study. *Journal of Behavior Therapy and Experimental Psychiatry, 6,* 79-82.

Nietzel, M. T., & Bernstein, D. A. (1981). Assessment of anxiety and fear. In M. Hersen & A. S. Bellack (Eds.), *Behavioral assessment: A practical handbook* (2nd ed., pp. 215-245). New York: Pergamon.

Ollendick, T. H. (1983). Anxiety-based disorders. In M. Hersen (Ed.), *Outpatient behavior therapy: A clinical guide* (pp. 273-305). New York: Grune & Stratton.

Ollendick, T. H. (in press). Assessment and treatment of internalizing problems: The role of longitudinal data. *Journal of Consulting and Clinical Psychology.*

Ollendick, T. H., & Cerny, J. A. (1981). *Clinical behavior therapy with children.* New York: Plenum.

Ollendick, T. H., & Francis, G. (1988). Behavioral assessment and treatment of childhood phobias. *Behavior Modification, 12,* 165-204.

Ollendick, T. H., & Gruen, C. E. (1972). Treatment of a bodily injury phobia with implosive therapy. *Journal of Consulting and Clinical Psychology, 38,* 389-393.

Ollendick, T. H., Hagopian, L. P., & Huntzinger, R. (1991). Cognitive behavior therapy with nighttime fearful children. *Journal of Behavior Therapy and Experimental Psychiatry, 22,* 113-121.

Ollendick, T. H., & Hersen, M. (1984). *Child behavioral assessment: Principles and procedures.* New York: Pergamon.

Ollendick, T. H., & Hersen, M. (Eds.). (1993). *Handbook of child and adolescent assessment.* Boston: Allyn & Bacon.

Ollendick, T. H., & Huntzinger, R. M. (1990). Separation anxiety disorders in childhood. In M. Hersen & C. G. Last (Eds.), *Handbook of child and adult psychopathology: A longitudinal perspective* (pp. 133-149). New York: Pergamon.

Ollendick, T. H., & King, N. J. (1991). Developmental factors in child behavioral assessment. In P. R. Martin (Ed.), *Handbook of behavior therapy and psychological science* (pp. 57-72). New York: Pergamon.

Ollendick, T. H., King, N. R., & Frary, R. B. (1989). Fears in children and adolescents in Australia and the United States. *Behaviour Research and Therapy, 27,* 19-26.

Ollendick, T. H., Matson, J. L., & Helsel, W. J. (1985). Fears in children and adolescents: Normative data. *Behaviour Research and Therapy, 23,* 465-467.

Ollendick, T. H., & Mayer, J. (1984). School phobia. In S. M. Turner (Ed.), *Behavioral treatment of anxiety disorders* (pp. 367-411). New York: Plenum.

Ollendick, T. H., Yule, W., & Ollier, K. (1991). Fears in British children and their relationship to manifest anxiety and depression. *Journal of Child Psychology and Psychiatry, 32,* 321-331.

Quay, H. C., & Peterson, D. R. (1983). *Manual for the Revised Behavior Problem Checklist.* Unpublished manuscript.

Reynolds, C. R., & Paget, K. D. (1981). Factor analysis of the Revised Children's Manifest Anxiety Scale for blacks, whites, males, and females with a national normative sample. *Journal of Consulting and Clinical Psychology, 49,* 352-359.

Reynolds, C. R., & Paget, K. D. (1983). National normative and reliability data for the Revised Children's Manifest Anxiety Scale. *School Psychology Review, 12,* 324-336.

Reynolds, C. R., & Richmond, B. O. (1978). What I think and feel: A revised measure of children's manifest anxiety. *Journal of Abnormal Child Psychology, 6,* 271-280.

Rutter, M., & Graham, P. (1968). The reliability and validity of the psychiatric assessment of the child. I. Interview with the child. *British Journal of Psychiatry, 114,* 563-579.

Ryall, M. R., & Deitikur, K. E. (1979). Reliability and clinical validity of the Children's Fear Survey Schedule. *Journal of Behavior Therapy and Experimental Psychiatry, 10,* 303-309.

Scherer, M. W., & Nakamura, C. Y. (1968). A Fear Survey Schedule for Children (FSSC-FC): A factor-analytic comparison with manifest anxiety (CMAS). *Behaviour Research and Therapy, 6,* 173-182.

Silverman, W. K., & Eisen, A. R. (1992). Age differences in the reliability of parent and child reports of child-anxious symptomatology using a structured interview. *Journal of the American Academy of Child and Adolescent Psychiatry, 31,* 117-124.

Silverman, W. K., & Nelles, W. B. (1988). A new semi-structured interview to assess childhood anxiety disorders. *Journal of the American Academy of Child and Adolescent Psychiatry, 27,* 772-778.

Smith, R. E., & Sharpe, T. M. (1970). Treatment of a school phobia with implosive therapy. *Journal of Consulting and Clinical Psychology, 35,* 239-243.

Sroufe, L. A., & Rutter, M. (1984). The domain of developmental psychopathology. *Child Development, 55,* 17-29.

Stefanek, M. E., Ollendick, T. H., Baldock, W. P., Francis, G., & Yaeger, N. J. (1987). Self-statements in aggressive, withdrawn, and popular children. *Cognitive Therapy and Research, 2,* 229-239.

Sternbach, R. (1962). Assessing differential autonomic patterns in emotions. *Journal of Psychosomatic Research, 6,* 87.

Tal, A., & Miklich, D. R. (1976). Emotionally induced decreases in pulmonary flow rates in asthmatic children. *Psychosomatic Medicine, 38,* 190-200.

Taylor, J. A. (1951). The relationship of anxiety to the conditioned eyelid response. *Journal of Experimental Psychology, 42,* 183-188.

Wolpe, J., & Lang, P. J. (1964). A fear survey schedule for use in behavior therapy. *Behaviour Research and Therapy, 2,* 27-30.

Zatz, S., & Chassin, L. (1983). Cognitions of test-anxious children. *Journal of Consulting and Clinical Psychology, 51,* 526-534.

Zatz, S., & Chassin, L. (1985). Cognitions of test-anxious children under naturalistic test-taking conditions. *Journal of Consulting and Clinical Psychology, 53,* 393-401.

6

Emotional Processing
in Anxiety Disorders

STANLEY J. RACHMAN

If a fear keeps returning, even in the absence of recurrent aversive events, it is difficult to evade the conclusion that a fragment or partial representation of that fear remains unabsorbed. Repeated nightmares about a disturbing experience, say an accident or painful rejection, also suggest the persistence of an unabsorbed "fragment" of emotion. This notion of the persistence of an unabsorbed emotional experience is strengthened by the fact that when reactions to the aversive material are deliberately reduced, the related nightmares, or other signs, decline in frequency. For example, when snake-phobic subjects overcome their fear, they report a marked decline in the number of snake-related dreams (Bandura, Jeffrey, & Gajdos, 1975). Similarly, patients who receive direct treatment for a fear of contamination report a significant decrease in the number of their unwanted and intrusive ideas and images about such threats to their well-being. War veterans who overcome their combat-related fears cease to experience nightmares or horrific flashbacks. Talking or writing about emotional experiences reduces their upsetting properties, and inhibition of the urge to relate such experiences can prolong disturbances (Pennebaker, 1993).

Attempts have been made to find connections between these phenomena. Do recurrent nightmares, the pressure to talk repeatedly about an unpleasant event, obsessional ideas and images, flashback experiences of terror, and the return of fear have anything in common? Possibly.

The concept of "emotional processing" was introduced in an attempt to accommodate a number of these disparate findings and account for the fact that a variety of techniques appear to be equally capable of reducing anxiety. Perhaps these various techniques achieve their effects by promoting emotional processing? The concept refers to the process whereby emotional disturbances are absorbed and decline to the extent that other behavior can proceed without disruption (Rachman, 1980). If an emotional disturbance is *not* absorbed satisfactorily, some signs become evident. These are likely to recur intermittently and may be direct and obvious or indirect and subtle. The central indispensable index of unsatisfactory emotional processing is the persistence or return of intrusive signs of emotional activity, such as obsessions, nightmares, pressure of talk, phobias, behavioral disruptions, hallucinations (e.g., after bereavement), unpleasant intrusive thoughts, or expressions of emotion that are out of proportion or simply inappropriate to time or place. Indirect signs may include subjective distress, fatigue, insomnia, preoccupations, resistance to distraction, an inability to concentrate, excessive restlessness, and irritability. As all of this suggests, it is easier to come to grips with *failures* of emotional processing than with successes. Broadly speaking, successful processing can be gauged from the person's ability to talk about, see, listen to, or be reminded of emotional events without experiencing distress or disruptions: Test probes fail to elicit disturbances, subjective distress and disturbed behavior decline, and "routine" behavior (e.g., concentration) returns.

Using emotional processing as a framework, we can connect apparently unrelated sets of events: the return of fear, incubation of fear, abnormal grief reactions, failures to respond to fear-reducing procedures, obsessions, and nightmares. All of these can be regarded as indices of incomplete emotional processing.

Part of the impetus for this concept of emotional processing came from the need to integrate the findings on fear reduction, and a more immediate prompt was provided by Lang's (1977, 1985) stimulating analysis of fear imagery. Lang found that phobic subjects who had minimal heart rate responses showed little improvement during desensitization. He concluded from these results, which contrasted with the concordance observed in the successfully treated subjects, that psychophysiological reactions to imagined scenes "may be a key to the emotional processing which the therapy is designed to accomplish" (Lang, 1977, p. 863).

The concept of emotional processing (Rachman, 1980) was then used to stitch together a variety of therapeutic procedures for reducing anxiety and if possible to detect the causes and passage of their common expression. As early as 1974 it had become apparent that several methods are capable of reducing anxiety, including desensitization, flooding, modeling, and habituation training (Rachman, 1974). Plausible explanations were offered to account for the effects of each method, and unsuccessful attempts were made to stretch the explanation for one method to encompass the four major techniques. The search for a unifying parsimonious explanation continued, and attempts were made to tidy and simplify the spreading facts and methods. The concept of emotional processing was formulated as an alternative to these attempts.

Before advancing to an account of emotional processing, a few observations are in order. Wolpe's (1958) original theory of reciprocal inhibition, which gives a plausible explanation of desensitization, had difficulty in accommodating the effects of flooding (and more recently of cognitive therapy). The theory proved surprisingly difficult to test in a rigorous manner, despite the clarity of Wolpe's exposition. The habituation model, introduced by Lader and Wing (1966) and elaborated by Lader and Mathews (1968), had the great merit of simplicity and was based on a widely observed phenomenon, but was unable to account for sudden and rapid changes in fear and for fears that decline in the absence of exposures. Moreover, in the continuing absence of an independent measure of habituation, the model is unfalsifiable (Clark, personal communication, 1988; Rachman, 1990). The related theory of extinction encountered the same difficulties. It has been suggested by Marks (1987) that the therapeutic changes are attributable to repeated exposures to the fearful stimulus. Controlled, repeated exposure is indeed a powerful reducer of fears, including panic. It is, however, a procedural description, not an explanation; therefore it cannot account for those instances in which fear persists despite many repetitions of exposure or explain the reductions of fear that occur without exposures (de Silva & Rachman, 1981). In the controlled treatment study of panic carried out by Margraf and Schneider (1991), for example, those patients who received pure cognitive therapy, without exposures, experienced large reductions in panic. No less than 86% of them were panic-free at the end of 15 sessions. Similarly, in their clinical experiment on the modification of claustrophobia, Booth and Rachman (1992) obtained significant reductions in fear using a form of cognitive therapy that specifically excluded exposure.

Lang construed fear as a set of three loosely coupled systems—verbal, behavioral, and psychophysiological. According to him, fear and anxiety are reduced when the structure of fear is evoked and new responses are introduced. The fear structure is evoked

> when a sufficient number of input concepts match those in the network. . . . The network activation is most likely when the phobic is confronted by the actual phobic objects which presumes a near-perfect stimulus match. However, phobic emotions may also be elicited by degraded input—pictures, verbal descriptions of context and the like. (Lang, 1986, p. 43)

A number of deductions can be drawn from this theory, and some of them have already been confirmed (e.g., that relatively speaking, agoraphobia has a less coherent structure than other anxiety disorders). Lang's theory, it should be said, is essentially a psychophysiological explanation and is an attempt to get at what he calls the deep structure of fear.

The model of emotional processing has some similarities to Lang's theory and was directly influenced by his work, but it is essentially psychological and is concerned with a broader, molar, level of explanation and description.

The initial aim of introducing the concept of emotional processing was to accommodate various forms of reducing anxiety, but there were also two subsidiary aims: to incorporate the fact that anxiety can be reduced without exposure to the anxiety-provoking situation or stimulus, and to include the growing evidence that anxiety can be modified directly by cognitive changes.

Most people successfully process the overwhelming majority of disturbing events that occur in their lives (Rachman, 1990). The emotional experiences that are processed smoothly include signaled events, mild events, prepared and controllable events, predictable events, and progressively incrementing events. Factors that promote a sense of increased controllability are particularly helpful, and people who have broad confidence and a high level of self-efficacy should successfully process most emotional experiences, including those in which anxiety is prominent. The state factors that impede processing include high arousal, dysphoria, illness, fatigue, and sleep deprivation. Personality factors associated with difficult processing include a sense of incompetence and high neurotic tendencies. Stimuli that give rise to difficulty include those that are intense, uncontrollable, unpredictable, and irregular and those that overload the system. Notable examples of incomplete emotional processing are seen in post-traumatic stress disorders and in the return-of-fear phenomenon.

From a therapeutic point of view, the factors that facilitate processing include engaged exposure to the disturbing material, calm rehearsals (especially of coping behavior), long presentations, repeated practice, the use of relaxation, vivid presentations, a sense of control, and the correction of critical misinterpretations of potential threats (see Table 6.1).

The most interesting recent development has been the widening use of and enthusiasm for cognitive forms of therapy, and it is therefore necessary to incorporate these new trends into the model of emotional processing. The most impressive recent advance of cognitive therapy has been its application to panic disorder. Controlled trials conducted in Oxford, Germany, Texas, Philadelphia, and Sweden have demonstrated that cognitive therapy effectively modifies the maladaptive cognitions, reduces the occurrence of panic, and diminishes anxiety to a marked degree. The evidence was recently summarized by Margraf, Clark, Telch, and Barlow (1993). The improvements tend to be stable, and there is evidence of a correlation between the reduction of negative cognitions and the maintenance of improvements.

The decline in cognitions observed after successful treatment is of course open to more than one interpretation. These cognitive shifts may be the cause of the therapeutic changes, or a consequence of change, or mere correlates (Rachman, 1991). The main reason for giving serious consideration to such alternative explanations arises from the fact that in the Margraf study, the patients who received *pure* exposure treatment without cognitive interventions showed improvements as large as those of patients receiving pure cognitive therapy. Moreover, the cognitions declined to the same extent in both groups.

Ost, Westling, and Hellstrom (1993) produced good results with panic patients using a relaxation technique, and here too the negative cognitions were substantially reduced after successful treatment, and to the same degree as that reported by patients who received cognitive therapy. Similarly, Booth and Rachman (1992) found that the fear and negative cognitions of claustrophobics showed large declines, regardless of whether they received exposure treatment or cognitive treatment (see Figure 6.1). It appears, therefore, that negative cognitions can decline after a direct attack or after an indirect attack.

Recent findings on the treatment of panic recall in an uncanny way one of the major observations that gave rise to the introduction of emotional

TABLE 6.1   Factors That Promote or Impede Emotional Processing

Promote	Impede
Engaged exposures	Avoidance behavior
Calm rehearsals (especially of coping)	Agitated rehearsals
Talk	Silence
Habituation training	Distractions
Extinction	Poorly presented material
No distractions	Excessively brief presentations
Catharsis	Inadequate practice
Vivid presentations	Excessively large "chunks"
Long presentations	Immobility
Repeated practice	Fatigue
Descending (?) presentations	Irregularity of stimulation
Relaxation	Unresponsive autonomic reactions
Autonomic reactivity (?)	Persisting misinterpretations of threat
Correction of critical misinterpretations of threat	

processing some 14 years ago. The fact that several procedures are dependably able to reduce anxiety inevitably gives rise to the question of whether these changes can best be accounted for by a single process or whether the therapeutic end is perhaps achieved by several different processes (see Barlow, 1988; Rachman, 1990). A possible interaction between the cognitive and exposure procedures was described by Rachman and Levitt (1988), who found that the persistence of negative cognitions impeded the extinction of claustrophobia. Interesting as this and similar interactions of the two processes might be, they should not obscure the fact that exposure, applied relaxation, and cognitive therapy all appear to be capable of achieving the same large reductions in anxiety. At the very least, the recent successes of cognitive therapy demand the incorporation of cognitive influences into the model of emotional processing. As suspected many years ago (Rachman, 1980), the provision of corrective information can indeed facilitate emotional processing—just as the introduction of threatening information can impede it.

Research on the treatment of circumscribed phobias has also given rise to the intriguing possibility that cognitive treatments might function by *initiat-*

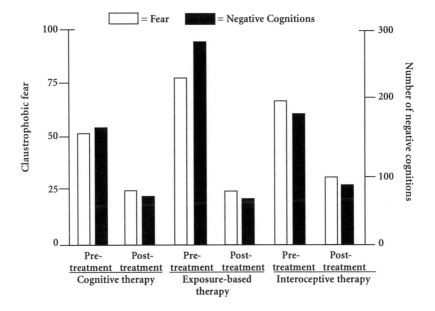

Figure 6.1. The reduction in claustrophobia and in negative cognitions observed after cognitive therapy, exposure therapy, and interoceptive therapy.

SOURCE: Booth & Rachman, 1992. Printed with permission.

ing emotional processing, and that such processing can reach completion even after an interval in which the fearful person has no contact with the stimulus and usually cannot recall any deliberate attempts to facilitate the fear reduction between sessions. This apparent delay in the effects of cognitive therapy was encountered in the experimental research on claustrophobia by Booth and Rachman (1992). The comparison group received exposure-only treatment and made rapid progress. The cognitive group made slow early progress but caught up with the gains of the exposure group directly after the retest in which the subjects were required to reenter the closet (to be reexposed). The immediacy with which the subjects in the cognitive group caught up to the subjects in the exposure group makes it clear that changes had been initiated during cognitive therapy that became apparent only after an experience in which the changes were in some sense validated.

The introduction of a cognitive perspective into the treatment of certain circumscribed phobias may facilitate treatment and ultimately lead to an improved understanding of the therapeutic processes involved (see Rachman, 1990, 1991, for fuller discussion). Much the same can be said for the treatment of obsessional disorders. Salkovskis' (1985) cognitive analysis has focused attention on the explanation that the affected person provides for his or her obsessional compulsive behavior and urges. The specific content of the obsessional ideas has for the first time become the focus of attention, with some interesting consequences. Salkovskis emphasizes the importance of the person's sense of responsibility, claiming that in most cases the obsessive-compulsive disorder is associated with an excessive and broad sense of responsibility (see Rachman, 1991, for discussion), and indeed the early trials of cognitive therapy with this disorder are looking promising. Emmelkamp and Beens (1993), van Oppen and Arntz (1994), and Salkovskis (1991) have all reported successful results.

Furthermore, there are early signs that the cognitive behavioral treatment of hypochondriasis will be equally rewarding. As in the cognitive analysis of panic disorder, the affected person is assumed to make catastrophic misinterpretations of his or her bodily sensations. Whereas the panic theory pertains to expectations of imminent catastrophe, the explanation of hypochondriasis pertains to threats to one's well-being or health that can be equally catastrophic but more remote.

In sum, the expansion of cognitive therapy into the full range of anxiety disorders is a welcome turn of events and one that initially, at least, adds to the complexity of attempting to find a unitary explanation for these changes. I am confident that the model of emotional processing has sufficient flexibility to incorporate this new evidence and indeed to benefit from it—bearing in mind that the model has from the start made provision for the effects of information on the processing of emotional experiences.

In conclusion, the concept of emotional processing provided and continues to provide a useful framework for connecting a number of phenomena and for organizing the data in a coherent fashion. It helps to make intelligible disparate emotional phenomena and provides an umbrella for the various fear reduction procedures in current use.

The weaknesses of the concept arise from the difficulty in establishing the borders of the phenomena and the slow progress in developing the technique of test probes to provide accurate and reliable measures of the extent of emotional processing. The concept must also incorporate the fact that fear, and other emotions, can be reduced or modified in the absence of "exposures."

In conclusion, progress in developing the concept of emotional processing will depend on the refinement of the test probe technique, firmer delineation of the borders of emotional processing, and the smooth incorporation of recent advances in cognitive therapy and the associated cognitive theory.

REFERENCES

Bandura, A., Jeffrey, R., & Gajdos, G. (1975). Generalizing change through participant modeling. *Behaviour Research in Therapy, 13,* 141-152.

Barlow, D. (1988). *Anxiety and its disorders.* New York: Guilford.

Booth, R., & Rachman, S. (1992). The reduction of claustrophobia. *Behaviour Research and Therapy, 30,* 207-221.

de Silva, P., & Rachman, S. (1981). Is exposure a necessary condition for fear-reduction? *Behaviour Research and Therapy, 19,* 227-232.

Emmelkamp, P., & Beens, H. (1993). Cognitive therapy with obsessive compulsive disorder. *Behaviour Research and Therapy, 31,* 62-71.

Lader, M., & Mathews, A. (1968). A physiological model of phobia anxiety and desensitization. *Behaviour Research and Therapy, 6,* 411-418.

Lader, M., & Wing, L. (1966). *Physiological measures, sedative drugs and morbid anxiety.* London: Oxford University Press.

Lang, P. (1977). Imagery in therapy: An information processing analysis of fear. *Behaviour Therapy, 8,* 862-886.

Lang, P. (1985). The cognitive psychophysiology of emotion: Fear and anxiety. In A. Tuma & J. Maser (Eds.), *Anxiety and the anxiety disorders* (pp. 143-156). Hillsdale, NJ: Lawrence Erlbaum.

Lang, P. (1987). Anxiety and memory. In B. Shaw, T. M. Vallis, & Z. Segal (Eds.), *Anxiety disorders: Psychological and Biological Perspectives* (pp. 217-234). New York: Plenum.

Margraf, J., Clark, D., Telch, M., & Barlow, D. (1993). Psychological treatment of panic. *Behaviour Research and Therapy, 31,* 1-8.

Margraf, J., & Schneider, S. (1991, July). *Outcome and ingredients of CBT for panic disorder.* American Association for Behavior Therapy Conference, New York.

Marks, I. (1987). *Fears, phobias, and rituals.* Oxford, UK: Oxford University Press.

Ost, L., Westling, B., & Hellstrom, K. (1993). Applied relaxation, exposure and cognitive methods in the treatment of panic disorder. *Behaviour Research and Therapy, 31,* 383-394.

Pennebaker, J. (1993). Social mechanisms of constraint. In D. Wegner & J. Pennebaker (Eds.), *Handbook of mental control* (pp. 539-548). New York: Prentice Hall.

Rachman, S. (1974). *The meanings of fear.* London: Penguin.

Rachman, S. (1980). Emotional processing. *Behaviour Research and Therapy, 18,* 51-60.

Rachman, S. (1990). *Fear and courage* (2nd ed.). New York: W. H. Freeman.

Rachman, S. (1991, July). *Cognitive therapy for anxiety disorders: Progress and problems.* American Association for Behavior Therapy Conference, New York.

Rachman, S., & Levitt, K. (1988). Panic, fear reduction and habituation. *Behaviour Research and Therapy, 26,* 199-206.

Salkovskis, P. (1985). Obsessional compulsive problems: A cognitive behavioral analysis. *Behaviour Research and Therapy, 23,* 511-583.

Salkovskis, P. (1991, July). *Cognitive treatment of OCD.* American Association for Behavior Therapy Conference, New York.

van Oppen, P., & Arntz, A. (1994). Cognitive therapy for obsessive compulsive disorder. *Behaviour Research and Therapy, 31,* 79-87.

Wolpe, J. (1958). *Psychotherapy by reciprocal inhibition.* Stanford, CA: Stanford University Press.

7

Anxiety and Somatic Awareness

DONALD BAKAL

KATHLYN HESSON

STEFAN DEMJEN

A middle-aged man presents to an emergency clinic with heart palpitations and chest pain, which upon ECG investigation prove to have no cardiac cause.

A young woman presents with symptoms of dizziness and nausea that begin upon awakening. The failure to resolve her symptoms has led to fears of an undiagnosed medical disease.

An elderly patient watching TV in hospital suddenly begins to sweat, and while attempting to make his way back to his room he falls in the corridor. No physical cause for the episode is found.

Patient presentations of somatic symptoms associated with dizziness, fainting, chest pain, and dyspnea are common occurrences in medical

AUTHORS' NOTE: This chapter was supported, in part, by an Alberta Mental Health Grant.

clinics and hospital departments. Kroenke (1992), an internal medicine specialist, remarked that "somatic symptoms are among the leading reasons patients visit doctors, yet are among the last things a doctor wants to see" (p. 3). Community data show a lifetime prevalence of close to 25% for chest pain, back pain, dizziness, headache, and abdominal pain. The incidence of these symptoms is much higher in the clinic, with at least 80% of patients surveyed admitting to at least one somatic symptom involving dyspnea, chest pain, abdominal pain, headache, dizziness, back pain, and fatigue. These symptoms account for almost one of every seven primary care outpatient encounters in the United States. Kroenke believes that the incidence may even be higher, in that many patients may not mention the symptoms when they present to clinics for diagnostic tests, examinations, and procedures.

Diagnostic testing for somatic symptoms seldom leads to a physical cause, and medical treatment seldom results in satisfactory resolution of the symptom. Kroenke (1992) reviewed data for 14 somatic symptoms based on patient reports of relief following medical treatment. These reports were available from only 54% of the total patient sample. Overall, just over 50% of the patients reported improvement following treatment. The percentage of patients who experienced improvement was less than 50% for patients with anxiety-related somatic symptoms such as dizziness, dyspnea, and insomnia. The fact that somatization symptoms are seldom resolved in medical settings explains much of the frustration that patients with symptoms feel toward health care professionals. Efforts to explain their symptoms as manifestations of psychological stress or anxiety, unconscious conflicts, family dysfunctions, or faulty thinking styles lead these patients to feel that their condition is not understood at all (Simon, 1991). They resent the inference that their bodily symptoms have no "real" basis and exist only in their head.

Our goal in the chapter is to provide a systematic framework for understanding patients who present with somatic symptoms associated with anxiety and to encourage the use of somatic awareness as a dimension for integrating therapeutic interventions with these patients. The framework has its origins in psychobiology and seeks to avoid the mind-body dualism inherent in present treatment approaches. The need for a better understanding of the somatic experiences of anxiety patients is evident from the familiar patient plea, "If something physical is not wrong, then what is? I have no reason to be anxious, and I don't think I am depressed."

The word *anxiety* has its origin in the Latin word *angere,* meaning "to choke" or "to strangle," suggesting that, at least for anxiety sufferers, significant physiological events are at the basis of their somatic sensations. Psychological theories of anxiety, however, have chosen to deemphasize the physiological origins of somatic symptoms in favor of identifying the subjective or cognitive determinants of the somatic symptoms. In the book *Anxiety Disorders and Phobias,* Beck and Emery (1985) presented a case for interpreting clinical occurrences of somatic symptoms in cognitive terms alone. For example, they described the case of a 40-year-old man who had gone on a skiing trip and while skiing began to experience shortness of breath, perspiration, faintness, and body weakness. He had difficulty focusing and eventually was taken from the slopes by stretcher and rushed to the hospital. Nothing abnormal was found, and he received the diagnosis of acute anxiety attack. The man was an experienced skier who had in the past simply "skied through" similar body symptoms (chest pain, feeling cold, sweaty). Why the difference this time? According to Beck and Emery, some cognitive circumstance led him to interpret these previously benign exercise sensations as having life-threatening significance. He had recently lost a brother due to a heart attack, and "If it could happen to my brother, it could happen to me. . . ." Although the skier may have been questioning his mortality as described, we need to be careful in assuming that his body experience was similar to the exercise state that he had previously "skied through" without anxiety. On this day, his body and mind were probably in a state of panic, and consequently he was correct in identifying within himself a condition that was different from the sensations resulting from overexercise.

In directing attention to the cognitive aspects of anxiety, Beck remained very aware of the somatic side of anxiety as a clinical condition. The Beck Anxiety Inventory (BAI; Beck, Epstein, Brown, & Steer, 1988; Beck & Steer, 1990) contains 21 items, with 6 items reflecting cognitive symptoms (unable to relax, fear of the worst happening, terrified, nervous, fear of losing control, scared) and the remaining 14 items reflecting somatic symptoms. The questionnaire was designed to separate anxiety from depression. A cluster analysis of the inventory identified four groups of symptoms. The items are presented in Table 7.1 in rank-order fashion to reflect their item-total correlations within each cluster. The dominant cluster is characterized by symptoms of dizziness that are presumed to have a neurophysiological origin. The second cluster is characterized by subjective symptoms that are consistent with the cognitive fear-of-fear hypothesis (fear of the worst happening, fear of losing control). The third cluster contains a mixture of cardiovascular, respiratory, and subjective symptoms. The two respiratory symptoms, feel-

TABLE 7.1   Subscales of the Beck Anxiety Inventory

Neurophysiological
  Shaky
  Unsteady
  ᴅizzy or lightheaded
  Faint
  Hands trembling
  Wobbliness in legs
  Numbness or tingling
Subjective
  Fear of the worst happening
  Fear of losing control
  Terrified
  Scared
  Nervous
  Unable to relax
Panic
  Difficulty breathing
  Fear of dying
  Feelings of choking
  Heart pounding or racing
Autonomic
  Feeling hot
  Sweating
  Face flushed
  Indigestion or discomfort in the abdomen

SOURCE: Beck & Steer, 1990.

ings of choking and difficulty breathing, and the racing heart symptom are extremely prevalent across anxiety disorders. The panic disorder symptoms of chest pain and/or chest tightness were not included in the questionnaire and their inclusion might have provided evidence for a distinct respiratory/chest pain symptom cluster. The fourth cluster is characterized by symptoms of feeling hot, sweaty, and flushed and, to a lesser extent, symptoms of abdominal discomfort.

We conducted a similar cluster analysis of the BAI, based on responses of 557 college students. The questionnaire was administered as part of a larger study dealing with somatic ratings of anxiety and depression symptoms in college students. The four BAI college student clusters were quite similar to those reported by Beck. The subjective cluster and the panic cluster of the student sample were identical to the clusters reported by Beck for the patient sample. A second analysis with the extraction criterion set to two clusters separated the items into 7 subjective symptoms and 14 somatic symptoms. The somatic symptoms contained in the cluster also corresponded to most common somatization disorders seen in medical practice.

SOMATIZATION

Within the recent somatization literature, there has been a shift away from the traditional view that somatization symptoms serve as a defense against emotional distress—that is, that somatizing patients express physical symptoms as a substitute for psychological distress. Theorists are placing greater emphasis on the fact that somatizing patients report both psychological and somatic symptoms in increasing proportion to the severity of their disorder.

Support for the positive relationship between expressions of psychological and physical symptoms comes from community survey studies. Simon and Von Korff (1991) used data from the NIMH Epidemiologic Catchment Area (ECA) Study to examine the relationship between somatization and the report of psychiatric symptoms in a multisite community survey. A structured clinical interview, the Diagnostic Interview Schedule (DIS), was used to assess the presence of *DSM-III* diagnoses. The version of the DIS used in the ECA study allowed diagnoses of mania, major depression, bipolar disorder, alcohol abuse or dependence, drug abuse or dependence, schizophrenia, obsessive-compulsive disorder, phobia, somatization disorder, panic disorder, and antisocial personality. The DIS symptoms that most clearly expressed emotional distress associated with anxiety and depression were identified and compared with the number of somatization symptoms endorsed. The percent of respondents reporting psychological distress increased with the number of reported somatic symptoms. In the group reporting five or more somatic symptoms, over 63% of the respondents endorsed one or more symptoms of emotional distress. Almost 50% of the high-somatization group met criteria for current depression or anxiety disorder. Respondents with the highest number of somatic symptoms had the highest risk for panic disorder relative to the other psychiatric disorders.

Costa and McCrae (1987) postulated that the distress-somatization covariation observed in normal and patient samples is due to neuroticism. They define *neuroticism* as a chronic condition of irritability and distress-proneness that operates independently from signs of real physical illness. That is, neuroticism or negative affectivity is associated with the verbal report of both psychological and physical problems but is not necessarily associated with the presence of physical disease. The anxious individual, in their words, has a perceptual bias and "seeks out and amplifies bodily sensations" (p. 307). In a similar fashion, Barsky (1992) hypothesized that the presentation of benign physical symptoms such as palpitation and chest pain is associated with somatosensory amplification and misattribution. That is, these individuals are prone to exaggerate or amplify sensations that would otherwise be experienced as benign and nonthreatening by the nonanxious individual.

Cognitive concepts like perceptual bias and misattribution parallel theoretical thinking in cognitive models of anxiety. Although the concepts have a degree of validity, they also foster a form of dualism by implying that the physiological component of a presenting symptom is not what determines the symptom. Symptom presentation depends not on physiological change but on how the patient interprets and reacts to normal physiological events. In short, these concepts imply that there are no physiological events necessarily taking place that match the patient's body experiences. We should not assume, however, that because a patient's phenomenological experiences with body symptoms are often difficult to describe, the physiologic origins of these experiences are unimportant. It is possible that the reverse is true—the more difficult it is for the patient to describe the experience, the more likely it is that something significant at a physiological level is taking place.

It is important to emphasize that not all patients who present with somatic symptoms also present with psychological symptoms. There are many patients with somatic symptoms who deny any evidence of psychological distress, in the form of either anxiety or depression. Beitman and colleagues (Kushner, Beitman, & Beck, 1989) noted that only half of a sample of chest pain cardiology patients with normal or near-normal coronary arteries verbalized anxiety, whereas the other half of the sample did not verbalize significant anxiety.

Engel, Baile, Costa, Brimlow, and Brinker (1985) conducted a behavioral assessment of chest pain episodes in 83 men and women who had been referred for cardiac catheterization for evaluation of chest pain. Prior to the examination, patients were asked to monitor the location and quality of chest pain episodes as well as to record the setting, the activity, and their mood when the pain episode occurred. The most frequent pain location was the sternum, and the most frequently reported mood prior to pain onset was contentment. Negative moods were not reported with any major frequency.

Awareness of body symptoms also varies tremendously across individuals, and the lack of awareness can have serious consequences. For example, although angina pectoris is the most common symptom of myocardial ischemia in patients with coronary artery disease, the majority of out-of-hospital ischemic episodes are asymptomatic. It is difficult to know why symptoms sometimes accompany ischemic episodes and sometimes do not. Some symptomatic patients tend to complain of chest pain early in the course of ischemic episodes even if their symptoms are relatively mild, whereas others endure prolonged ischemia before reporting any symptoms. Freedland et al. (1991) identified a group of patients with chest pain and reversible myocardial ischemia and a group of patients with silent ischemia during an exercise stress test. At the start of the exercise, patients were instructed to report any chest discomfort, fatigue, or other symptoms. All patients were asked to report the time at which they expected to be able to continue exercising only one more minute. The onset of chest pain was recorded in the majority of symptomatic cases. There were no significant differences between the groups with respect to total exercise duration or time from onset of electrocardiographic indications of ischemia to the end of exercise. Whereas chest discomfort was the most common reason for stopping among symptomatic patients, 48% of the silent ischemia patients exercised until they were too fatigued to do so.

Another example of differences in body perception of symptom onset and development is found with asthmatics. It is known that some asthmatic individuals fail to recognize both the presence of anxiety within themselves and changes in airflow obstruction (Yellowlees & Kalucy, 1990). Lack of awareness of symptom onset has also been linked to occurrences of fatal asthmatic attacks in both children and adults (Fritz, Rubinstein, & Lewiston, 1987).

Historically, concepts such as masked depression and alexithymia have been invoked to explain individuals who experience somatic symptoms in the absence of psychological distress. Although these concepts have failed to generate strong empirical findings, clinical observations would suggest that individuals who fail to verbalize psychological distress accompanying somatic symptom presentation are as prevalent as individuals who verbalize distress.

Barsky (1992) suggested that there may be an individual difference continuum that reflects sensitivity to visceral stimuli. At one end of the continuum are "minimizing" patients who underreport body sensations, and at the other end are "amplifying" patients who are very sensitive to and aware of visceral stimuli. Such a continuum, if present, probably would reflect learned coping styles for dealing with stress, emotion, and body sensations rather than innate biologic traits.

DIZZINESS AS A SYMPTOM
OF ALTERED CONSCIOUSNESS

Unexplained sensations of dizziness as well as wobbliness, unsteadiness, and feeling faint are some of the most frequently reported somatic symptoms experienced by anxiety sufferers. Initially, the definition of *dizziness* was restricted to vertigo and implied a vestibular dysfunction with an associated rotating sensation. The dizziness experienced by anxiety sufferers and somatizing patients is more nonspecific in experience, and patients with this symptom have difficulty putting into words the sensations that they are experiencing. Common descriptors include lightheadedness, feelings of detachment, and fuzziness and suggest an altered state of consciousness.

Fewtrell and O'Connor (1988) observed that individuals who experience dizziness have a preoccupation with being unable to cope in public with the symptom as well as concern with possible serious physical illness, making it important to recognize the meaning aspect of the symptom. Dizziness episodes, like other anxiety symptoms, sometimes occur during periods of relaxation or inactivity and resemble the state of relaxation-induced anxiety (Heide & Borkovec, 1984). Fewtrell and O'Connor provided an example of a teacher who was prone to dizzy bouts that were restricted to relaxing weekends and holidays, but were never experienced in the classroom. They proposed that abrupt arousal shifts upward or downward may provoke dizziness.

Some instances of dizziness may be experienced as a form of depersonalization. Fewtrell and O'Connor (1988) defined depersonalization as "an unpleasant change in the quality of consciousness in which there is a reduction of intensity of feeling, accompanied by a curious change of self-awareness" (p. 204). Slater and Roth (1969) described depersonalization phenomena as a form of constriction of consciousness that is activated by severe anxiety and that serves to attenuate the effects of anxiety on behavior. Depersonalization serves, then, to protect the individual during periods of intolerable distress. To illustrate the relationship between fear, anxiety, and depersonalization, they provided an incident of a psychiatrist who was involved in a road traffic accident on his way to work:

> The man in question was driving at some speed on a wet road surface and as he cornered fast the car skidded. He immediately experienced a dream-like detachment and found himself steering mechanically and aware of his actions as if he were contemplating some unfortunate victim from a distance. After spinning round several times and narrowly avoiding on-coming traffic, the car finally came to a halt facing in the opposite direction. The driver felt quite calm but when by-standers spoke to him their voices seemed muffled and the surrounding countryside appeared still, remote and unreal. His own voice sounded unfamiliar. He drove on feeling quite calm, arrived at his clinic and rang for his first patient. As the patient entered the psychiatrist's depersonal-ization suddenly lifted and he became quite aware that he was perspiring and trembling severely and his heart was pounding at a rapid rate. (pp. 122-123)

Fewtrell and O'Connor hypothesized that dizziness and depersonalization may be phenomenologically identical and reflect variation in patients' choice of semantics in describing the same perceptual disturbance.

Clinical occurrences of dizziness in public settings first led to the identi-fication of agoraphobia as an anxiety disorder. In 1870 Benedikt reported a clinical state called *Platzschwindel,* which means "dizziness in public places." This observation was followed by Westphal's publication a year later using the term *agoraphobia* for the same phenomenon (Boyd & Crump, 1991). Westphal presented the cases of three men who had a strong fear of crossing open spaces. One individual experienced both dizziness and heart palpitations; the second individual described a "feeling of heat beginning in the lower part of the abdomen and rising toward the head, accompanied by heart palpitations also more often with general tremor and a feeling of bewilderment of the highest degree"; the third individual felt chest tightness in the region of the heart, followed by heat sensations in the face and feelings of derealization (pp. 81-82). All patients reported "absolutely no reason for the fear that befalls them" (p. 82), and all were able to benefit from having someone accompany them and/or a drink of alcohol prior to entering the open space. Westphal noted that dizziness was a common symptom of these individuals, and he felt that its origins were purely cerebral or mental.

Ottaviani and Beck (1987) asked subjects to recall the thoughts and images that were present during an episode of panic and also to indicate the situational context in which the attack occurred. The qualitative data suggested that panic sufferers may report dizziness and disorientation sensations when the attacks occur in public situations (shopping, caught in a crowd, talking to a boss) and chest pain and shortness of breath sensations when the attacks occur in private, usually at home. There was considerable overlap of the two categories of symptoms, in that the majority of subjects identified symptoms associated with the chest and/or breathing as being present at panic onset, regardless of the situation. These were retrospective and uncontrolled accounts, making it impossible to know the degree to which dizziness and dyspnea occurred together and were noticed differently depending on the patient's situational circumstance.

A connection between fear of social situations and dizziness has been suggested by Telch, Brouillard, Telch, Agras, and Taylor (1989). They observed that the main physical symptom that differentiated panic disorder patients with agoraphobia from panic patients without agoraphobia was fear of fainting. In addition, the two *DSM-III-R* symptoms that significantly differentiated panic disorder patients with agoraphobia from panic disorder patients without it were feeling faint and dizziness. A number of cognitive symptoms related to social embarrassment and loss of control also differentiated the two groups, but it is interesting that the physical symptom of dizziness clearly separated the groups in terms of their situational avoidance.

Dizziness leading to loss of consciousness and postural tone is called *syncope* (Linzer et al., 1991). Like agoraphobics, individuals who experience syncope often develop a fear of fainting and consequent functional impairment. Syncope often leads to interference with daily activities, driving, employment, and interpersonal relationships. The loss of consciousness is believed to result from anxiety-generated sympathetic tone followed by a homeostatic parasympathetic response associated with bradycardia and hypotension. It also seems to occur for no apparent reason to the sufferer.

A 72-year-old patient was admitted to a hospital with longstanding pain secondary to Mellaril. The majority of pain occurred around the perineal region and the mouth and gums. The individual had received a diagnosis of PTSD during World War II and had been receiving anxiolytic medications for over 40 years. He had experienced numerous episodes of being angry with the medical system for prescribing phenothiazines. He was admitted to a rehabilitation unit for the purpose of withdrawing him from phenothiazines and benzodiazepines. The patient had one activity for reducing pain and that was watching TV. One evening he was having difficulty sleeping so he went to the TV room to watch late night shows. After an hour he began to sweat and decided to make his way to bed. On the way he lost consciousness and fell to the floor. He insisted, after the episode, that he could recall no reason for the event. This is a common observation of syncope patients, in that they all believe that the episodes are unexplained, even though there is often evidence of emotional tension or apprehension within the period prior to an episode. This particular patient was extremely sensitive to perceived staff criticism of his actions, and on this night he was watching TV in the same room that the night staff used for their coffee-rest breaks. The awareness that he was preventing the staff from using the room may have generated anxiety, although he never acknowledged that this was the case.

This patient also noted the presence of chest pain during his dizziness, in that he felt as if "I could not open my lungs up." This indicates that there may be a respiratory and/or ventilatory component to syncope, the extent of which is unknown. Hyperventilation, for example, is known to lead to vasoconstriction of the cerebral vasculature and accompanying dizziness and depersonalization (Drachman & Hart, 1972).

DYSPNEA AND CHEST PAIN

Dyspnea and chest pain/tightness represent two of the most prevalent somatic symptoms seen in medical practice. Dyspnea has received the most attention in the anxiety literature because of its significance to ventilatory explanations of panic disorder. Chest tightness is also a very common symptom, and its physiologic origins are only beginning to be investigated. In the past, symptoms of dyspnea and chest tightness were assumed to have a cardiac origin, but current research is directed more toward a ventilatory, a respiratory, or some ventilatory-respiratory explanation. Ventilatory models deal primarily with central mechanisms (e.g., brainstem chemoreceptors) that regulate breathing, whereas respiratory models focus more on the psychophysiological variables involved in breathing.

The leading advocate of a ventilatory explanation of dyspnea and other chest symptoms is Klein (1993). His interest in these symptoms is in their unique contribution to panic anxiety. He believes that ventilatory symptoms (changes in minute ventilation) are specific to panic anxiety, whereas cardiac symptoms (palpitations) can be found with both panic disorder and generalized anxiety patients. Klein has refined the hyperventilation theory of panic anxiety with the postulation of a biologic suffocation alarm system. He suggests that the brain abnormalities of panic disorder might be thought of as constituting a derangement of the "suffocation centers" of the brain. The idea is that our brain naturally has a way of sounding an alarm if we are being suffocated, and in some people that regulatory thermostat may have an incorrectly low threshold such that alarm bells go off internally, causing the person to gasp for air. Breathlessness is, in his words, a preliminary phase of panic that initiates hyperventilation. Breathlessness itself is initiated by the suffocation alarm—that is, an internal or endogenous danger signal.

Biologic theorists are able to martial considerable evidence for centrally determined ventilatory changes associated with panic anxiety. There remains the possibility, however, that the respiratory symptoms of panic have a peripheral rather than central origin. This belief is based on some pilot observations of panic sufferers during a laboratory carbon dioxide provocation study (Lynch, Bakal, Whitelaw, & Fung, 1991). The study was designed to examine, within a hyperventilation framework, the minute ventilation characteristics of panic sufferers and controls when exposed to different concentrations of carbon dioxide inhalations. Hyperventilation theory predicts that panic sufferers should show greater changes than normals in minute ventilation because of their hypersensitivity to carbon dioxide. The physiological measures of heart rate, forehead EMG, and chest wall EMG were also used in the study. Chest wall EMG was recorded from the sternum region to determine if there might be a peripheral musculoskeletal correlate of the symptoms of chest tightness, pressure, and/or heaviness. The subjects were divided on the basis of how anxious or "panicky" they became during the course of the experiment, as determined by several administrations of a 10-point Likert scale. The physiologic data were analyzed across the baseline, carbon dioxide inhalation, and recovery phases. The group means for these data are presented in Figure 7.1. The primary ventilatory measure, minute ventilation, failed to discriminate the groups and provided no evidence for the hyperventilation hypothesis. However, Klein (personal communication, August 21, 1991) noted that the 5-minute inhalation period used in this study may not have been sufficient for subjects to have reached asymptotic levels of minute ventilation. The heart rate data were also non-significant but were consistent with the findings of other investigators who use this measure. Generally, tonic heart rate is higher for panic sufferers than

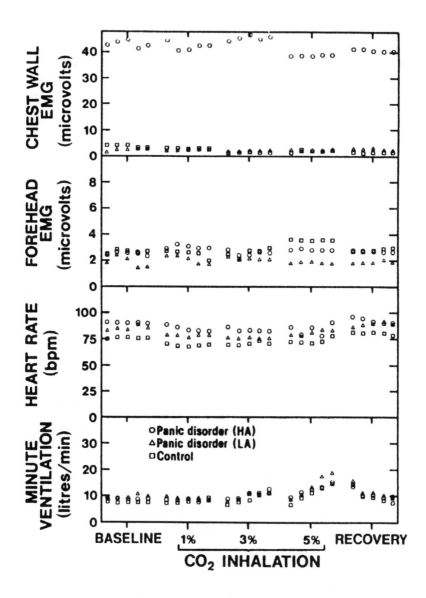

Figure 7.1. Physiologic average scores of high-anxious (HA) panic disorder subjects, low-anxious (LA) panic disorder subjects, and controls.

SOURCE: P. Lynch, D. A. Bakal, W. Whitelaw, & T. Fung. Chest muscle activity and panic anxiety: A preliminary investigation. *Psychosomatic Medicine, 1991, 53*(1), 80-89. Copyright by American Psychosomatic Society. Reprinted by permission.

for controls, with the group differences sometimes being significant and sometimes not. There were significant differences in chest EMG, with the high-anxiety panic subjects exhibiting the greatest activity. Heightened chest muscle activity was observed only in the panic disorder subjects who were also showing evidence of anxiety and/or panic. We could not determine whether the heightened chest EMG activity was chronic in nature or specific to the experimental situation. Our suspicion is that the activity was specific to the situation and that the pulmonary laboratory proved to be highly provoking for the more severe agoraphobic patients. The hallmark characteristic of agoraphobic avoidance is "the fear of being in places or situations from which escape might be difficult (or embarrassing) or in which help might not be available in the event of a panic attack" (American Psychiatric Association, 1987, p. 238).

There is a need for further study of the precise role of respiratory muscles and breathing patterns in anxiety disorders. Respiratory physiologists have observed wide individual differences in breathing patterns, and these patterns may be not be easily alterable. Requiring subjects to breathe in a fashion that deviates too far from their natural breathing style may be more anxiety provoking than relaxing. In addition, the significance of chest muscle activity requires study as an independent contributory factor to the anxiety sensations of chest tightness, chest heaviness, and chest pain. Our observations of sustained chest wall EMG activity were made during periods of end-expiration and were therefore indicative of inspiratory effort that was maintained throughout the whole breathing cycle. Thus the muscles were holding the chest in a tonic fashion at a volume higher than its relaxed volume, in addition to making repeated inspiratory efforts to increase volume further with each breath. Such activity is abnormal and serves no physiological purpose.

A number of studies are currently examining the relationship of chest pain in cardiology patients and panic anxiety. The focus is on patients with chest pain and no evidence of coronary artery disease. Claims are made that between 30 and 40% of chest pain cardiology patients with normal or near-normal coronary arteries have panic disorder (Kushner et al., 1989). Eifert (1992) views chest pain as a form of cardiophobia—a form of health anxiety that is present in consciousness only when there is chest pain. He recommends that the chest muscles be targeted specifically in behavioral treatment.

INTEGRATING SOMATIC AWARENESS

A case has been presented for the incorporation of somatic sensations and associated physiological processes into explanatory models of anxiety. Somatic awareness can be used as a therapeutic strategy for all anxiety patients, although the mode of use will have to be individually determined for each patient. Respiratory and chest wall muscle changes appear to be of particular importance and may not only account for dyspnea and chest pain but also contribute to symptoms of dizziness and depersonalization. It is important that the psychobiological determinants of these symptoms be integrated into cognitive-behavioral treatments of anxiety symptoms. Otherwise, we are left with the impression that cognitive and physiological events are independent of one another and that there are different types of anxiety conditions, some with a physiological substrate and some without. Ley (1992), for example, proposed that there are different types of panic disorder and that each type requires a different intervention. He described one type of panic as being characterized by high-intensity dyspnea, heart palpitations, and terror and stated that patients with this type of condition would be expected to benefit from breathing retraining. A second type of panic attack was characterized by low levels of chronic anxiety that wax and wane and produce symptoms of anxiety that on occasion are sufficiently strong to alarm the sufferer and lead to a catastrophic interpretation. According to Ley, patients with this type of panic would not be discernible from normal subjects on standard psychophysiological measures with the symptom either absent or present, and these patients would require cognitive intervention. Further study, however, is required before adopting typologies to resolve apparent discrepancies between physiologic signs and sensory symptoms. Had respiratory measures been obtained, it might have been possible to detect physiologic similarities in these two "types" of patients.

Our approach to intervention is based on an intraindividual systemic model with an emphasis on psychobiological processes that regulate anxiety symptoms. Systemic models are increasingly being used to conceptualize health and illness and are especially useful for conceptualizing the sensory-physiological factors of anxiety symptoms within the context of ongoing cognitive, personality, and interpersonal factors. Somatic awareness is viewed as the critical system parameter, use of which will reduce the presenting somatic symptom.

Defining *somatic awareness* is not a simple matter; as a concept it is rich in surplus meaning, an advantage in the clinical situation, but very difficult for teaching. It has been defined by Cioffi (1991) as the process by which we perceive, interpret, and act on the information from our bodies. To be effective, the awareness needs to be accompanied by an alteration of the sensory symptoms. This state is variously described as letting go, the relaxation response, the quieting response, and passive relaxation.

If one were to characterize the various levels of variables controlling anxiety in terms of layers or levels, then somatic awareness would constitute the core of the discovery process. Although the concept often does not find its way into treatment plans, it is not a completely novel concept either historically or in nonmedical situations. It seems to be best understood in sports psychology, in which athletes use somatic awareness to enhance performance. Morgan and Pollock (1977) reported a number of years ago that elite marathon runners, when compared to their less experienced counterparts, used an associative rather than a dissociative cognitive strategy in dealing with sensations while running. Dissociative strategies had no relation to the sensory experiences of running and included techniques such as recalling early experiences, working mathematical exercises, and hearing favorite music. These strategies were also accompanied by efforts to "run or fight through" the pain when it became noticeable, a strategy that led to increased discomfort, pain, and discouragement. Elite runners, on the other hand, paid especially close attention to bodily sensations arising in their feet, calves, and chest. They repeatedly reminded themselves to "stay loose" during the run. They also dismissed the marathon concept of "the wall" as myth—they simply did not come up against the wall during the run. Morgan and Pollock speculated that elite runners are able to associate (monitor) their sensory input and to adjust their pace and technique accordingly.

Hanna (1988) coined the term *sensory motor amnesia* to describe the lack of body awareness that often characterizes patients with somatic complaints. Even when instructed to relax, the bodies often show no sign of following the mental command. Although most human functioning takes place in the absence of body awareness, there are suggestions in the literature that subjects, when directed to bodily sensations associated with their head, heart, respiration, and chest, can become quite accurate in the perception of such information.

Experimental literature on body awareness was discouraged for a number of years following demonstrations that subjects could be readily deceived into misreading or mislabeling bodily information. Following the lead of Schachter and Singer (1962), a number of experiments appeared that were designed to show, using falsified feedback, that it is the cognitive information provided about bodily events rather than direct perception of the events themselves that determines a subject's understanding of what is taking place within him- or herself. Similar experiments using placebo study designs repeatedly demonstrated that subjects can readily be persuaded to experience sensations that have no obvious bodily counterpart, such as sensations of excitement when they are actually calm or sensations of an elevated blood alcohol level even when their alcohol intake has been minimal (Fisher, 1986).

In a recent study, Steptoe and Vögele (1992) presented volunteer female students with three stressful tasks involving a nonverbal mental arithmetic task, mirror drawing, and the cold pressor test and required the subjects to provide ratings of bodily sensations experienced as "racing heart," "sweaty hands," "high blood pressure," and "shortness of breath." Heart rate, electrodermal activity, blood pressure, and respiration rate were recorded as the corresponding physiological measures. There was a close association between the contour of responses in each physiological parameter and its corresponding sensation rating, making it apparent that the subjects were able to identify bodily sensations in a laboratory setting. The graphs for heart rate (HR), skin conductance (SCL), and palmar sweat index (PSI) are presented in Figure 7.2. The mean within-subject correlations were highest for heart rate (.76) followed by systolic BP/high BP (.55), SCL/sweaty hands (.47), PSI/sweaty hands (.64), and respiration rate/shortness of breath (.48). There were, however, major differences in the accuracy-of-perception correlation coefficients across the 30 subjects. These differences were not due to differences in autonomic lability or measured trait anxiety. There was no association between accuracy of somatic perception across the different physiological parameters, a finding that "casts doubt on any general tendencies towards sensitivity and accuracy of somatic perception and on the notion that people vary on a dimension of visceral sensitivity" (p. 605).

Fisher (1986) noted that the puzzling aspect of the body perception literature is that people without training do little better than chance in identifying their own visceral experiences, yet with training they can become quite accurate in identifying such experiences. Why, he asked, would the infinite body experiences that people have not provide them with comparable opportunities to learn? Self-awareness theorists believe that direct body perception is too threatening to the individual's self-esteem to be used on a

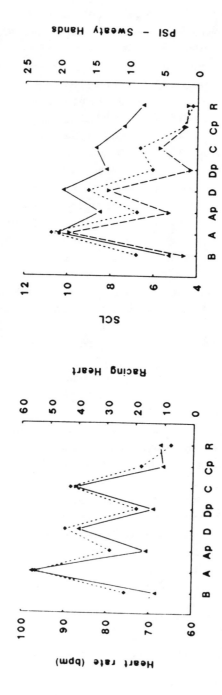

Figure 7.2 (a) Mean levels of heart rate (00) and ratings of racing heart (00) over the experimental session. B = baseline, A = peak response to mental arithmetic, Ap = end of postarithmetic recovery, D = peak response to mirror drawing, Dp = end of postdrawing recovery, C = peak response to cold pressor, Cp = end of postcold recovery, R = relaxation. (b) Mean levels of skin conductance levels (00), palmar sweat count (00), and ratings of sweaty hands (00).

SOURCE: A. Steptoe & C. Vögele. Individual differences in the perception of bodily sensations: The role of trait anxiety and coping style. *Behaviour Research and Therapy*, 1992, 30, 597-607. Copyright © 1992 Pergamon Press. Reprinted by permission.

regular basis. Wicklund (1991) hypothesized that any form of self-induction brought about by hearing one's voice or seeing oneself in a mirror can generate entire arrays of unpleasant psychological states. For Wicklund, self-focused attention of any type sets up awareness of personal discrepancies or shortcomings. The awareness may then cut the person off from a system of immediate social support and guidance, leaving him or her to cope with life on the basis of a handful of internalized values.

At a clinical level, patients generally prefer to ignore sensations associated with symptom development, for fear that attending to their presence will make the condition worse. They often prefer to manage their condition by staying busy or "clogging" their mind with other thoughts. In the clinical pain literature, active avoidance through distraction is often encouraged as a coping strategy. Straight distraction in the absence of somatic changes is generally not effective for coping with clinical pain. Research using cold-pressor tasks and reaction time attention diversion tasks has shown that distraction alone is not sufficient to reduce experimental pain (McCaul, Monson, & Maki, 1992). Leventhal (1992) noted that the belief that distraction works is very common and is also very difficult to reverse. During a childbirth study, he found that repeated revision and weeks of testing were necessary in order to develop instructions that were effective in getting women to monitor the somatic sensations of their contractions.

> These mothers wanted to distract, not to monitor; we had no trouble encouraging another group of mothers to distract. After giving birth, several of those who were monitored expressed surprise that monitoring actually reduced distress! In sum, it is counterintuitive to monitor sensations in order to reduce pain and distress and intuitively consistent to distract. (Leventhal, 1992, p. 208)

The attainment of somatic awareness constitutes a viable therapeutic objective and serves to coordinate different interventions for anxiety patients who present with somatic symptoms. Therapists, by using somatic awareness as the core element of therapy, can organize their therapeutic interventions to deal systemically with psychological issues and the mind-body symptom interface.

Treatment should be directed toward increasing rather than decreasing the patient's awareness of the sensations that are associated with the symptoms of the disorder. Somatic symptoms have a physiologic substrate, and it is inappropriate to view their presence as "usual noise made by the body." Making subjects with these types of symptoms perform stress tests or other activation responses to prove to them that no harm will result seems a questionable method of treatment if the goal of treatment is to help patients acquire a better understanding of themselves through their symptoms.

Because of active-avoidant coping styles, anxiety patients may initially report that attending directly to their body is unpleasant and anxiety producing, but with encouragement and practice, they can be brought to achieve a degree of awareness:

> Mrs. C. was referred to the hospital clinic for behavioral management of panic attacks, generalized anxiety disorder, and multiple phobias. She is 38 years old, married with four children, and working as an office manager responsible for nine staff. She did not respond to pharmacological treatment mainly because of adverse reactions to anxiolytics. She underwent several years of psychodynamic therapy and attended self-help/growth groups for the past 10 years. She experienced physical abuse as a child and was battered by a husband in a previous marriage.
>
> In the initial session she identified panic attacks as the most pressing problem. She was experiencing four to five attacks a day, mostly at work. The attacks were associated with a fear of heart failure, sensations of choking, and thoughts of looking foolish. Initially she refused to do breathing relaxation because she thought that attending to her breathing would make her more anxious. She was introduced to autogenic relaxation (arms and legs) and encouraged to identify anxiety-provoking thoughts and generate alternate ways of looking at the problem. She took a leave of absence so that she could focus her attention on learning to cope with the panic attacks. Within weeks she experienced control of the panic and felt the problem was behind her. However, within days of returning to work the panic attacks had returned. She reluctantly agreed to start focusing on her breathing and to practice abdominal breathing exercises. She noticed that when she was overwhelmed she stopped breathing and held her breath. When excited or emotional she would breathe in a shallow fashion and begin to feel dizzy. She began observing these breathing irregularities in everyday life and slowly corrected these respiratory reactions as well as her panicky thoughts.

Somatic awareness is usually very difficult to integrate into the patient's day-to-day life experiences. Patients will state that they are completely relaxed following the listening of an appropriate relaxation tape, and yet they may have no understanding of how bodily relaxation is to be used to reduce episodes of anxiety. Most somatization patients do not readily accept, at an experiential level, the therapeutic importance of monitoring their body sensations in the context of ongoing thoughts, feelings, and behaviors. Why this is so requires theoretical explanation, but at an applied level we see the difficulty in the limited success of technique-oriented approaches such as biofeedback and relaxation training when used in isolation. Patients are often amazed at the magnitude of psychobiological change that is required during the 24-hour day to effect therapeutic change.

The psychobiologic approach advocated uses some elements of the stepwise systemic emotional awareness model advocated by Lane and Schwartz (1992). They hypothesized that patients often present emotional difficulties at different emotional levels, the lowest being bodily distress and somatic sensations. Cognitive distress and conflicts over different emotions represent respectively higher levels of emotional difficulty. Their highest level represents a form of existential crisis. They made three treatment recommendations that are relevant to the present approach:

1. Intervention should be directed to the level of emotion information processing at which the patient currently functions.
2. Intervention should proceed from the bottom up rather than the top down.
3. Additional modalities targeted for higher levels should be added incrementally when those aimed at lower levels are not fully adequate to resolve the problem.

We are proposing less of a stepwise intervention strategy and a more integrated management of the various factors that are maintaining the symptom by focusing throughout therapy on the interplay of situational, interpersonal, personality, and emotional characteristics of the symptom. The enhancement of somatic awareness is not restricted to biofeedback or relaxation training, but remains at the basis of all therapeutic issues that are addressed during the course of therapy.

In difficult patient cases of somatization symptoms, especially when the patient exhibits excessive use of medical facilities and medication, symptom management may be best attained through patient admission to an inpatient psychiatric unit. Otherwise, the patient will continue to seek and receive alternate explanations and treatments for his or her condition, making it nearly impossible to achieve significant changes through self-regulation strategies alone. Once admitted, the patient can be encouraged to participate in a wide variety of interventions including group therapy, psychotherapy, stress management, medication management, and physiotherapy. Initially the patient may resent having to sit and listen to other patients, believing that his or her condition is not psychiatric in origin. However, by having a team therapist stay with the symptom and listen to the patient's good and bad experiences on the unit (e.g., does the symptom get better or worse during group therapy), it is possible to have the patient come to understand his or her symptom in the context of experiences resembling day-to-day life events. By including the participation of a health care team, the patient is more likely to develop a shift in his or her symptom perspective.

What the patient learns through somatic awareness interventions is not necessarily known. Unlike the athlete who is learning a specific skill for a particular application, the patient needs to use this awareness in all aspects of waking and sleeping life. In some instances, patients simply cannot develop the concept within themselves to a significant degree. The elderly syncope patient cited earlier could not easily identify somatic cues that marked the onset of syncope. As an inpatient he was intellectually fascinated with passive relaxation and with EMG biofeedback, yet during training sessions there was no experiential awareness of changing EMG levels. At the beginning of session, he could raise the levels higher only by making a fist followed by opening his fist and watching the EMG meter levels fall. He could not experience these changes beyond watching the values rise and fall on the meter. He also found it impossible to breathe diaphragmatically. The patient attributed his difficulties to the lifelong use of medication. During the course of therapy he was able to identify external situations in which he was "uptight," and he became better, in his words, at "walking away" from these situations.

We have outlined a systemic psychobiological approach to therapy that places somatic awareness at the core. The concept provides therapists with an understanding that incorporates physiological, cognitive, behavioral, and interactional processes. The key to symptom management remains becoming more rather than less aware of body sensations that accompany thoughts, feelings, and behaviors. Somatization patients have an especially difficult time grasping the distinction between preoccupation with their symptom and appropriate somatic awareness. Unresolved medical concerns, fears of functioning without medication, personality and self-esteem issues, and interpersonal problems all add to the difficulty but can still be addressed with the goal of increasing awareness in mind. The more complex the patient, the more multidimensional the interventions need to be.

The heuristic value of somatic awareness lies in its ability to integrate a number of determinants of somatic symptoms within a single framework. In seeking medical intervention, somatizing patients often believe that they have no role to play in the alleviation of their symptoms. Efforts to explain their symptoms as a result of anxiety or depression often fare no better, as patients resent the implication that they have a psychological problem. They must come to understand that their symptoms have a physiological substrate and that the symptoms are inextricably tied to their thoughts, feelings, and bodily sensations. Regulating the complex processes involved is best guided by developing enduring and overriding habits of somatic awareness.

REFERENCES

American Psychiatric Association. (1987). *Diagnostic and statistical manual of mental disorders* (3rd ed., rev.). Washington, DC: Author.

Barsky, A. J. (1992). Palpitations, cardiac awareness, and panic disorder. *American Journal of Medicine, 92* (Suppl. 1A), 31-35.

Beck, A. T., & Emery, G. (1985). *Anxiety disorders and phobias: A cognitive perspective.* New York: Basic Books.

Beck, A. T., Epstein, N., Brown, G., & Steer, R. A. (1988). An inventory for measuring clinical anxiety: Psychometric properties. *Journal of Consulting and Clinical Psychology, 56,* 893-897.

Beck, A. T., & Steer, R. A. (1990). *Manual for the Beck Anxiety Inventory.* San Antonio, TX: The Psychological Corporation.

Boyd, J. H., & Crump, T. (1991). Westphal's agoraphobia. *Journal of Anxiety Disorders, 5,* 77-86.

Cioffi, D. (1991). Beyond attentional strategies: A cognitive-perceptual model of somatic interpretation. *Psychological Bulletin, 109,* 25-41.

Costa, Jr., P. T., & McCrae, R. R. (1987). Neuroticism, somatic complaints, and disease: Is the bark worse than the bite? *Journal of Personality, 55,* 299-316.

Drachman, D. A., & Hart, C. W. (1972). An approach to the dizzy patient. *Neurology, 22,* 323-334.

Eifert, G. H. (1992). Cardiophobia: A paradigmatic behavioural model of heart-focused anxiety and non-anginal chest pain. *Behaviour Research and Therapy, 30,* 329-345.

Engel, B. T., Baile, W. F., Costa, P. T., Brimlow, D. L., & Brinker, J. (1985). A behavioral analysis of chest pain in patients suspected of having coronary artery disease. *Psychosomatic Medicine, 47,* 274-284.

Fewtrell, W. D., & O'Connor, K. P. (1988). Dizziness and depersonalization. *Advances in Behaviour Research and Therapy, 10,* 201-218.

Fisher, S. (1986). *Development and structure of the body image* (Vol. 1). Hillsdale, NJ: Lawrence Erlbaum.

Freedland, K. E., Carney, R. M., Krone, R. J., Smith, L. J., Rich, M. W., Eisenkramer, G., & Fischer, K. C. (1991). Psychological factors in silent myocardial ischemia. *Psychosomatic Medicine, 53,* 13-24.

Fritz, G. F., Rubinstein, S., & Lewiston, N. J. (1987). Psychological factors in fatal childhood asthma. *American Journal of Orthopsychiatry, 57,* 253-257.

Hanna, T. (1988). *Somatics.* Reading, MA: Addison-Wesley.

Heide, F. J., & Borkovec, T. D. (1984). Relaxation-induced anxiety: Mechanisms and theoretical implications. *Behavior Research and Therapy, 22,* 1-12.

Klein, D. F. (1993). False suffocation alarms, spontaneous panics, and related conditions: An integrative hypothesis. *Archives of General Psychiatry, 50,* 306-317.

Kroenke, K. (1992). Symptoms in medical patients: An untended field. *American Journal of Medicine, 92* (Suppl. lA), 1-7.

Kushner, M. G., Beitman, B. D., & Beck, N. C. (1989). Factors predictive of panic disorder in cardiology patients with chest pain and no evidence of coronary artery disease: A cross-validation. *Journal of Psychosomatic Research, 33,* 207-215.

Lane, R. D., & Schwartz, G. E. (1992). Levels of emotional awareness: Implications for psychotherapeutic integration. *Journal of Psychotherapy Integration, 2,* 1-18.

Leventhal, H. (1992). I know distraction works even though it doesn't! *Health Psychology, 11,* 208-209.

Ley, R. (1992). The many faces of Pan: Psychological and physiological differences among three types of panic attacks. *Behaviour Research and Therapy, 30,* 347-357.

Linzer, M., Pontinen, M., Gold, D. T., Divine, G. W., Felder, A., & Brooks, W. B. (1991). Impairment of physical and psychosocial function in recurrent syncope. *Journal of Clinical Epidemiology, 44,* 1037-1043.

Lynch, P., Bakal, D. A., Whitelaw, W., & Fung, T. (1991). Chest muscle activity and panic anxiety: A preliminary investigation. *Psychosomatic Medicine, 53,* 80-89.

McCaul, K. D., Monson, N. & Maki, R. (1992). Does distraction reduce pain-produced distress among college students? *Health Psychology, 11,* 210-217.

Morgan, W. P., & Pollock, M. L. (1977). Psychologic characterization of the elite distance runner. *Annals of the New York Academy of Sciences, 301,* 382-403.

Ottaviani, R., & Beck, A. T. (1987). Cognitive aspects of panic disorders. *Journal of Anxiety Disorders, 1,* 15-28.

Schachter, S., & Singer, J. E. (1962). Cognitive, social, and physiological determinants of emotional state. *Psychological Review, 69,* 379-399.

Simon, G. E. (1991). Somatization and psychiatric disorders. In L. J. Kirmayer & J. M. Robbins (Eds.), *Current concepts of somatization: Research and clinical perspectives* (pp. 37-62). Washington, DC: American Psychiatric Press.

Simon, G. E., & Von Korff, M. (1991). Somatization and psychiatric disorder in the NIMH Epidemiologic Catchment Area Study. *American Journal of Psychiatry, 148,* 1494-1500.

Slater, E., & Roth, M. (1969). *Clinical psychiatry* (3rd ed.). London: Bailliere, Tindall & Cassell.

Steptoe, A., & Vögele, C. (1992). Individual differences in the perception of bodily sensations: The role of trait anxiety and coping style. *Behaviour Research and Therapy, 30,* 597-607.

Telch, M. J., Brouillard, M., Telch, C. F., Agras, W. S., & Taylor, C. B. (1989). Role of cognitive appraisal in panic-related avoidance. *Behaviour Research and Therapy, 27,* 373-383.

Wicklund, R. A. (1991). Introduction. In R. Schwarzer & R. A. Wicklund (Eds.), *Anxiety and self-focused attention* (pp. ix-xii). New York: Harwood Academic Publishers.

Yellowlees, P. M., & Kalucy, R. S. (1990). Psychobiological aspects of asthma and the consequent research implications. *Chest, 97,* 629-634.

8

Anxiety Management Training

RICHARD M. SUINN

For the Twenty-Fifth Banff International Conference on Behavioural Science, a workshop was presented on anxiety management training (AMT), a behavior therapy for anxiety states. The workshop provided detailed coverage of the rationale, content of each session, logs, and homework assignments. A videotape illustrated some of the major components of the AMT methodology. This chapter summarizes material that was presented, along with an extended survey of pertinent research. For more information, including case examples and instructions for anger management training, the reader is directed to the book *Anxiety Management Training: A Behavior Therapy* (Suinn, 1990).

THEORETICAL MODEL AND RESEARCH

Principles of Anxiety Management Training

Examination of the theory and method of desensitization makes clear the inadequacy of this treatment model in dealing with generalized anxiety states. According to the usual desensitization method, an anxiety hierarchy is constructed that is dependent upon the client's ability to identify the stimulus conditions precipitating the anxiety response. In generalized anxiety disorder, the client is not able to be so precise; hence desensitization, which is so powerful with phobias, is inapplicable to conditions such as general anxiety disorder.

In 1971 AMT was developed to provide a behavior therapy for treatment of generalized anxiety disorders (Suinn & Richardson, 1971). Its theoretical foundation was based upon the premise that clients can be taught first to identify the internal signs, both cognitive and physical, that signal the presence of anxiety and then to react to these signs using responses that remove them (Suinn, 1975). This formulation was based upon the learning principles that conceptualized anxiety as a drive state and postulated that behaviors can be learned that eliminate the drive (Brown, 1961; Dollard & Miller, 1950; Mowrer, 1950). In essence, anxiety might be viewed as having stimulus properties. If so, then anxiety as a stimulus can become associated with new responses, such as coping responses. As an example of the general formulation about drive states, hunger as a drive can become associated with search for specific foods, with the foods sought reflecting one's specific culture or learning history. For some, an increase in anxiety precipitates smoking behaviors or increased eating or alcohol intake.

In AMT, clients are not required to identify the causes or stimuli that precipitate their anxieties. In other words, a client suffering from generalized anxiety disorder need not be able to say clearly, "I have an anxiety attack whenever I have the spotlight on me and I think I have to speak out assertively" or "I suffer severe anxiety each time I have finished an argument with my spouse that implies who is dominant and in control." Instead, the experience of anxiety itself is used to train the client. Specifically, the client need only recall the last time he or she experienced an anxiety attack. The client is then directed to recall how the experience felt—for example, through the onset of gloom and doom thoughts or other cognitive experiences or through increased sweating or other such physical experiences. In effect, the client is now being taught to pay attention to symptoms that reflect the presence of anxiety. AMT sessions then proceed to train the client in the initiation of relaxation responses when anxiety arousal is perceived, with the relaxation serving to reduce and eliminate the anxiety state. As AMT sessions progress, AMT clients are taught to identify those cognitive or bodily cues that signal the *beginning stages* of anxiety arousal. Relaxation responses are again used and now serve as a method for preventing more severe anxiety arousal. In effect, the client is being taught a coping method, relaxation, to eliminate anxiety once it is precipitated. Homework is assigned for several objectives: to strengthen the relaxation skill in a variety of settings, to increase generalization to situations outside the therapy environment, and as a step in learning prevention. In theoretical terms, AMT trains the client in responding to anxiety cues (symptoms) with relaxation, leading to the development of a new, self-managed coping habit pattern. Thus the AMT sessions are educational sessions, involving opportunities for practice in self-control, with a view toward real-life applications. Such anxiety management can be used as an adjunct to other therapies that would be enhanced if the client could first decrease his or her anxiety levels.

Because clients suffering from generalized anxiety disorder or panic disorder cannot identify the stimuli that precipitate their anxiety, and because AMT does not require such identification, AMT is especially appropriate for such clients. In addition, AMT is appropriate for any conditions in which anxiety plays a major symptomatic role: for instance, when anxiety is the source of medical symptoms such as hypertension or is an obstacle to performance, as in performance anxiety. AMT also appears to have value for training clients in the control of other arousal states, such as anger.

Among the basic or core characteristics of the AMT method are guided imagery, anxiety arousal, and relaxation for self-control. The guided imagery involves introduction of relaxation imagery to strengthen the relaxation response, and anxiety imagery to precipitate an anxiety arousal. Anxiety arousal is precipitated during the sessions in order to aid the client in use of relaxation to reduce an actual experience of anxiety. Thus the client can first practice controlling his or her anxiety in the safe setting of the treatment environment before being assigned homework in real-life applications.

Consistent with some other behavioral approaches, AMT also relies upon self-monitoring and recognizes that clients may differ in their cognitive versus physiological patterns. In regards to self-monitoring, AMT encourages such behaviors by requiring clients to keep daily logs. For instance, the relaxation log involves writing down each time relaxation is practiced at home, the depth of relaxation achieved, and its success in reducing anxiety. Later on, application of relaxation to cope with anxiety is recorded in a similar manner. One advantage of such reports is that they permit the therapist to determine compliance, whether the client is practicing what is being learned in therapy, and what progress seems to be occurring. These logs are reviewed at the start of each session to determine how well the client has been doing and to plan the session. For instance, if the logs or interview suggest that the client has not yet developed control over relaxation after the first session, then the contents of the first session may be repeated. If the later logs suggest that the client is not successful in controlling anxiety in real-life applications, then the appropriate AMT sessions are repeated.

Time is also allocated at the end of each session for an interview on how the session went. During such interviews, the therapist ascertains indications of progress and other matters. For instance, in a session using imagery for anxiety arousal, was the client actually able to experience the arousal? During relaxation training, what instructions helped the client to develop the relaxation? In developing imagery, were there some parts of the description that enhanced retrieval of the imagery?

In regard to cognitive versus physiological patterns, it is recognized that some clients experience anxiety mainly through cognitive responses but have very few physiological symptoms. On the other hand, other clients have very severe physiological symptoms but few cognitive ones. AMT provides steps aimed at helping clients of both types, as well as clients whose anxiety experiences or responses include a combination of cognitive and physical reactions.

Characteristics of AMT

Although some of the AMT procedures may appear similar to other behavioral therapy methods that rely upon relaxation, AMT has several unique characteristics.

AMT aims at self-management through gradually requiring the client to assume more and more responsibility. For example, in earlier sessions the therapist specifically tells the client when to visualize an anxiety scene to obtain anxiety arousal, when to terminate the scene, and when to initiate the relaxation. In later sessions, the client is given responsibility for both the anxiety arousal and the relaxation control. In general, this increase of self-control occurs through a graduated fading out of therapist activity in favor of client activity. The procedure for fading is systematically described in the therapist manual (Suinn, 1990), as are other aspects of the AMT method.

Another characteristic of AMT is the use of homework to promote generalization. Such assignments require the client to transfer skills being acquired in the treatment sessions themselves to their life settings outside treatment.

That is, clients must demonstrate anxiety control not only within sessions but also in real life before therapeutic goals have been fully achieved.

A third characteristic is the continuing emphasis on self-control. The instructions, fading, and homework assignments are all ultimately aimed at communicating that clients are to learn a skill that they will possess. So treatment is not an occasion where something *done* by a therapist *to* the client transforms the client. Rather, the client is taught a skill that, when acquired, is possessed by the client and within his or her own control.

A fourth characteristic of AMT is the recognition that cognitions may be involved as part of the anxiety reactions or as part of the initial sequence of cues prompting the anxiety. Hence part of the training permits attention to cognitive elements.

One by-product of AMT, because of the self-control aspect, is an increase in self-efficacy. AMT is structured such that the client experiences not only anxiety arousal but also an ability to eliminate the anxiety through use of relaxation. In experiencing this control, the client acquires a firsthand knowledge that indeed he or she has developed a new skill. As this skill is also applied through homework, efficacy is further increased.

Finally, AMT is unique in that each session follows carefully prescribed steps. In this way, any new therapist is able to determine what is expected at each session. The full treatment manual (Suinn, 1990) provides information on how to introduce the rationale of AMT, samples of instructions for relaxation training and for anxiety arousal, copies of the various logs, and case illustrations for each session as well as for different disorders.

Research

AMT has proven effective in reducing specific anxieties—for example, math anxiety (Smith, Ingram, & Brehm, 1983; Suinn & Richardson, 1971), test anxiety (Deffenbacher, Michaels, Daley, & Michaels, 1980; Deffenbacher, Michaels, Michaels, & Daley, 1980; Deffenbacher & Shelton, 1978), public speaking anxiety (Deffenbacher, Michaels, Daley, & Michaels, 1980), and vocational indecision anxiety (Mendonca & Siess, 1976). AMT has also proven of value with general anxiety disorders (Cragan & Deffenbacher, 1984; Daley, Bloom, Deffenbacher, & Stewart, 1983; Hutchings, Denney, Basgall, & Houston, 1980; Jannoun, Oppenheimer, & Gelder, 1982), for which it was developed. AMT has also been a useful adjunctive treatment for schizophrenics, helping them to reduce anxiety, anger, and anxiety medication and to use psychotherapy more profitably (van Hassel, Bloom, & Gonzales, 1982). Furthermore, AMT has been effective with a number of stress-related medical problems—for example, Type A behavior (Jenni & Wollersheim, 1979; Kelly & Stone, 1987; Suinn & Bloom, 1978), high blood pressure (Drazen, Nevid, Pace, & O'Brien, 1982; Jorgensen, Houston, & Zurawski, 1981), ulcers (Brooks & Richardson, 1980), dysmenorrhea and other gynecological problems (Deffenbacher & Craun, 1985; Quillen & Denney, 1982), and diabetes (Rose, Firestone, Heick, & Faught, 1983). A recent application has been the adapting of AMT for anger management, with significantly positive outcomes (Deffenbacher, Demm, & Brandon, 1986; Deffenbacher, McNamara, Stark, & Sabadell, 1990; Deffenbacher & Stark, 1992). Given the associations between anger, Type A behaviors, and cardiovascular disease, the work of Deffenbacher on anger management is highly important. Equally relevant is a study by Nakano (1990) using AMT for anger management for Type A persons. Following treatment only for anger, the Type A characteristics of the clients diminished. This study from Japan is actually a replication of very similar findings by Hart (1984) conducted in Canada.

Outcome research shows a number of other positive features as well for AMT. For example, AMT was generally as effective as other behavioral treatments at short-term follow-up. Such studies compared AMT with desensitization (Deffenbacher & Shelton, 1978; Suinn & Richardson, 1971), self-control desensitization (Deffenbacher, Michaels, Michaels, & Daley, 1980), relaxation as self-control (Cragan & Deffenbacher, 1984), and cognitive interventions (Hazaleus & Deffenbacher, 1986; Jenni & Wollersheim, 1979). However, long-term follow-up studies (e.g., Deffenbacher & Craun, 1985; Deffenbacher et al., 1986; Deffenbacher & Michaels, 1981a, 1981b; Hazaleus & Deffenbacher, 1986; Hutchings et al., 1980; Quillen & Denney, 1982) demonstrated maintenance of therapeutic gains over a period of at least a year or two for AMT. Moreover, clients appeared to be learning generalized coping skills, for generalization to nontargeted problems was noted in several studies (e.g., Cragan & Deffenbacher, 1984; Deffenbacher et al., 1986; Deffenbacher, Michaels, Daley, & Michaels, 1980; Deffenbacher, Michaels, Michaels, & Daley, 1980; Deffenbacher & Shelton, 1978).

One interesting generalization has been to depression. Several studies have been aimed at treatment of anxiety and not directed toward depression, yet depression scores have showed reductions post therapy with AMT (Cragan & Deffenbacher, 1984; Jannoun et al., 1982). Although Jannoun et al.'s subjects were not clinically depressed, Cragan and Deffenbacher's subjects initially showed high depression scores. By posttherapy, these latter subjects' scores on depression had decreased to a normal level, even though AMT was being used solely for anxiety management. Given observations by Kendall and Ingram at this Banff Conference on comorbidity, one speculation would be that AMT's success with anxiety also generalizes where a comorbid state of depression exists.

In summary, the research on AMT suggests its applicability to a broad range of clinical problems and in a variety of settings in which applied psychologists work. These include the following applications:

1. Anxiety state disorders, such as generalized anxiety disorder
2. Phobias or situation-specific anxieties—for example, test or speech or mathematics anxiety
3. Multiple situational stressors or anxieties—for example, simultaneous vocational, marital, and financial stress, or simultaneous test, speech, and heterosocial anxieties
4. Anxiety intense enough to disrupt performance—for example, athletic or musical performance—particularly when the environmental conditions vary from performance to performance
5. Anxiety that disrupts counseling or is an obstacle to the effective use of other counseling methods—for example, inability to make career decisions, to use counseling or psychotherapy profitably, or to self-disclose and explore concerns due to anxiety
6. Anxiety- or stress-related health issues—for example, essential hypertension, ulcers, dysmenorrhea, tension headaches, or Type A behavior patterns

TREATMENT PROCEDURES
FOR INDIVIDUAL AMT

AMT involves a structured set of five basic sessions plus intake, with the actual number of sessions individually tailored to the specific client's progress (Suinn, 1990).

AMT relies heavily upon the use of imagery either to arouse anxiety or to enhance relaxation. In the first instance, the client is required to recall an event in which moderate or high levels of anxiety were experienced. Using imagery, the client recalls this event, thereby reexperiencing the anxiety itself. For relaxation, the client identifies an event that involved being relaxed, such as "last summer, sitting in the sun on my deck, eyes closed, with my favorite CD playing the song ——— softly." By focusing on this image, the client is helped to retrieve the same sense of relaxation.

All sessions take about 60 minutes, with the interval between sessions averaging about 1 week (shorter intervals can be used pending progress shown in the session and by homework and daily logs). After the first session, each session also begins with a brief preinterview to determine whether the client has been practicing the homework that has been assigned and any progress the client is experiencing in reducing anxieties. At the end of each session, a brief postinterview is also conducted to determine how well the client is acquiring the skills initiated in the session and what appears to enhance these skills.

Intake Interview

Although the intake interview is not a formal part of the AMT treatment sessions, a few comments are important. There are a number of approaches to doing assessment of anxiety conditions, depending upon the disorder. Among some of the procedures are the Anxiety Disorders Interview Schedule for generalized anxiety disorder or panic disorder, the Hamilton Rating Scale for observational ratings, and questionnaires such as the Multiple Affect Adjective Check List and the Spielberger State-Trait Personality Inventory.

There are several ways of assessing the severity of the symptoms being reported beyond the use of norms. One way of conceptualizing involves considering time variables and magnitude variables regarding the symptoms. Using time, we infer greater severity if:

1. The anxiety reactions appear more often per unit of time (i.e., are of high frequency).
2. The anxiety reactions last for longer periods once initiated (i.e., have a slower recovery time).
3. The period elapsing before the next anxiety reaction appears shorter (i.e., there are diminishing periods of time free from anxiety).

Using magnitude, we infer greater severity if

1. The symptoms within any response modality (autonomic, behavioral, cognitive) are severe in magnitude (e.g., excessive heart rate, severe speech disruption, or extreme distractibility).

2. There are numerous severe symptoms within or across several response modalities (e.g., severe diarrhea plus nausea and elevated blood pressure, or consuming negative thoughts of doom plus fatigue plus headaches).

3. The symptoms have a major impact on life adjustment (e.g., they cause great disruptions in employment or major expenditures of energies).

Session 1

Session 1 involves four steps—rationale, development of a relaxation scene, relaxation training, and the assignment of homework.

Rationale. A brief rationale of AMT describes AMT as a method that provides training (a) in identifying early signs of the presence of anxiety and (b) in using relaxation to eliminate the anxiety. The client is informed that imagery will be used to enable the client to reexperience anxiety, with the anxiety being eliminated through the use of relaxation. Finally, the client is told that AMT involves the development of a skill and that, as with other skills, practice is essential at home.

The following is an example of an AMT rationale:

> You've been having experiences with anxiety, and they often seem to come from nowhere, they're so unpredictable. These attacks bring that fast-beating heart rate, sometimes so fast you think you're having a heart attack. What can be done is some training to lower the anxiety and short-circuit its effects. One way we can do this is through a procedure called anxiety management training. In it, we will go through several basic steps. First, I will teach you an exercise to achieve relaxation. Then we will arrange for you to practice applying relaxation to reduce anxiety. Within the sessions, we will have you reexperience anxiety by using imagery to recall a situation that made you anxious— maybe that time you were so worried about explaining to your supervisor why you were late. Then you'll kick in the relaxation and relax away the tension. We will practice over and over until you have control over this method. We'll start with moderate anxiety and work our way up as you get better at getting rid of the tension. As you gain skill here in the sessions, we will have you apply it to your everyday life to manage anxiety whenever and wherever it appears. Do you have any questions about the general idea?

Relaxation Scene. The session next focuses on the development of a relaxation scene. The relaxation scene should describe a real event that was associated with feelings of relaxation or calmness. Scene details should be concrete and should attend to sensory aspects that help make the scene vivid, such as vision, sound, temperature, tactile, emotional, and other sensations. Relaxation scenes are identified in the same way as they are in desensitization.

Information that helps confirm that the scene is a real one and therefore not subject to "drifting" when presented includes statements about an exact date or time of day of the event, a name for the location, detailed description of the activity, and other concrete details, such as the name of the book being read or the melody being played on the CD.

Relaxation Training. Relaxation training relies upon the standard Jacobson deep muscle method (1938), whereby muscle groups are first tensed, then relaxed. A cognitive emphasis is added by alerting the client to "pay attention" to the tension and to the contrast between the tensed and the relaxed muscle sensations. This instruction helps to prevent distraction and increases client awareness of somatic tension. Muscle groups reviewed include each hand, forearm, upper arm, forehead, facial area, neck and shoulders, chest, stomach, each leg, and feet. Typically, this relaxation training takes about 30 minutes. It is useful to have the client take a few deep breaths once the muscle relaxation procedure is completed. The intent is to permit the deep breathing to become a method for inducing relaxation (e.g., "Now take a slow, deep breath, and use this to increase your level of relaxation; with each breath, just loosen up more of your muscle groups").

Once the relaxation exercise is completed, the client is instructed to "switch on" the relaxation scene and to use the scene to further increase the level of relaxation. A hand signal is used by the client to indicate when the relaxation scene is being experienced: "Signal me by raising your right hand if you are reasonably relaxed."

Following termination of the relaxation scene, the therapist reviews the muscle groups: "Pay attention to the sense of relaxation in your hands, . . . in both upper arms, . . . [etc.]" The relaxation scene is repeated, followed by relaxation review, with this sequence repeated until there are about 10 minutes left in the session. In the remaining minutes, a postinterview is done to determine how well the client did in relaxing and how clear the relaxation imagery had been. Homework is also assigned.

Homework. The homework assignment is to practice the tension-relaxation exercise without the relaxation scene. The exercise should be for about 5 of the next 7 days in a quiet place at home. Although the exercise itself will probably take about 30 to 40 minutes to complete, the client is instructed to set aside 1 hour when there will not be any interruptions. Relaxation logs are provided to monitor this practice, and stress logs are assigned to obtain a record of daily stresses or anxiety experiences. The relaxation log covers details on practice times and level of relaxation accomplished in order to gauge progress. The relaxation log is printed on a single page and might have headings that appear as follows:

Date/Time of Practice	Tension Before (0-100)	Tension After (0-100)	Easy Areas to Relax	Difficult Areas to Relax

The stress logs involve monitoring situations and times associated with stress and appear as follows:

Date/Time	Stress Situation	Stress Level (0-100)

Session 2

This session involves four steps—identification of an anxiety scene, relaxation, anxiety arousal followed by relaxation, and homework.

Anxiety Scene. Session 2 begins with the development of an anxiety scene (see below for example). This scene involves a real experience that has been associated with a moderately high level of anxiety (about 60 on a scale with 100 as extreme anxiety). This anxiety scene must be a real event and concretely described; in this way the procedure is similar to that for the relaxation scene. In fact, if the client has done well in identifying a concrete relaxation scene, he or she should require little further instruction about how to identify an anxiety scene. The scene should be a real event rather than a fantasized one, again in order to keep the client from drifting during visualization. A fantasy event would permit the client to make up details in a storytelling way, thereby permitting the scene to change or drift. In turn, if the scene is allowed to change, the level of anxiety being aroused may also shift out of control.

Scene-setting details are included that identify the circumstances of the event—for example, location, time, and persons involved. The scene should contain anxiety-arousing details, that is, situational, emotional, physiological, and cognitive details to maximize vivid involvement with the scene for greatest arousal. Behavioral elements may be included, such as "I'm beginning to be aware that I'm anxious and notice that I'm biting my jaws tightly." On the other hand, events with elements involving avoidance, escape, or other defensive behaviors should not be included. For instance, the following would be unacceptable: "I'm beginning to be aware that I'm anxious, and I can't tolerate it all, so I leave the room" or "I'm so anxious with what's going on that I just think about something else. . . . I stop listening, pretend I am somewhere else." In these latter examples, the client is using inappropriate ways of dealing with the anxiety; using such scenes would only strengthen these inappropriate solutions. It would, however, be acceptable to include a scene where the feeling tone expresses a desire, but not an actual activity: for instance, "I'm so anxious, I am feeling I want to leave the room."

The following is a sample anxiety scene (60 level):

[Scene-setting detail] It is May, outside of the Shell building in Denver. You're standing on the windy corner with friends at lunch hour. You were feeling pretty comfortable, but now you suddenly look up and see all the tall buildings, their height, the closed sensation of being surrounded . . . and you start feeling real scared and apprehensive [anxiety-arousing detail]. You have that tight sensation across your chest and stomach and that sinking, heavy feeling in your stomach. You have tension in your neck, especially at the base of the skull, your neck is stiff. You're feeling dizzy and lightheaded, a bit wobbly. Your heart is beating much harder and faster and you feel out of control [physiological and emotional detail]. You start to think that your friends will notice your anxiety [cognitive detail], and that makes it even worse, you're self-conscious, thinking you need to get out of that spot, but "How to do this without everyone figuring something's wrong with me?"

Relaxation. After the anxiety scene is identified, the therapist provides relaxation instructions, without use of the tensing component. Instead a muscle review is used, calling attention to letting each muscle group relax. This takes about 20 minutes. Slow, deep breaths are used to aid in the relaxation, followed by the relaxation scene. Hand signals continue to be the means for obtaining information—for example, when the client has achieved a comfortable level of relaxation, when the relaxation scene is clearly developed, and later, when anxiety is being experienced and when anxiety has been replaced by relaxation.

Anxiety Arousal and Relaxation. When the client is relaxed through the above procedure, anxiety arousal is initiated through the therapist's instruction (see below for example) to switch on the anxiety scene, to use the scene to reexperience the anxiety, and to signal the onset of this anxiety. The instructions include description of both scene-setting and anxiety-arousing details, as well as appropriate voice emphasis (volume, tone) to aid in anxiety arousal. After about 10 to 15 seconds of exposure, that is, after the client signals anxiety, the anxiety scene is terminated, and the therapist reintroduces the relaxation scene. The client signals when he or she has retrieved a comfortable relaxation level. A brief muscle review is also conducted to further the level of relaxation. This sequence of anxiety arousal and relaxation control is repeated until the end of the session. After the first exposure, the anxiety arousal is kept for a longer interval, about 20 to 30 seconds. The postinterview reviews initial relaxation, relaxation scene clarity and involvement, anxiety scene clarity and involvement, anxiety arousal, and relaxation retrieval after anxiety arousal.

The following are sample instructions:

> [Client is relaxed.] In a moment, I am going to have you switch on that scene involving the lunch break in Denver. When I do that, I want you to put yourself right back into that situation, experience it as if it was happening to you right now. When you are experiencing that anxiety, signal me by raising your right hand. So, right now, switch on that scene and really reexperience the anxiety again. You're standing with friends. . . .

Homework. Homework involves practicing relaxation in quiet places, other than in the home, once daily. For instance, the client may use the relaxation exercise, without tensing, while riding on the bus or sitting in a waiting room. Anxiety experiences are also monitored as before.

Session 3

This session follows the steps used in Session 2, with the addition of two major new steps, self-initiated relaxation and attention to the anxiety-arousal symptoms so that the client can identify his or her personal signs associated with anxiety. Thus the steps involved in Session 3 are self-initiated relaxation, anxiety arousal, attending to anxiety symptoms during this arousal, return of relaxation, repeating this cycle of arousal, attention to symptoms, relaxation (three to five repetitions), and homework.

Relaxation. The first step in this session is self-initiated relaxation. Instead of the therapist giving the instructions, the client goes through the relaxation exercise on his or her own. This is one step toward the client's assuming responsibility for self-management and the fading out of therapist control. When relaxation is signaled (usually in about a minute or two), the therapist provides the instruction to switch on the anxiety scene.

Anxiety Arousal. As in the prior session, anxiety arousal is achieved through the use of the 60-level-intensity anxiety scene. As before, the client signals when the scene has produced a return of anxiety. At this point, the therapist introduces the new instructions about attending to anxiety symptoms.

Attending to Anxiety Symptoms. In order to train the client to attend to the symptoms that indicate the presence of anxiety, the following instructions are given: "Pay attention to how you experience anxiety; perhaps it is in body signs such as your neck muscles tensing, or your heart rate, or in some of your thoughts." These instructions might include symptoms based upon those the client described during the construction of the anxiety scene.

Relaxation Return. Relaxation is again retrieved through the relaxation scene, with the therapist taking responsibility for switching on the scene and describing the details. This is followed by a brief muscle review for increasing the level of relaxation.

This cycle of anxiety arousal, attention to anxiety signs, and retrieval of relaxation is continued to the end of the hour—a cycle of about three to five repetitions. By training the client in becoming aware of the signs of anxiety, AMT not only teaches the client how to identify the presence of anxiety but also makes it possible for the client to prevent anxiety in the future. The therapist discusses these anxiety signs as "early warning signals" to tell the client in the future that tension or anxiety is building and to initiate self-controlled relaxation-coping skills.

Homework. Homework continues the relaxation practice. Although the client should avoid confronting major anxiety-provoking situations, he or she is instructed to initiate relaxation under situations of minor stress. Using the stress log, clients also continue to monitor stress, with increased attention to the physiological, cognitive, and behavioral cues of anxiety within themselves. A column is added to the log format for the client to write in the nature of these early warning signals (i.e., specific physical or cognitive cues). Attempts to cope should also be recorded, and a "coping outcomes" column should be added to the log in which client attempts and outcomes at coping are listed. In this column, the client records a "yes" or "no" regarding whether he or she was able to successfully control the anxiety during each of the experienced anxiety situations.

Session 4

This session adds two new major components. First a 90-level-intensity anxiety scene is identified. During this session, this scene will be alternated with the 60-level scene used in Sessions 2 and 3. A new 60-level scene is sometimes needed if the initial scene has lost its anxiety-arousing capacity. Next, the session requires the client to assume more responsibility for regaining self-control after anxiety arousal. Instead of the therapist terminating the anxiety scene and reinitiating the relaxation, the client decides when to end the anxiety scene and takes responsibility for relaxation retrieval by using a relaxation scene, relaxation muscle review, or cue-controlled (deep breath) relaxation. To accommodate this change, the hand signal system is revised. The client is now instructed, "Raise your hand when you reexperience the anxiety, keeping your hand up while you experience the anxiety. . . . When you're ready, switch off the anxiety scene and reinitiate the relaxation. When you're reasonably comfortable again, signal by lowering your hand."

Homework continues with self-monitoring through logs. In addition, the client is instructed to routinely check for the early warning signals of impending stress arousal and to initiate relaxation coping skills if stress is perceived. *Time monitoring* and *situational monitoring* are used. In time monitoring, the client checks for signs of building stress in the morning, at midday, in the afternoon, and in the evening. For clients with tension headaches, this monitoring is done every 2 hours to abort any beginnings of muscle tension buildup. In situational monitoring, the client checks his or her stress level prior to any activity that has a known association with stress arousal—for example, studying for a test or waiting for the dentist. In all cases, relaxation control is applied if there is any evidence of anxiety increasing. Attempts at anxiety control are recorded in the stress log.

In summary, Session 4 repeats a general pattern, once a 90-level scene is constructed and the client self-initiates relaxation. The therapist instructs the client to switch on the 90-level scene and pay attention to the cognitive, emotional, and behavioral cues of anxiety arousal. After the client signals anxiety and when he or she is ready, he or she switches the anxiety scene off, retrieves relaxation by whatever method works best, and signals the therapist when the relaxation is retrieved. This same pattern is repeated with the 60-level scene, then with the 90-level scene, and so forth until the session is over. As before, the session ends with a brief postinterview and homework assignment of self-monitoring of anxiety and coping efforts through logs plus time and situational monitoring.

Session 5

This session completes the fading out of therapist control and the completion of client self-control. At the start of the session, the client self-initiates relaxation, signaling its achievement. Although the therapist switches on the anxiety scene, all activities from this point are client controlled. Hence the client uses the anxiety scene to experience anxiety arousal and, while still in the scene, initiates relaxation control. When relaxation is gained, the client then terminates the anxiety scene, signals its termination, and continues the relaxation until the next anxiety scene is called for by the therapist. As before, the 60-level and 90-level scenes are alternated. Hand signaling is as before, with the hand raised being indicative of anxiety arousal and hand lowering indicating that relaxation has been retrieved. The latency between signals provides evidence for the progress of the client in anxiety management. Homework is the same as for Session 4.

In summary, Session 5 also repeats a pattern once self-initiated relaxation has taken place. The therapist instructs the client to switch on the 90-level scene and pay attention to the internal cues of anxiety arousal, signaling when anxiety is experienced. When anxiety is experienced and signaled, the client initiates relaxation while remaining with the scene in imagery, signaling when relaxation is again retrieved. The client terminates the anxiety scene. The cycle begins again with the 60-level scene. The 90- and 60-level scenes are alternated in this manner until the end of the session. Homework of coping with all anxiety and stress is repeated as in Session 4.

Sessions 6 to 8

The AMT Session 5 format is repeated until self-control appears complete, typically 6 to 8 sessions. New anxiety scenes may be employed as needed. Termination is best handled by the therapist's suggesting that "we're at the stage now where it would be helpful to obtain some progress checks." The therapist then seeks an in vivo situation whereby the client can "test" his or her progress in managing anxiety. With such a test, the client can observe firsthand the level of the improvement and recovery. The client is then more confident that change has indeed taken place and he or she can make personal decisions to terminate instead of relying only upon the therapist's opinion that change has occurred. In work with clients, this approach seems to lead to more straightforward terminations than when the therapist simply tells the client that the sessions are at an end. When the therapist announces termination, clients sometimes do not feel ready for termination. However, when a "test" is agreed upon, clients seem more able to see for themselves that they are ready for terminating.

TREATMENT PROCEDURES FOR GROUP AMT

The basic AMT technique is also suitable for group work and may be provided within a group format for 6 to 8 clients. Several modifications of individual AMT are suggested.

First, training times are extended. The pace is geared to that of the slowest client in order to ensure that all clients have gained the necessary coping skills. For example, if a client has not acquired the ability to achieve relaxation, then movement to Session 2 will prove valueless. Also, because relaxation scenes must be identified for each client, Session 1 will require more time for this phase. In general, Session 1 may take about 75 minutes to complete. To ensure that all clients have developed relaxation skills, Session 1 should be repeated.

This rule of extending the length of a session and of repeating a session also holds for later AMT sessions. Hence 75 minutes should be allotted for sessions that involve the identification of the 60-level anxiety scene (individual AMT Session 2) and the 90-level anxiety scene (individual AMT Session 4).

With the exception of the first anxiety arousal/relaxation control session (individual AMT Session 2), all other sessions are repeated. A typical group format would therefore involve

Session 1 (75 minutes): rationale, relaxation scene identification, and relaxation training
Session 2 (60 minutes): repetition of Session 1
Session 3 (75 minutes): anxiety scene identification (60-level), relaxation instructions directed by therapist, and anxiety arousal followed by relaxation control
Session 4 (60 minutes): self-initiated relaxation by clients, anxiety arousal followed by relaxation control—attention to early warning signs
Session 5 (60 minutes): repetition of Session 4
Session 6 (75 minutes): anxiety scene identification (90-level), self-initiated relaxation by clients, anxiety arousals followed by clients' termination of anxiety scene and clients' self-initiation of relaxation control, 60- and 90-level scenes alternated
Session 7 (60 minutes): repetition of Session 6
Session 8 to termination (60 minutes): self-initiated relaxation, anxiety arousal followed by client self-initiation of relaxation while remaining in anxiety scene, 60- and 90-level scenes alternated

Relaxation and anxiety scenes are written down. In individual AMT, the therapist describes the scene-setting and anxiety-arousal details when the scene is switched on. Because groups of clients have different anxiety content, this detailed verbal description is not possible. Instead, clients are interviewed to identify the details and are told to write these on index cards. When the therapist instructs the clients to switch on their relaxation scene, each client now knows that this refers to the scene on his or her index card, referring to a relaxation event. Similarly, the anxiety scene refers to the scene on each person's index card that describes an anxiety event.

Hand signals are especially useful for obtaining information. For example, if a client fails to signal anxiety arousal, the therapist can say, "If you were able to experience about a 60 level of anxiety in your last scene, signal me by raising your right hand." Such use of signals enables the therapist to monitor the progress of each client during the session.

With a group it is likely that one or more members may profit from generalizing relaxation to reduction of other dysfunctional affective states— for example, anger or dysphoria (Cragan & Deffenbacher, 1984). In later sessions these issues should be elicited and discussed, and the application of relaxation coping to them encouraged and monitored. If a common theme emerges—for example, anger—then 60-level and 90-level scenes could be developed and employed in the individual AMT Session S format. Many of the studies in the research review earlier showed that AMT may be profitably applied in small groups. Mixing in the same group clients with different anxiety and stress disorders (e.g., Cragan & Deffenbacher, 1984; Hutchings et al., 1980; Jannoun et al., 1982) did not appear to impede progress or outcome. In fact, in one study (Deffenbacher, Michaels, Daley, & Michaels, 1980) some clients appeared to benefit more from the mix. Thus group AMT should allow for the efficient, timely delivery of anxiety/stress/anger reduction services in settings with significant numbers of such clients—for example, counseling centers, mental health clinics, and general medical clinics or organizations. The efficacy of extending AMT to large group or workshop formats should not, however, be assumed. One study (Daley et al., 1983) that investigated the large group format found that small group AMT was effective, whereas large group AMT was not. Thus caution should be exercised and program evaluation required as AMT (or other methodologies for that matter) is extended into larger psychoeducational group interventions.

REFERENCES

Brooks, G., & Richardson, F. (1980). Emotional skills training: A treatment program for duodenal ulcer. *Behavior Therapy, 11,* 198-207.

Brown, J. (1961). *The motivation of behavior.* New York: McGraw-Hill.

Cragan, M. K., & Deffenbacher, J. L. (1984). Anxiety management training and relaxation as self-control in the treatment of generalized anxiety in medical outpatients. *Journal of Counseling Psychology, 1,* 123-131.

Daley, P. C., Bloom, L. J., Deffenbacher, J. L., & Stewart, R. (1983). Treatment effectiveness of anxiety management training in small and large group formats. *Journal of Counseling Psychology, 30,* 104-107.

Deffenbacher, J. L., & Craun, A. M. (1985). Anxiety management training with stressed student gynecology patients: A collaborative approach. *Journal of College Student Personnel, 26,* 513-518.

Deffenbacher, J., Demm, P., & Brandon, A. (1986). High general anger: Correlates and treatment. *Behavioural Research and Therapy, 24,* 481-489.

Deffenbacher, J., McNamara, J., Stark, R., & Sabadell, P. (1990). A combination of cognitive, relaxation, and behavioral coping skills in the reduction of general anger. *Journal of College Student Development, 69,* 167-172.

Deffenbacher, J. L., & Michaels, A. C. (1981a). Anxiety management training and self-control desensitization—15 months later. *Journal of Counseling Psychology, 28,* 459-462.

Deffenbacher, J. L., & Michaels, A. C. (1981b). A twelve-month follow-up of homogeneous and heterogeneous anxiety management training. *Journal of Counseling Psychology, 28,* 463-466.

Deffenbacher, J. L., Michaels, A. C., Daley, P. C., & Michaels, T. (1980). A comparison of homogeneous and heterogeneous anxiety management training. *Journal of Counseling Psychology, 27,* 630-634.

Deffenbacher, J. L., Michaels, A. C., Michaels, T., & Daley, P. C. (1980). A comparison of anxiety management training and self-control desensitization in reducing test and other anxieties. *Journal of Counseling Psychology, 27,* 232-239.

Deffenbacher, J. L., & Shelton, J. L. (1978). A comparison of anxiety management training and desensitization in reducing test and other anxieties. *Journal of Counseling Psychology, 25,* 277-282.

Deffenbacher, J., & Stark, R. (1992). Relaxation and cognitive-relaxation coping skills in the reduction of general anger. *Journal of Counseling Psychology, 39,* 158-167.

Dollard, J., & Miller, N. (1950). *Personality and psychotherapy.* New York: McGraw-Hill.

Drazen, M., Nevid, J., Pace, N., & O'Brien, R. (1982). Worksite-based behavioral treatment of mild hypertension. *Journal of Occupational Medicine, 24,* 511-514.

Hart, K. (1984). Stress management training for Type A individuals. *Journal of Behavioral Medicine, 12,* 133-140.

Hazaleus, S. L., & Deffenbacher, J. L. (1986). Relaxation and cognitive treatments of anger. *Journal of Consulting and Clinical Psychology, 54,* 222-226.

Hutchings, D., Denney, D., Basgall, J., & Houston, B. (1980). Anxiety management and applied relaxation in reducing general anxiety. *Behavior Research and Therapy, 18,* 181-190.

Jacobson, E. (1938). *Progressive relaxation.* Chicago: University of Chicago Press.

Jannoun, L., Oppenheimer, C., & Gelder, M. (1982). A self-help treatment program for anxiety state patients. *Behavior Therapy, 13,* 103-111.

Jenni, M. A., & Wollersheim, J. P. (1979). Cognitive therapy, stress management training, and the Type A behavior pattern. *Cognitive Therapy and Research, 3,* 61-73.

Jorgensen, R. S., Houston, B. K., & Zurawski, R. M. (1981). Anxiety management training in the treatment of essential hypertension. *Behavior Research and Therapy, 19,* 467-474.

Kelly, K., & Stone, G. L. (1987). Effects of three psychological treatments and self-monitoring on the reduction of Type A behaviors. *Journal of Counseling Psychology, 34,* 46-54.

Mendonca, J. D., & Siess, T. F. (1976). Counseling for indecisiveness: Problem-solving and anxiety-management training. *Journal of Counseling Psychology, 23,* 339-347.

Mowrer, O. H. (1950). *Learning theory and personality dynamics.* New York: Ronald.

Nakano, K. (1990). Effects of two self-control procedures on modifying Type A behavior. *Journal of Clinical Psychology, 46,* 652-657.

Quillen, M. A., & Denney, D. R. (1982). Self-control of dysmenorrheic symptoms through pain management training. *Journal of Behavior Therapy and Experimental Psychiatry, 13,* 123-130.

Rose, M., Firestone, P., Heick, H., & Faught, A. (1983). The effects of anxiety management training on the control of juvenile diabetes mellitus. *Journal of Behavioral Medicine, 27,* 381-395.

Smith, T., Ingram, R., & Brehm, S. (1983). Social anxiety, anxious self-preoccupation, and recall of self-relevant information. *Journal of Personality and Social Psychology, 44,* 1276-1283.

Suinn, R. M. (1975). Anxiety management training for general anxiety. In R. M. Suinn & R. G. Weigel (Eds.), *The innovative psychological therapies: Critical and creative contributions* (pp. 66-70). New York: Harper & Row.

Suinn, R. M. (1990). *Anxiety management training (AMT): A behavior therapy.* New York: Plenum.

Suinn, R. M., & Bloom, L. J. (1978). Anxiety management training for Pattern A behavior. *Journal of Behavioral Medicine, 1,* 25-35.

Suinn, R., & Richardson, F. (1971). Anxiety management training: A non-specific behavior therapy program for anxiety control. *Behavior Therapy, 2,* 498-512.

van Hassel, J., Bloom, L. J., & Gonzales, A. C. (1982). Anxiety management training with schizophrenic outpatients. *Journal of Clinical Psychology, 38,* 280-285.

PART III

Depression

ASSESSMENT AND MANAGEMENT

9

Psychotherapies for Depression

LYNN P. REHM

This review focuses on therapy programs for depression that have been empirically studied and validated, a recent field of study that has come a long way in its development (Kaslow & Rehm, 1984; Rehm, 1981; Rehm & Kornblith, 1979). The first studies with homogeneous depressed subject samples and controlled outcome designs were published in 1973 (McLean, Ogston, & Grauer, 1973; Shipley & Fazio, 1973). In more recent years the number and quality of studies have increased dramatically. Empirically studied therapies tend to be cognitive-behavioral programs, and I will limit my review to these. With few exceptions, cognitive-behavioral therapies tend to be carefully "manualized" programs. That is, they are structured, they tend to have scheduled components, and to some extent, their procedures are spelled out in manual scripts. I will note later some additional commonalities among them.

I have four aims in this review: (a) to describe briefly the rationale and procedures of currently researched therapy programs; (b) to summarize the research on the particular programs and highlight some particular and

AUTHOR'S NOTE: An earlier version of this chapter was presented at the Boulder Symposium on Clinical Psychology: Depression, University of Colorado at Boulder, April 24-26, 1989.

unexpected findings; (c) to try to put these findings together and make some assertions and speculations regarding the state of our knowledge about effective therapy for depression; and (d) to suggest some directions in which this research should go in the future.

Categorizing these therapies is not a simple task. There are many independently developed programs. The programs are quite complex, and most are composed of multiple units, lessons, or modules that overlap and duplicate one another. In addition, there are variations in the application of the same program from one researcher to another, and even in the research clinics of the originators, the programs have evolved and changed. In many instances the effect is that the programs have become more similar to one another. When closely examined, the basic structures of most of the programs are surprisingly similar. Many of the programs contain similar procedures, though the rationale and the label for the procedure may vary from one program to another.

As would be expected, the studies vary in quality on dimensions such as the nature and criteria for defining depression. Samples are not convincingly comparable, although the trend is toward greater commonality of assessment procedures and instruments so that differences are often clear. Most recent studies use diagnostic criteria based on standardized structured interviews and severity criteria based on a clinician rating scale or self-report instrument. Individual versus group format varies within and among the programs. The number and duration of sessions are also quite variable, though all programs reviewed are short-term by traditional standards.

I have settled on dividing the current literature into four primary categories. These are

1. *Behavioral programs,* in which the rationale is to increase the person's level of activity so as to increase obtained reinforcement. These studies are most associated with Peter Lewinsohn (e.g., 1974) of the University of Oregon.

2. *Social skills programs,* based on the assumption that depression is caused by a deficiency in certain interpersonal skills. These programs overlap with the behavioral programs in that in some instances the goal of increasing skills is explicitly to increase reinforcement. However, they are characterized by an emphasis on the mastery of specific skills, such as assertion skills, problem-solving skills, and marital communication skills.

3. *Cognitive therapy,* based on the assumption that negative cognitive distortion of experience underlies depression. This approach is identified with Aaron Beck (1972), but it includes some additions and variations by others.

4. *Self-management therapy,* which assumes that depressed persons have deficiencies in self-control skills. These studies are primarily associated with my program and the self-control model of depression (Rehm, 1977).

I have chosen for review studies that use control or comparison groups and are published in a form that allows fairly close inspection of results. I have attempted to tabulate the results of these studies in four areas:

1. Efficacy of psychotherapy in comparison to no therapy (no-therapy control group—waiting list, therapy on demand, delayed therapy, etc.)
2. Efficacy of psychotherapy in comparison to a placebo psychotherapy. Definition here is a problem, but placebos include nonspecific therapies, therapy as usual, and therapy without theoretically effective components.
3. Efficacy of one psychotherapy in comparison to another—for example, a cognitive versus a behavioral approach
4. Efficacy of psychotherapy in comparison to pharmacotherapy, usually with tricyclics such as amitriptyline or imipramine

Studies comparing variations or components of the program have not been reviewed as systematically, but I will comment on what research evidence exists concerning the effective components of the therapies.

BEHAVIORAL THERAPY:
REINFORCEMENT-INCREASE PROGRAMS

Peter Lewinsohn was the first to develop a behavioral approach to depression in the late 1960s (e.g., Lewinsohn, Weinstein, & Shaw, 1969). Lewinsohn's theory states that depression can be seen as analogous to the learning phenomenon of extinction or reinforcement ratio strain. The basic deficit posited is a loss or lack of response-contingent positive reinforcement. The analogy is that the loss of a relationship, job, or other important objective in life is loss of a source of gratification or reinforcement that organizes behavior and motivates daily activity. When reinforcement is lost or is insufficient, a decrease in activity is the primary behavioral result, which then produces the other symptoms of depression as secondary effects.

The theory posits that this can occur in three ways. First, the environment can change, producing a loss or lack of reinforcement from the outside. The environment does not, or no longer does, supply the necessary reinforcement to motivate and sustain normal rates of adaptive behavior. Second, a lack of social skills may result in an inability to obtain sufficient motivating reinforcement. Third, the person may have an inability to experience reinforcement because anxiety interferes with the positive experience of reinforcement from others, even though it occurs.

Each situation leads logically to a different therapy strategy. For a lack of external reinforcement, the patient is encouraged to increase reinforcing activities. To increase activity, pleasant events are identified that are associated with improvements in mood. These are then scheduled for increased occurrence so as to provide lacking reinforcements. When interpersonal skill deficits are indicated, social skill training is provided to improve ability to obtain higher rates of response-contingent reinforcement. If anxiety seems to be interfering with experiencing reinforcement as positive, relaxation and desensitization procedures are used to reduce anxiety.

At an earlier point in the development of the program, Lewinsohn developed criteria for matching assessments of deficits with specific therapy modules (Lewinsohn, 1976). His current program, however, is a psychoeducational course in coping with depression that stacks the various therapy modules in sequence (Lewinsohn, Antonuccio, Breckenridge, & Teri, 1987). The course materials include an instructor's manual, a text (Lewinsohn, Muñoz, Youngren, & Zeiss, 1978), and a workbook (Brown & Lewinsohn, 1984b). The current program consists of 12 "classes" that include an introduction to the rationale, an activity increase unit, a cognitive "constructive thinking" unit, a social skills unit, and a self-change program.

Behavioral therapy studies are summarized in Tables 9.1 and 9.2. Comparisons to no treatment are generally quite positive for behavior therapy in seven of nine individual comparisons. Comparisons to placebo therapy conditions are less positive, with behavior therapy superior in only two of six comparisons. Comparisons with alternative types of therapy find behavior therapy equal in effectiveness to four alternative therapies in a total of eight comparisons. The most common comparison has been to cognitive therapy, but equivalence has also been found in comparisons to social skills therapy, to short-term dynamic therapy, and to relaxation, which has been considered a placebo in some instances. Several other findings from these studies are of interest. Individual, group (including class presentation), and self-administration of the coping course seem equally effective. Elderly and adolescent versions have been developed. Measures of pleasant events, presumably assessing the deficiency in level of reinforcement, do not predict

TABLE 9.1   Behavior Therapy/Reinforcement Increase Programs for Depression

Reference	Subjects	Selection Criteria	Outcome Criteria	Results
Padfield (1976)	24 outpts 24 female	ZSDS GFCC	SADS DACL	BT = PL
Turner, Ward, & Turner (1979)	56 outpts 28 female	Interview DACL	DACL	BT > PL = PL = NT
Barrera (1979)	20 outpts 10 female	MMPI	MMPI	BT = NT
Zeiss, Lewinsohn, & Muñoz (1979)	44 outpts 35 female	MMPI GFCC	MMPI GFCC	BT = SST = CT > NT
Zielinski (1979)	36 inpts, alcoholic 9 female	ZSDS BDI MMPI	SADS BDI MMPI	BT = PL = NT No effect
Wilson (1982)	64 volunteers 42 female	Interview BDI	BDI DIS	BT + Drug = Rlx + Drug = PL + Drug = BT + PLDrug = Rlx + PLDrug = PL + PLDrug
Wilson et al. (1983)	25 volunteers 20 female	Interview BDI	BDI HRSD	BT = CT > NT
Brown & Lewinsohn (1984a)	63 outpts 44 female	SADS/RDC	SADS BDI ZSDS	BT(Class) = BT(Individvual) = BT(Self) > NT
McNamara & Horan (1986)	40 outpts	DX BDI HRSD	DX BDI HRSD	BT = CT = Combined = PL
Thompson, Gallagher, & Breckenridge (1987)	91 elders	SADS/RDC HRSD BDI	SADS HRSD GDS	BT = CT = PD > NT

NOTE: *Therapy Conditions:* BT = behavior therapy; CT = cognitive therapy; Drug = pharmacotherapy (usually tricyclic antidepressant); NT = no treatment (waiting list, delayed treatment, etc.); PD = psychodynamically oriented therapy; PL = placebo psychotherapy; PLDrug = placebo pharmacotherapy; Rlx = relaxation; SST = social skills therapy. *Depression Assessment Instruments:* BDI = Beck Depression Inventory; DX = diagnosis; DIS = Diagnostic Interview Schedule; DACL = Depression Adjective Checklist; GFCC = Grinker Feelings and Concerns Checklist; HRSD = Hamilton Rating Scale for Depression; MMPI = Minnesota Multiphasic Personality Inventory (D30 is a separate depression scale within the MMPI); SADS/RDC = Schedule for Affective Disorders and Schizophrenia, used for the Research Diagnostic Criteria; ZSDS = Zung Self-Rating Depression Scale; GDS = Geriatric Depression Scale.

TABLE 9.2   Summary of Comparisons With Behavior Therapy Programs for Depression

Compared to	More Effective	Equal	Less Effective
No treatment	7	2	0
Placebo	2	4	0
Social skill	0	1	0
Cognitive therapy	0	4	0
Self-management	0	0	0
Psychodynamic	0	1	0
Relaxation	0	2	0

outcome. That is, various methods of trying to increase reinforcement seem to be effective regardless of initial level of reinforcement.

SOCIAL SKILLS TRAINING

This category of therapy studies includes several variations on theory and therapy rationale. Theory overlaps in part with Lewinsohn's low-reinforcement model of depression in that one of the posited causes of insufficient reinforcement would be insufficient skills to obtain it. Other theorists posit a lack of various specific interpersonal skills. A major study by Hersen, Bellack, Himmelhoch, and Thase (1984) employed a traditional social skill training program plus activity scheduling and self-control procedures (Becker, Heimberg, & Bellack, 1987). McLean (McLean et al., 1973; McLean & Hakstian, 1979) selected among behavioral skill modules, including marital communication skill training and assertion training. Jacobson (1984) and Beach and O'Leary (1986) have investigated marital therapy as an approach to therapy for depression. Nezu, Nezu, and Perri (1989) describe a problem-solving skills program for depression that includes units on problem orientation and definition, problem identification, generation of alternatives, decision making, implementation and verification of solutions, and maintenance and generalization plans. Gotlib and Colby (1987) present a case for an interpersonal systems view of therapy for depression.

An approach by Klerman, Weissman, Rounsaville, and Chevron (1984) derives from the interpersonal therapy approach of Sullivan (1953) and

Meyer (1948). This approach has been evaluated in several studies. It shares an orientation toward treating depression by trying to resolve interpersonal difficulties, but does so from a generally dynamic viewpoint. Because of its different theoretical perspective, it is included in this review as a specific alternative comparison different from the four major approaches.

Social skill therapy studies are summarized in Tables 9.3 and 9.4. Comparisons to no treatment are positive for social skills therapy in four of five individual comparisons. Comparisons to placebo therapy conditions are again less positive, with social skill treatments superior in only four of seven comparisons. Comparisons with alternative types of therapy find social skill treatments superior to relaxation and equivalent to behavior therapy or cognitive therapy in three studies, but inferior to cognitive therapy in another study and inferior to self-management in yet another. In one study, the combination of social skill treatment and cognitive therapy was superior to either alone. No group design studies of components or alternative formats of social skill programs have been reported to date. Social skill approaches have been applied to therapy with children (for a review of this area see Rehm & Kaslow, 1984).

COGNITIVE THERAPY

Although a cognitive paradigm may be a generic approach to therapy, in the area of depression, research has focused almost exclusively on Aaron Beck's Cognitive Therapy (Beck, Rush, Shaw, & Emery, 1979). Beck (1972) sees the essence of depression to be the cognitive triad of negative views of self, world, and future. He posits that the basis for depression is the cognitive distortion of experience based on negatively biased cognitive schemata that are activated when the person becomes depressed. He describes specific mechanisms of distortion such as selective abstraction, arbitrary inference, magnification, minimization, over- and undergeneralization, inexact labeling, and all-or-none thinking. Automatic thoughts are the result of depressive schemata operating in situations. Schemata, in the form of underlying assumptions, form the automatic thoughts. Latent schemata are activated by loss or perception of loss. Modern cognitive theory and research on memory and information processing support important parts of Beck's theory (Rehm & Naus, 1990).

Beck's therapy is described in a manual (Beck et al., 1979). It is an individual approach with many individual decisions and therapist choices of

TABLE 9.3   Social Skill Programs for Depression

Reference	Subjects	Selection Criteria	Outcome Criteria	Results
McLean, Ogston, & Grauer (1973)	20 outpts 16 female	DACL	DACL	SST > PL
Shaw (1977)	32 college	BDI HRSD VAS Interview	BDI HRSD VAS	CT > SST = PL > NT
Taylor & Marshall (1977)	28 college 20 female	BDI MMPI Interview	BDI MMPI-D30 MAACL VAS	SST + CT > SST = CT > NT
McLean & Hakstian (1979)	154 outpts 72% female	MMPI BDI DACL	MMPI BDI DACL	SST > Drug = Rlx > PL
Rehm et al. (1979)	22 volunteers all female	MMPI Interview	MMPI-D BDI	SMT > SST
Teri & Leitenberg (1979)	22 outpts	Cl. Dx.	BDI	SST + PL > PL
Zeiss, Lewinsohn, & Muñoz (1979)	44 outpts 35 female	MMPI GFCC	MMPI GFCC	SST = BT = CT > NT
Hayman & Cope (1980)	44 outpts 35 female	BDI ZSDS	BDI ZSDS	SST = NT
Sanchez, Lewinsohn, & Larson (1980)	32 outpts 21 female	MMPI GFCC	MMPI-D BDI	SST = PL
Hersen et al. (1984)	125 outpts All female	SADS/RDC BDI HRSD DACL Raskin	SADS/RDC BDI HRSD DACL Raskin	SST + Drug = SST + PLDrug = Drug = PL + PLDrug
Nezu (1986)	26 com. volunteers 20 female	SADS/RDC BDI MMPI-D	BDI MMPI	SST > PL = NT
Miller et al. (1989)	46 inpts 34 female	DIS/DSM-III BDI HRSD	DIS/DSM-III BDI HRSD	CT = SST > Std Treatment (all with drugs)

NOTE: *Therapy Conditions:* BT = behavior therapy; CT = cognitive therapy; Drug = pharmacotherapy (usually tricyclic antidepressant); NT = no treatment (waiting list, delayed treatment, etc.); PD = psychodynamically oriented therapy; PL = placebo psychotherapy; PLDrug = placebo pharmacotherapy; Rlx = relaxation; SMT = self-management therapy; SST = social skills therapy. *Depression Assessment Instruments:* BDI = Beck Depression Inventory; Cl. Dx. = clinical depression; DIS = Diagnostic Interview Schedule; DACL = Depression Adjective Checklist; GFCC = Grinker Feelings and Concerns Checklist; HRSD = Hamilton Rating Scale for Depression; MAACL = Multiple Affect Adjective Checklist; MMPI = Minnesota Multiphasic Personality Inventory (D30 is a separate depression scale within the MMPI); Raskin = 3-item depression rating scale; SADS/RDC = Schedule for Affective Disorders and Schizophrenia, used for the Research Diagnostic Criteria; VAS = Visual Analog Scale; ZSDS = Zung Self-Rating Depression Scale.

TABLE 9.4   Summary of Comparisons With Social Skills Therapy Programs
for Depression

Compared to	More Effective	Equal	Less Effective
No treatment	4	1	0
Placebo	4	3	0
Behavior therapy	0	1	0
Cognitive therapy	0	3	1
Self-management	0	0	1
Relaxation	1	0	0

techniques in a traditional one-to-one psychotherapy format. Nevertheless, the manual suggests a typical structure for the sequence of sessions. Activity scheduling is the first strategy. For inactive, severe cases, the use of graded activities is suggested. Recording cognitions by the triple-column technique is a variation on the self-monitoring techniques common to many cognitive-behavioral therapies. Later sessions discuss "shoulds and wants" and deal with self-criticism. The process can be considered a progression from activity, to automatic thoughts, to underlying assumptions. Another basic therapy process is assumed to be collaborative empiricism, the mode of operation between therapist and client. The structuring of therapy sessions with feedback from the client as to the agenda is also a component of cognitive therapy.

Cognitive therapy studies are summarized in Tables 9.5 and 9.6. Comparisons to no treatment are positive for cognitive therapy in seven of nine individual comparisons. Comparisons to placebo therapy conditions are positive, however, in only one of four comparisons. Quite a few studies have compared cognitive therapy to alternative approaches. A total of 11 comparisons with behavior therapy, social skill, self-management, interpersonal psychodynamic, and relaxation find them equally effective. In two comparisons, one with social skill training and one with a psychodynamic approach, cognitive therapy was superior.

Disassembly studies are only beginning to be done in the area. Group and individual formats were equivalent in the one controlled study, but another uncontrolled study found the individual format superior (Rush & Watkins, 1981). Adaptations of cognitive therapy have been applied to depressed adolescents and elderly individuals. Several additional studies are in progress.

TABLE 9.5 Cognitive Therapy for Depression

Reference	Subjects	Selection Criteria	Outcome Criteria	Results
Shaw (1977)	32 college	BDI	BDI	CT >
	22 female	HRSD	HRSD	SST = PL
		VAS	VAS	> NT
		Interview		
Taylor & Marshall	28 college	BDI	BDI	SST + CT >
(1977)	20 female	MMPI	MMPI-D30	SST = CT
		Interview	MAACL	> NT
			VAS	
Fleming &	35 volunteers	MMPI-D30	MMPI-D30	CT = SMT = PL
Thornton	25 female	BDI	BDI	
(1980)		Interview		
Wilson et al.	25 volunteers	Interview	BDI	CT = BT > NT
(1983)	20 female	BDI	HRSD	
Steuer et al.	33 outpts	DX	DX	CT > PD
(1984)	25 female	HDRS	HDRS	
			BDI	
Teasdale et al.	34 outpts	SADS/RDC	SADS/RDC	CT + PL > PL
(1984)		BDI	BDI	
		MADS	MADS	
			ZSDS	
Beach & O'Leary	8 couples	DX		CT = Marital > NT
(1986)		Marital discord		
McNamara &	40 outpts	DX	DX	BT = Combined = PL
Horan (1986)		BDI	BDI	
		HDRS	HDRS	
Reynolds & Coats	30 adolescents	BDI	BDI	CT = Rlx > NT
(1986)		BDI	BDI	
		RADS	RADS	
Thompson,	91 elders	SADS/RDC	SADS	CT = BT = PD > NT
Gallagher, &		HRSD	HRSD	
Breckenridge		BDI	GDS	
(1987)				
Wierzbicki &	18 outpts	DX	DX	CT (Individual) >
Bartlett (1987)		BDI	BDI	CT (Group) =
				NT
Hogg & Deffen-	37 college outpts	DX	BDI	CT = IP = NT
bacher (1988)			MMPI-D	
Elkin et al.	239 outpts	SADS/RDC	SADS/RDC	CT = IP = Drug
(1989)	168 female	HRSD	HRSD	IP = Drug > PLDrug
			BDI	CT = PLDrug
Miller et al.	46 inpts	DIS/DSM-III	DIS/DSM-III	CT = SST >
(1989)	34 female	BDI	BDI	Std treatment
		HRSD	HRSD	(all with drugs)

NOTE: *Therapy Conditions:* BT = behavior therapy; CT = cognitive therapy; Drug = pharmacotherapy (usually tricyclic antidepressant); NT = no treatment (waiting list, delayed treatment, etc.); IP = interpersonal therapy; PD = psychodynamically oriented therapy; PL = placebo psychotherapy; PLDrug = placebo pharmacotherapy; Rlx = relaxation; SMT = self-management therapy; SST = social skills therapy. *Depression Assessment Instruments:* BDI = Beck Depression Inventory; DX = diagnosis; DIS = Diagnostic Interview Schedule; HRSD = Hamilton Rating Scale for Depression; MAACL = Multiple Affect Adjective Checklist; MMPI = Minnesota Multiphasic Personality Inventory (D30 is a separate depression scale within the MMPI); RADS = Reynolds Adolescent Depression Scale; SADS/RDC = Schedule for Affective Disorders and Schizophrenia, used for the Research Diagnostic Criteria; VAS = Visual Analog Scale; ZSDS = Zung Self-Rating Depression Scale; MADS = Montgomery-Asberg Depression Scale; GDS = Geriatric Depression Scale.

TABLE 9.6   Summary of Comparisons With Cognitive Therapy Programs for Depression

Compared to	More Effective	Equal	Less Effective
No treatment	7	2	0
Placebo	1	3	0
Behavior therapy	0	3	0
Social skill	1	3	0
Self-management	0	1	0
Interpersonal	0	2	0
Psychodynamic	1	1	0
Relaxation	0	1	0

SELF-MANAGEMENT THERAPY

Self-management therapy is derived from my self-control model of depression (Rehm, 1977). Studies include those from my labs, others with my manuals, and a few independent but similar programs. My 1977 model followed from a review of then current theoretical models of Lewinsohn, Beck, and Seligman. It was an effort to employ Kanfer's model of self-control as framework for incorporating multiple factors from other theories that seem to be basic to depression. The basic assumption is that the problems of depression can be seen as problems in regulation or management of behavior toward long-term goals.

The model suggests that depressed persons show one or more deficits in self-control behavior. Specifically, six deficits are postulated:

1. Depressed persons attend to negative events in their experience to the relative exclusion of positive events.
2. Depressed persons attend to the immediate, relative to the delayed, consequences of their behavior.
3. Depressed persons set stringent standards for the self-evaluation of their behavior.
4. Depressed persons make negative attributions consistent with low self-esteem.
5. As a consequence, depressed persons self-administer insufficient contingent reinforcement to maintain behavior to obtain long-term goals.
6. They self-administer excessive punishment that suppresses activity and initiative.

The symptoms of depression reflect these deficits.

The unpublished therapy manual for this program (Rehm, 1980) describes a group format, didactic approach that involves presentation of principles, discussion of application to individuals, exercises to enhance understanding of the principles, and homework assignments to put the principles into practice. The program includes units on self-monitoring of positive activities, recognizing immediate versus delayed consequences of behavior, appropriate attributions for success and for failure, goal setting with appropriate self-evaluation and activity scheduling, and both overt and covert self-reinforcement.

Research findings with self-management therapy for depression are shown in Tables 9.7 and 9.8. Self-management therapy is superior to no treatment in nine specific condition comparisons. Comparisons to placebo show self-management therapy superior in two of six specific comparisons. In one comparison self-management therapy was superior to social skill training, and in another they were equally effective. One comparison with cognitive therapy found them to be equal in outcome.

Several studies of the self-management program have attempted to disassemble the program and evaluate its components. Uniformly these studies have not shown specific additive effects for components of the program. Also, targeted outcome measures are not differentially affected by versions of the therapy program matched or mismatched to the target. The program has been adapted for adolescents (Reynolds & Coats, 1986), children (Stark, Reynolds, & Kaslow, 1987), and the elderly (Barlow, 1986; Rokke, 1985).

PHARMACOTHERAPY COMPARISONS

Tricyclic antidepressant drugs are the most frequently used treatment of depression, and their efficacy is well established in outcome research (Morris & Beck, 1974). Because the efficacy of pharmacotherapy is so well established, comparisons of the cognitive-behavioral therapies to drugs and to placebo drug conditions provide a standard for assessing the efficacy of the cognitive-behavioral approaches. Assessing cognitive-behavioral therapies as an alternative or as an adjunct to drugs has significant practical importance in that many people are averse to taking antidepressant medications either philosophically or because of negative side effects of the medications. It would also be of great importance to know whether the effects are different or whether the types of treatment are effective for different groups of people.

TABLE 9.7 Self-Management Therapy Programs for Depression

Reference	Subjects	Selection Criteria	Outcome Criteria	Results
Hilford (1975)	46 inpts all female	Cl.Dx	ZSDS DACL	SMT > PL = NT
Fuchs & Rehm (1977)	36 female volunteers	MMPI Interview	MMPI BDI	SMT > PL > NT
Rehm et al. (1979)	24 female volunteers	MMPI BDI Interview	MMPI	SMT > SST
Fleming & Thornton (1980)	35 volunteers 25 female	MMPI-D30 BDI Interview	MMPI-D30 BDI	SMT = CT = PL
Rehm et al. (1981)	45 female volunteers	SADS/RDC MMPI	SADS/RDC BDI MMPI HRSD Raskin	SMT = SMT(−SR) = SMT(−SE) = SMT(SM) > NT
Kornblith et al. (1983)	49 female volunteers	SADS/RDC BDI	SADS/RDC BDI MMPI HRSD Raskin	SMT = SMT(−SR) = SMT(−H) = PL
Rehm et al. (1985)	44 female volunteers	SADS/RDC BDI MMPI	SADS/RDC BDI MMPI HRSD Raskin	SMT(BT) = SMT(CT) = SMT(COMB.) > NT
Rehm et al. (1987)	103 female volunteers	SADS/RDC BDI MMPI	SADS/RDC BDI MMPI HRSD Raskin	SMT(BT) = SMT(CT) = SMT(COMB.)
Rude (1986)	48 female volunteers	SADS/RDC BDI MMPI	BDI MMPI-D	SMT = SST SMT + SST > NT

NOTE: *Therapy Conditions:* BT = behavior therapy; CT = cognitive therapy; NT = no treatment (waiting list, delayed treatment, etc.); PD = psychodynamically oriented therapy; PL = placebo psychotherapy; SMT = self-management therapy (components: SM = self-monitoring, SE = self-evaluation, SR = self-reinforcement, H = homework, BT = behavioral target, CT = cognitive target, Comb. = combined target); SST = social skills therapy. *Depression Assessment Instruments:* BDI = Beck Depression Inventory; DACL = Depression Adjective Checklist; HRSD = Hamilton Rating Scale for Depression; MMPI = Minnesota Multiphasic Personality Inventory (D30 is a separate depression scale within the MMPI); Raskin = 3-item depression rating scale; SADS/RDC = Schedule for Affective Disorders and Schizophrenia, used for the Research Diagnostic Criteria; ZSDS = Zung Self-Rating Depression Scale; Cl. Dx. = clinical diagnosis.

TABLE 9.8   Summary of Comparisons With Self-Management Therapy
              Programs for Depression

Compared to	More Effective	Equal	Less Effective
No treatment	9	0	0
Placebo	2	4	0
Behavior therapy	0	0	0
Social skill	1	1	0
Cognitive therapy	0	1	0

   Enough studies have now been conducted so that we can begin to draw some conclusions about the cognitive-behavioral therapies and pharmacotherapy. Among the therapies reviewed in this chapter, cognitive therapy has most frequently been compared in one way or another with drug conditions. The other therapies have not been included in a sufficient number of studies to warrant separate analysis, so all studies are included in Tables 9.9 and 9.10.

   Although a placebo drug condition is the standard reference in pharmacotherapy studies, only one study, the recently completed national collaborative treatment of depression study (Elkin et al., 1989), provided a direct comparison to a placebo drug condition. In this case cognitive therapy was not significantly different in outcome. Interestingly, interpersonal therapy was superior to drug placebo in this study, even though cognitive and interpersonal therapy were not significantly different from one another. On the other hand, in direct comparisons between cognitive-behavioral therapies and active drug therapy, the cognitive-behavioral programs have been superior in one half of the six available comparisons. The combination of drug and cognitive-behavioral therapy has been shown to be superior to the psychological treatment alone in two of seven studies. In comparisons of the combination to the drug alone, the combination is superior in two of five studies. Several studies have compared different combinations of psychological therapy or placebo combined with drug or drug placebo. When combined with an active cognitive-behavioral therapy, drugs were equal to drug placebo in three studies. Active cognitive-behavioral therapy was equal to placebo psychotherapy when both were combined with either placebo drug therapy (two studies) or active drug therapy (three studies).

   Some other initial conclusions can be drawn from these studies. Although the cognitive-behavioral therapies are often superior in outcome of the complete trial, there is some evidence that drugs may work faster, especially

TABLE 9.9 All Programs in Comparison With Pharmacotherapy Conditions

Reference	Subjects	Selection Criteria	Outcome Criteria	Results
Wilson (1982)	64 volunteers 42 female	Interview BDI	BDI DIS	BT + Drug = Rlx + Drug = PL + Drug = BT + PLDrug = Rlx + PLDrug = PL + PLDrug
McLean & Hakstian (1979)	154 outpts 72% female	MMPI BDI DACL	MMPI BDI DACL	SST > Drug = Rlx > PL
Hersen et al. (1984)	125 outpts All female	SADS/RDC BDI HRSD DACL Raskin	SADS/RDC BDI HRSD DACL Raskin	SST + Drug = SST + PLDrug = Drug = PL + PLDrug
Rush et al. (1977)	41 outpts 26 female	SADS/RDC BDI HRSD	SADS/RDC BDI HRSD	CT > Drug
Dunn (1979)	20 outpts 14 female	Prior Dx	BDI Ratings	CT + Drug > PL + Drug
Blackburn et al. (1981)	88 outpts (Hospital & Practice)	SADS/RDC BDI	SADS/RDC BDI	Hosp. CT + Drug > CT = Drug Prac. CT + Drug = CT > Drug
Rush & Watkins (1981)	44 outpts 38 female	SADS/RDC BDI HRSD	BDI HRSD	CT(Indiv.) = CT(Indiv.) + Drug > CT(Group)
Roth et al. (1982)	26 volunteers 17 female	SADS/RDC BDI HRSD	BDI HRSD	SMT = SMT + Drug
Murphy et al. (1984)	70 outpts 52 female	DIS BDI HRSD	DIS BDI HRSD	CT + Drug = CT = CT + PLDrug = Drug
Beck et al. (1985)	33 outpts 24 female	Feighner BDI HRSD	Feighner BDI HRSD	CT = CT + Drug
Beutler et al. (1987)	56 elder outpts 31 female	DSM-III HRSD	DSM-III HRSD BDI	CT + Drug = CT + PLDrug = Drug = PLDrug
Elkin et al. (1989)	239 outpts 168 female	SADS/RDC HRSD	SADS/RDC HRSD BDI	CT = IP = Drug IP = Drug > PLDrug CT = PLDrug
Hollon et al. (1992)	107 outpts	SADS/RDC BDI HRSD	SADS/RDC BDI HRSD RADS GAS	CT = Drug = CT + Drug

NOTE: *Therapy Conditions:* BT = behavior therapy; CT = cognitive therapy; Drug = pharmacotherapy (usually tricyclic antidepressant); PL = placebo psychotherapy; PLDrug = placebo pharmacotherapy; Rlx = relaxation; SMT = self-management therapy; SST = social skills therapy. *Depression Assessment Instruments:* BDI = Beck Depression Inventory; DIS = Diagnostic Interview Schedule; DACL = Depression Adjective Checklist; Feighner = Diagnostic criteria by Feighner et al.; HRSD = Hamilton Rating Scale for Depression; MMPI = Minnesota Multiphasic Personality Inventory (D30 is a separate depression scale within the MMPI); Raskin = 3-item depression rating scale; RADS = Reynolds Adolescent Depression Scale; SADS/RDC = Schedule for Affective Disorders and Schizophrenia, used for the Research Diagnostic Criteria; GAS = Global Adjustment Scale; Dx = diagnosis; DIS = Diagnostic Interview Schedule; IP = Interpersonal Therapy.

TABLE 9.10 Summary of Comparisons of All Therapy Programs for Depression to Pharmacotherapy Conditions

Compared to	More Effective	Equal	Less Effective
Placebo Drug	0	1	0
Drug	3	4	0
Combination	0	6	2
Treatment + drug versus treatment + placebo drug	0	3	0
Treatment + placebo drug versus placebo therapy + placebo drug	0	2	0
Treatment + drug versus placebo therapy + placebo drug	0	3	0

on vegetative symptoms such as insomnia. On the other hand, cognitive-behavioral therapy may be more effective in decreasing relapse or recurrence of episodes. Taking these two findings together suggests that initial pharmacotherapy combined with, or followed by, cognitive-behavioral therapy might be the best overall strategy for treating depression. Although there are relatively few data on differential effectiveness for subsets of patients, two findings have appeared. When patients are separated by initial severity of depression, it appears that more severe patients respond better to pharmacotherapy, whereas mildly to moderately depressed persons may respond as well or better to cognitive-behavioral treatment (Elkin et al., 1989). Simons, Lustman, Wetzel, and Murphy (1985) found that subjects scoring high on the Self-Control Schedule (also known as the Learned Resourcefulness Scale; Rosenbaum, 1980) did better in cognitive therapy, whereas those who scored low on the scale did equally well in cognitive therapy or pharmacotherapy.

SUMMARY AND SOME ADDITIONAL FINDINGS

Let me summarize the findings that I have reviewed. Cognitive-behavioral therapy programs are well established in terms of efficacy. All four types of programs are clearly better than no treatment. We are able to help depressed people make clinically significant improvements in a high proportion of cases.

The picture is less clear in comparisons to placebo conditions. The cognitive-behavioral treatments are superior to placebo psychotherapy in only about 40% of the relevant comparisons. The meaning and function of placebo psychotherapy conditions are troublesome at best, and it is hard to interpret these findings. A large part of the effect of the cognitive-behavioral therapies may be due to nonspecific placebo effects such as the therapy setting, expectancies, and a confiding relationship. It is notable that when both placebo psychotherapy and no-treatment conditions are included, placebo does usually show a significant therapeutic effect. Many of the placebos are fairly active and may include processes that are helpful to depressed persons. It may be informative to study some of these therapies more closely in order to learn the specifics of these apparent nonspecific effects. Although the cognitive-behavioral programs do have somewhat of an edge over the psychotherapy placebos (at least there are no instances of placebo being superior), the paucity of differences begins to suggest that therapy components other than those related to the specific theories may be important.

Comparisons among these four types of programs demonstrate no clear winners. The modal finding by far is no differences in outcome (86% of comparisons). The few differences found and comparisons to placebos seem to give an edge to the cognitive and self-management programs. Although all these programs are complex, the cognitive and self-management programs may be more comprehensive in the problems addressed.

The modal finding of no differences among active treatments is in many ways the most puzzling result of the review. What are the implications for our understanding of the mechanisms of change, that programs with seemingly very different contents are equally effective? Let me add to the puzzle by enumerating some additional findings that appear with some consistency in this depression therapy literature.

First, as partly reviewed above, disassembly studies largely fail to support the independent contribution of specific components of therapy. For example, two studies by my research group (Kornblith, Rehm, O'Hara, & Lamparski, 1983; Rehm et al., 1981) found that removing the self-evaluation, self-reinforcement, or homework components of the self-management therapy program did not lead to significant differences in outcome. Differences due to specific elements of therapy may be quite subtle, and large numbers of subjects may be needed to detect them. The research problem is that greater effort is needed to answer smaller questions. Yet again this result suggests that the effective elements of the therapy programs may be other than the theoretical components that have been manipulated in research.

Second, therapies are nonspecific in terms of targeted outcomes. Subjects improve on nontargeted outcome measures as much as they do on targeted measures of the deficits that are the focus of the therapy. For example, Rehm, Kaslow, and Rabin (1987) measured negative cognitions and activity levels for subjects who were randomly assigned to a cognitive target, a behavior-increase target, or a combined target version of the self-management therapy. Subjects in all three conditions improved equally in depression but also improved equally on cognitions and behavior. Similarly, Zeiss, Lewinsohn, and Muñoz (1979) found improvement on activity, social skill, and cognition equally whether subjects were assigned to behavioral, social skills, or cognitive therapy conditions. Findings of specificity or target outcome are rare but do occur (e.g., Rehm, Fuchs, Roth, Kornblith, & Romano, 1979). In general, however, it appears that with various treatments, people improve on diverse related dimensions whether or not these dimensions were the target of therapy.

Third, studies of predictors of outcome do not support the idea that these therapies compensate for targeted deficits. Stephanie Rude and I (Rude & Rehm, 1991) surveyed all prediction studies that assessed a deficit theoretically targeted by the specific cognitive-behavioral therapy programs. We separated studies into behavioral (reinforcement increase and social skills programs) versus cognitive (cognitive therapy and self-management therapy) along lines similar to the categorization in the review above. By far the modal finding is again nonspecificity: that is, initial status on a deficit measure is unrelated to outcome in therapy that targets the construct being measured.

The positive findings were uniformly not as expected. Among the 10 behavioral studies, 6 different scales of social adjustment or skill predicted outcome, but in the direction opposite to that expected. Better initial levels of adjustment and skill were related to better outcome! Among the 13 cognitive studies, 2 scales, the Dysfunctional Attitudes Scale (Weissman & Beck, 1978) and the Self-Control Schedule (Rosenbaum, 1980), each predicted outcome in two separate studies. Again, they demonstrated that those who began with more positive cognition did better in the cognitive therapy programs! Rather than the compensation effect predicted by the idea that these therapies compensate for a deficit, the evidence suggests a capitalization effect whereby these therapies capitalize on strengths of their participants.

It is important to note, however, that these measures predict a good therapy prognosis generally but are not prescriptive. That is, there is no evidence that these measures suggest that the person will do better in one cognitive-behavioral therapy over another. The skills or attitudes on which the programs capitalize may be very general therapy utilization factors. The only prescriptive finding is the one cited above that self-control or learned resourcefulness (Rosenbaum, 1980) may differentially predict response to cognitive therapy versus drugs (Simons et al., 1985). Low psychotherapy utilization skills may predict a better response to the more passive pharmacotherapy. The available evidence suggests that an initial match between the subject's general skills and beliefs about therapy and the general nature of the therapy yields a positive prognosis.

A fourth finding relevant to understanding the factors making for effective therapy for depression comes from our study of evaluations of the rationales for therapies for depression (Rokke, Carter, Rehm, & Veltum, 1990). College students were asked to rate the rationales for the most common therapy programs for depression on a number of dimensions of expected efficacy and desirability. Correlations with personality measures suggested that students' preferences were related to their own personality characteristics. For example, students who scored higher on extraversion were more likely to favor a social skill approach to therapy for depression. Again, perhaps a fit between either general or specific skills and beliefs, and the nature of the therapy produced an optimism about outcome.

Fifth, in a study of the course of change during cognitive-behavioral therapy, we (Rabin, Kaslow, & Rehm, 1984) found that the biggest changes occurred early in therapy and, in fact, that a major improvement occurred between screening and Session 1! Apparently subjects respond with relief and hopefulness when they have the expectancy of help and a clear rationale for how therapy is going to proceed. The majority of improvement occurs before many of the specific component interventions are introduced.

Overall then, therapy for depression seems to be effective, but this effectiveness seems unrelated to differences in theoretical rationales or to specific intervention strategies or components. The therapies do not seem to operate by remediating specific deficits and may not differentially affect the dimensions they target. Having healthier cognitions and social adjustment seems to make one more likely to improve successfully in any one of these therapies, and perhaps this is because of a compatibility between personal approaches to life and the rationale of the therapy.

SOME ATTEMPTS AT INTEGRATION

What is going on here? These therapies do not seem to be effective for the reasons we think make them effective. Our cherished theories about depression do not seem to have much to do with helping people overcome depression. Let me try to develop some interpretations of these findings.

As I have suggested elsewhere (Rehm et al., 1987), these programs share four characteristics that may account for their success. First, each program has a clear rationale. Each is based on a well-developed, sophisticated, credible theory. Each devotes time and effort to teaching the rationale and theory. Thus the programs provide the person with an alternative view of the nature of their depression. The therapies reconceptualize the person's problem in a more workable language: for example, "Your depression is due to a lack of reinforcement, a deficit in social skill, a process of cognitive distortion, or poor self-management." Psychologists find these rationales to be helpful ways to think about depression, and patients find them helpful too. What are the limits on this? What does it take for a rationale to be helpful or not helpful?

Part of the answer may lie in the second similarity among these programs. Specifically, each program is highly structured. Each program is sequenced. The rationale leads directly to action. "Because of deficit X you need to do Y to remediate it," these programs say. The programs offer not just a rational reconceptualization of the problem but an action plan as well.

Third, all of these programs are instigative. They are active, motivating, and homework oriented. Behavior change between sessions is presented as the central and essential focus of the programs from the start. Research needs to focus on getting people to do their homework effectively.

Fourth, all of these programs provide progress feedback. Recording procedures, periodic ratings, and self-monitoring provide credible evidence that actual change is occurring consistent with the rationale. Such feedback may change both beliefs about the nature of depression and expectations about the patient's ability to effect change based on these beliefs.

When looked at in terms of these common factors, specific theories and interventions become important, but for common reasons. They are useful to people to get them active in changing the conditions responsible for their depression. Alternate conceptualizations and behavioral strategies can be effective for attacking the same problems.

FUTURE DIRECTIONS FOR RESEARCH

It is about time we give up doing studies of "horse race" comparisons between forms of psychotherapy for depression. Although there may be times when we want to use an established therapy as a standard against which to evaluate a new therapy, we can generally expect that almost any therapy with the general characteristics described above will be helpful for many people and that comparison between any two such programs is unlikely to produce important differences in effectiveness. We should turn our attentions in other directions.

We should think about therapy presentation in terms of effective teaching. How well do we teach our rationale and our concepts about how to change depressed behavior? How can we better ensure that patients will be able to put into practice what we teach? We should probably be concerned more with issues of modes of presentation, pacing, and levels of practice in psychotherapy research. The structures of current therapies are remarkably consistent—for example, four or five "units" in 10 to 16 weeks of therapy. Are these natural or intuitive limits on teaching or learning? Are we effectively conveying the content and implementation of each unit in a 2- or 3-week presentation?

We could look much more closely at the learning process. What beliefs or skill levels does the person start with, and how well do we improve them? When we present an idea or skill, does the person understand that specific point? Does the person believe it is applicable to his or her depression and that making a change in that area will be beneficial? What is the relationship between specific changes in depressive symptoms and the acquisition of new knowledge and skills?

We should also ask questions about whether we should try to apply our therapies to subjects who already have consistent belief and behavior patterns or whether we can be successful in persuading or teaching new patterns. It seems clear that we have a head start on teaching when people come into therapy with attitudes, beliefs, skills, or approaches to life that are generally compatible with the nature of the therapy. What about those individuals who do not have positive approaches to therapy?

We should be investigating whether alternative therapies might match alternative personal approaches. We should also study our nonresponders. If they did not find one approach useful, is there another approach more compatible? Perhaps we need to put even more effort into our initial efforts to persuade or teach our rationales so that even those with inconsistent views may better avail themselves of the interventions offered. Perhaps we should construct therapies compatible with the outlooks of groups of nonresponders.

We should look at more innovative questions concerning the interaction between cognitive-behavioral therapies and pharmacotherapies. The two modalities provide us with the widest possible contrast in approaches. Again, rather than looking at horse race comparisons, we should be trying to find out which modality or combination of modalities is most effective for which depressed people. The Simons et al. (1985) finding of differential response as a function of self-control scores is intriguing and needs to be replicated. Initial severity of depression may also predict response differentially. Are there any other scales or dimensions that might help us to prescribe one therapy versus another?

On the biological side, there are a number of measures associated with depression. The biological markers are often conceptualized as indicating a different type of endogenous depression. It would be informative to investigate how these measures relate to outcome in both broad therapy modalities. Will these variables show more specificity in outcome or prediction than the psychological deficit markers? Evidence to date suggests they may be just as nonspecific.

We should look at different ways of using both modalities. We need to know who are the nonresponders to both types of intervention. Are they the same or different people in the two approaches? We need crossover designs to see if we can better treat nonresponders to a single intervention with a second intervention.

If drugs work faster on some symptoms and for more severe depression, but cognitive-behavioral approaches provide more resistance to relapse, then perhaps the optimal treatment is to begin with the medication and then shift to cognitive-behavioral therapy. It would be interesting to see if medication increased activity, skill, and cognition to a point at which the person's patterns become more compatible with the second therapy format.

Studying the interaction of cognitive-behavioral therapies and pharmacotherapy for depression is important not only for the practical reason of finding effective treatment strategies but also because it informs us about depression itself and about our theories of depression. We have much to learn, and new approaches to therapy research for depression are needed to advance our knowledge.

REFERENCES

Barlow, J. (1986). *A group treatment for depression in the elderly.* Unpublished doctoral dissertation, University of Houston.

Barrera, M., Jr. (1979). An evaluation of brief group therapy for depression. *Journal of Consulting and Clinical Psychology, 47,* 413-415.

Beach, S. R. H., & O'Leary, K. D. (1986). The treatment of depression occurring in the context of marital discord. *Behavior Therapy, 17,* 43-49.

Beck, A. T. (1972). *Depression: Causes and treatment.* Philadelphia: University of Pennsylvania Press.

Beck, A. T., Hollon, S. D., Young, J. E., Bedrosian, R. C., & Budenz, D. (1985). Treatment of depression with cognitive therapy and amitriptyline. *Archives of General Psychiatry, 42*(2), 142-152.

Beck, A. T., Rush, A. J., Shaw, B. F., & Emery, G. (1979). *Cognitive therapy for depression.* New York: Guilford.

Becker, R. E., Heimberg, R. G., & Bellack, A. S. (1987). *Social skills training treatment for depression.* New York: Pergamon.

Beutler, L. E., Scogin, F., Kirbish, P., Schretlen, D., Corbishley, A., Hamblin, D., Meredith, K., Potter, R., Bamford, C. R., & Levenson, A. I. (1987). Group cognitive therapy and alprazolam in the treatment of depression in older adults. *Journal of Consulting and Clinical Psychology, 55,* 550-556.

Blackburn, I. M., Bishop, S., Glenn, A. I. M., Whalley, L. J., & Christie, J. E. (1981). The efficacy of cognitive therapy in depression: A treatment trial using cognitive therapy and pharmacotherapy, each alone and in combination. *British Journal of Psychiatry, 139,* 181-189.

Brown, R. A., & Lewinsohn, P. M. (1984a). A psychoeducational approach to the treatment of depression: Comparison of group, individual, and minimal contact procedures. *Journal of Consulting and Clinical Psychology, 52,* 774-783.

Brown, R. A., & Lewinsohn, P. M. (1984b). *Participant workbook for the coping with depression course.* Eugene, OR: Castalia.

Dunn, R. J. (1979). Cognitive modification with depression-prone psychiatric patients. *Cognitive Therapy and Research, 3,* 307-317.

Elkin, I., Shea, M. T., Watkins, J. T., Imber, S. D., Sotsky, S. M., Collins, J. F., Glass, D. R., Pilkonis, P. A., Leber, W. R., Docherty, J. P., Fiester, S. J., & Parloff, M. B. (1989). National Institute of Mental Health treatment of depression collaborative research program: General effectiveness of treatments. *Archives of General Psychiatry, 46,* 971-982.

Fleming, B. M., & Thornton, D. W. (1980). Coping skills training as a component in the short-term treatment of depression. *Journal of Consulting and Clinical Psychology, 48,* 652-655.

Fuchs, C. Z., & Rehm, L. P. (1977). A self-control behavior therapy program for depression. *Journal of Consulting and Clinical Psychology, 45,* 206-215.

Gotlib, I. H., & Colby, C. A. (1987). *Treatment of depression: An interpersonal systems approach.* New York: Pergamon.

Hayman, P. M., & Cope, C. S. (1980). Effects of assertion training on depression. *Journal of Clinical Psychology, 36,* 534-543.

Hersen, M., Bellack, A. S., Himmelhoch, J. M., & Thase, M. E. (1984). Effects of social skill training, amitriptyline, and psychotherapy in unipolar depressed women. *Behavior Therapy, 15,* 21-40.

Hilford, N. G. (1975). Self initiated behavior change by depressed women following verbal behavior therapy. *Behavior Therapy, 6,* 703.

Hogg, J. A., & Deffenbacher, J. L. (1988). A comparison of cognitive and interpersonal-process group therapies in the treatment of depression among college students. *Journal of Counseling Psychology, 35,* 304-310.

Hollon, S. D., DeRubeis, R. J., Evans, M. D., Wiener, M. J., Garvey, M. J., Grove, W. M., & Tuason, V. B. (1992). Cognitive therapy and pharmacotherapy for depression: Singly and in combination. *Archives of General Psychiatry, 49,* 774-781.

Jacobson, N. S. (1984). Marital therapy and the cognitive-behavioral treatment of depression. *Behavior Therapist, 7,* 143-147.

Kanfer, F. H. (1970). Self-regulation: Research, issues and speculations. In C. Neuringer & J. L. Michael (Eds.), *Behavior modification in clinical psychology* (pp. 178-220). New York: Appleton-Century-Crofts.

Kaslow, N. J., & Rehm, L. P. (1984). Childhood depression. In R. J. Morris & T. R. Krathochwill, *The practice of child therapy: A textbook of methods* (2nd ed., pp. 27-51). New York: Pergamon.

Klerman, G. L., Weissman, M. M., Rounsaville, B. J., & Chevron, E. S. (1984). *Interpersonal psychotherapy for depression.* New York: Basic Books.

Kornblith, S. J., Rehm, L. P., O'Hara, M. W., & Lamparski, D. M. (1983). The contribution of self-reinforcement training and behavioral assignments to the efficacy of self-control therapy for depression. *Cognitive Therapy and Research, 7,* 499-527.

Lewinsohn, P. M. (1974). A behavioral approach to depression. In R. M. Friedman & M. M. Katz (Eds.), *The psychology of depression: Contemporary theory and research* (pp. 157-185). New York: John Wiley.

Lewinsohn, P. M. (1976). Activity schedules in treatment of depression. In J. D. Krumboltz & C. E. Thoresen, *Counseling methods* (pp. 74-82). New York: Holt, Rinehart & Winston.

Lewinsohn, P. M., Antonuccio, D. O., Breckenridge, J., & Teri, L. (1987). *The coping with depression course: A psychoeducational intervention for unipolar depression.* Eugene, OR: Castalia.

Lewinsohn, P. M., Muñoz, R. F., Youngren, M. A., & Zeiss, A. M. (1978). *Control your depression.* Englewood Cliffs, NJ: Prentice Hall.

Lewinsohn, P. M., Weinstein, M. S., & Shaw, D. (1969). Depression: A clinical-research approach. In R. D. Rubin & C. M. Franks (Eds.), *Advances in behavioral therapy.* New York: Academic Press.

McLean, P. D., & Hakstian, A. R. (1979). Clinical depression: Comparative efficacy of outpatient treatments. *Journal of Consulting and Clinical Psychology, 47,* 818-836.

McLean, P. D., Ogston, K., & Grauer, L. (1973). A behavioral approach to the treatment of depression. *Journal of Behavior Therapy and Experimental Psychiatry, 4,* 323-330.

McNamara, K., & Horan, J. J. (1986). Experimental construct validity in the evaluation of cognitive and behavioral treatments for depression. *Journal of Counseling Psychology, 33,* 23-30.

Meyer, A. (1948). *The commonsense psychiatry of Dr. Adolf Meyer.* New York: McGraw-Hill.

Miller, I. W., Norman, W. H., Keitner, G. I., Bishop, S. B., & Dow, M. G. (1989). Cognitive-behavioral treatment of depressed inpatients. *Behavior Therapy, 20,* 25-47.

Morris, J. B., & Beck, A. T. (1974). The efficacy of antidepressant drugs: A review of research (1958-1972). *Archives of General Psychiatry, 30,* 667-674.

Murphy, G. E., Simons, A. D., Wetzel, R. D., & Lustman, R. J. (1984). Cognitive therapy and pharmacotherapy singly and together, in the treatment of depression. *Archives of General Psychiatry, 41,* 33-41.

Nezu, A. M. (1986). Efficacy of a social problem-solving therapy approach for unipolar depression. *Journal of Consulting and Clinical Psychology, 54,* 196-202.

Nezu, A. M., Nezu, C. M., & Perri, M. G. (1989). *Problem-solving therapy for depression: Theory, research and clinical guidelines.* New York: John Wiley.

Padfield, M. (1976). The comparative effects of two counseling approaches on the intensity of depression among rural women of low-socioeconomic status. *Journal of Counseling Psychology, 23,* 209-214.

Rabin, A. S., Kaslow, N. J., & Rehm, L. P. (1984). Changes in symptoms of depression during the course of therapy. *Cognitive Therapy and Research, 8,* 479-487.

Rehm, L. P. (1977). A self-control model of depression. *Behavior Therapy, 8,* 787-804.

Rehm, L. P. (1980). *Self-management therapy for depression: Therapist's manual VIII.* Photocopy manuscript, University of Houston.

Rehm, L. P. (Ed.). (1981). *Behavior therapy for depression: Present status and future directions.* New York: Academic Press.

Rehm, L. P., Fuchs, C. Z., Roth, D. M., Kornblith, S. J., & Romano, J. M. (1979). A comparison of self-control and assertion skills treatments of depression. *Behavior Therapy, 10,* 429-442.

Rehm, L. P., & Kaslow, N. J. (1984). Behavioral approaches to depression: Research results and clinical recommendations. In C. M. Franks (Ed.), *New developments in behavior therapy: From research to clinical application* (pp. 155-230). New York: Haworth.

Rehm, L. P., Kaslow, N. J., & Rabin, A. S. (1987). Cognitive and behavioral targets in a self-control therapy program for depression. *Journal of Consulting and Clinical Psychology, 55,* 60-67.

Rehm, L. P., & Kornblith, S. J. (1979). Behavior therapy for depression: A review of recent developments. In M. Hersen, R. M. Eisler, & P. M. Miller (Eds.), *Progress in behavior modification* (Vol. 7, pp. 277-318). New York: Academic Press.

Rehm, L. P., Kornblith, S. J., O'Hara, M. W., Lamparski, D. M., Romano, J. M., & Volkin, J. (1981). An evaluation of major components in a self-control behavior therapy program for depression. *Behavior Modification, 5,* 459-490.

Rehm, L. P., Lamparski, D., Romano, J. M., & O'Hara, M. W. (1985). *A comparison of behavioral, cognitive and combined target versions of a self-control therapy program for depression.* Unpublished study, University of Pittsburgh.

Rehm, L. P., & Naus, M. J. (1990). A memory model of emotion. In R. E. Ingram (Ed.), *Contemporary psychological approaches to depression: Theory, research and treatment* (pp. 23-35). New York: Plenum.

Reynolds, W. M., & Coats, K. I. (1986). A comparison of cognitive-behavioral therapy and relaxation training for the treatment of depression in adolescents. *Journal of Consulting and Clinical Psychology, 54*(5), 653-660.

Rokke, P. D. (1985). *Processes of change in depression: A self-control perspective.* Unpublished doctoral dissertation, University of Houston.

Rokke, P. D., Carter, A. S., Rehm, L. P., & Veltum, L. G. (1990). Comparative credibility of current treatments for depression. *Psychotherapy: Theory, Research and Practice, 27,* 235-242.

Rosenbaum, M. (1980). A schedule for assessing self-control behaviors: Preliminary findings. *Behavior Therapy, 11,* 109-121.

Roth, D., Bielski, R., Jones, M., Parker, W., & Osborn, G. (1982). A comparison of self-control therapy and combined self-control therapy and antidepressant medication in the treatment of depression. *Behavior Therapy, 13,* 133-144.

Rude, S. S. (1986). Relative benefits of assertion or cognitive self-control treatment for depression as a function of proficiency in each domain. *Journal of Consulting and Clinical Psychology, 54,* 390-394.

Rude, S. S., & Rehm, L. P. (1991). Cognitive and behavioral predictors of response to treatments for depression. *Clinical Psychology Review, 11,* 493-514.

Rush, A. J., Beck, A. T., Kovacs, M., & Hollon, S. (1977). Comparative efficacy of cognitive therapy and pharmacotherapy in the treatment of depressed outpatients. *Cognitive Therapy and Research, 1,* 17-38.

Rush, A. J., & Watkins, J. T. (1981). Group versus individual cognitive therapy: A pilot study. *Cognitive Therapy and Research, 5,* 95-104.

Sanchez, V. C., Lewinsohn, P. M., & Larson, D. W. (1980). Assertion training: Effectiveness in the treatment of depression. *Journal of Clinical Psychology, 36,* 526-529.

Seligman, M. E. P. (1981). A learned helplessness point of view. In L. P. Rehm (Ed.), *Behavior therapy for depression: Present status and future directions.* New York: Academic Press.

Shaw, B. F. (1977). Comparative of cognitive therapy and behavior therapy in the treatment of depression. *Journal of Consulting and Clinical Psychology, 45,* 543-551.

Shipley, C. R., & Fazio, A. F. (1973). Pilot study of a treatment for psychological depression. *Journal of Abnormal Psychology, 82,* 372-376.

Simons, A. D., Lustman, P. J., Wetzel, R. D., & Murphy, G. E. (1985). Predicting response to cognitive therapy of depression: The role of learned resourcefulness. *Cognitive Therapy and Research, 9,* 79-90.

Stark, K. D., Reynolds, W. M., & Kaslow, N. J. (1987). A comparison of the relative efficacy of self-control therapy and a behavioral problem-solving therapy for depression in children. *Journal of Abnormal Child Psychology, 15,* 91-113.

Steuer, J. L., Mintz, J., Hammen, C. L., Hill, M. A., Jarvik, L. F., McCaney, T., Motoike, P., & Rosen, R. (1984). Cognitive-behavioral and psychodynamic group psychotherapy in treatment of geriatric depression. *Journal of Consulting and Clinical Psychology, 52,* 180-189.

Sullivan, H. S. (1953). *The interpersonal theory of psychiatry.* New York: Norton.

Taylor, F. G., & Marshall, W. L. (1977). Experimental analysis of a cognitive-behavioral therapy for depression. *Cognitive Therapy and Research, 1,* 59-72.

Teasdale, J. D., Fennell, M. J., Hibbert, G. A., & Amies, P. L. (1984). Cognitive therapy for major depressive disorder in primary care. *British Journal of Psychiatry, 144,* 400-406.

Thompson, L. W., Gallagher, D., & Breckenridge, J. S. (1987). Comparative effectiveness of psychotherapies for depressed elders. *Journal of Consulting and Clinical Psychology, 55,* 385-390.

Turner, R. W., Ward, M. F., & Turner, J. D. (1979). Behavioral treatment for depression: An evaluation of therapeutic components. *Journal of Clinical Psychology, 55,* 166-175.

Weissman, A. N., & Beck, A. T. (1978, November). *Development and validation of the Dysfunctional Attitudes Scale.* Paper presented at the annual meeting of the Association for the Advancement of Behavior Therapy, Chicago.

Wierzbicki, M., & Bartlett, T. S. (1987). The efficacy of group and individual cognitive therapy for mild depression. *Cognitive Therapy and Research, 11,* 337-342.

Wilson, P. H. (1982). Combined pharmacological and behavioral treatment of depression. *Behavior Research and Therapy, 20,* 173-184.

Wilson, P. H., Goldin, J. C., & Charbonneau-Powis, M. (1983). Comparative efficacy of behavioral and cognitive treatments of depression. *Cognitive Therapy and Research, 7,* 111-124.

Zeiss, A. M., Lewinsohn, P. M., & Muñoz, R. (1979). Nonspecific improvement effects in depression using interpersonal, cognitive and pleasant events focused treatments. *Journal of Consulting and Clinical Psychology, 47,* 427-439.

Zielinski, J. L. (1979). Behavioral treatments of depression with alcoholics receiving pharmacological aversion. *Behavior Therapist, 2*(5), 25-27.

10

Cognitive-Behavioral Therapy
for Unipolar Depression

STEPHEN R. SWALLOW

ZINDEL V. SEGAL

Unipolar depression is a serious mental health problem that, according to one recent estimate, may afflict 4 to 5% of the general population at any given point in time (Paykel, 1989). Its reputation as the "common cold" of psychopathology, though warranted with respect to incidence, is certainly misleading in terms of the severity of the impact that depression can have upon its sufferers and their friends and families (Gilbert, 1991). Suicide, for example, is one lethal and alarmingly frequent consequence of depression (Minkoff, Bergman, Beck, & Beck, 1973). However, even episodes of milder levels of depression are associated with significantly diminished quality of life in a variety of domains (de Jong & Verhage, 1985). Furthermore, depression is a potentially recurrent disorder, often taking a chronic and progressively more intractable course (Keller et al., 1986).

Among the various approaches, both psychological and biological, to the treatment of unipolar depression, cognitive-behavioral therapy (CBT) has emerged as an increasingly popular and highly effective intervention modality. A number of outcome studies consistently indicate that CBT is at least as effective as pharmacological intervention for acute treatment of depressive symptomatology (e.g., Elkin et al., 1989; Murphy, Simons, Wetzel, & Lustman, 1984). Interestingly enough, several follow-up studies suggest that CBT may be associated with lower rates of relapse than pharmacological treatment (e.g., Blackburn, Eunson, & Bishop, 1986; Evans et al., 1992; Simons, Murphy, Levine, & Wetzel, 1986). Overall, CBT represents a useful modality of treatment for unipolar affective disorder.

The aim of this chapter is to provide a "state-of-the-art" overview of CBT for depression in terms of both theory and practice. We begin by presenting a cognitive-behavioral formulation of unipolar depression, thus providing a conceptual foundation for CBT. Building on this foundation, we go on to consider clinically relevant procedures for assessing depression and planning treatment. Next we will focus on the clinical application of CBT, describing some defining characteristics of CBT and then highlighting specific intervention strategies. In the final section, we will address the increasingly salient issue of patient selection. Working from the observation that depressed individuals do not uniformly benefit from short-term CBT, we present guidelines for identifying those most likely to experience a favorable therapeutic outcome.

COGNITIVE-BEHAVIORAL
FORMULATIONS OF UNIPOLAR DEPRESSION

Clinical researchers generally concur that unipolar depression is most accurately viewed as a multifactorial phenomenon, involving a complex and dynamic interaction of social, biological, and psychological (e.g., cognitive, behavioral, affective, motivational, personality) variables. Though acknowledging this complexity, cognitive-behavioral models of depression tend to emphasize the role of dysfunctional thinking patterns in the development and maintenance of the depressive syndrome. Most typically, these models posit some form of vicious cycle of cognition, affect, and behavior resulting in what has been termed the *downward spiral* of depression. To illustrate, having the thought "I am a hopeless loser" in response to some unfavorable life event could generate feelings of dysphoria or apathy. In turn, these emotions could stimulate withdrawal or efforts to avoid situations involving risk taking and challenge. Ultimately, such behavior could reinforce the plausibility of the original self-disparaging belief.

Cognitively oriented psychopathologists have identified a number of levels at which dysfunctional thinking may occur in depression (Hollon & Kriss, 1984; Segal, 1988; Segal & Swallow, 1994). At the most manifest, symptomatic level are automatic thoughts. These are thoughts or visual images that occur in a seemingly involuntary fashion as part of an individual's ongoing stream of consciousness. In depression, the content of these automatic thoughts is predominantly negative. More specifically, Beck (1967) has noted a negative "triad" of depressive cognition involving highly critical and disparaging thoughts about the self (e.g., "I am a loser"), a negative view of the world (e.g., "People will hurt me if I give them the chance"), and a pessimistic outlook on the future (e.g., "Things will never get better"). Despite the fact that these automatic thoughts typically reflect a negatively distorted construction of reality, they nevertheless tend to hold an almost unquestioned plausibility for depressed individuals. Consequently negative automatic thoughts are hypothesized to play an important proximal role in the development and maintenance of emotional distress.

In turn, the content of negative automatic thoughts is hypothesized to reflect the outworking of dysfunction occurring at the level of information processing. In Beck's (1967) model of depression, for example, special emphasis is given to the systematic errors in logic and reasoning that purportedly culminate in negative automatic thoughts. Examples of such errors include overgeneralization (e.g., "I failed this exam; therefore I will fail all my exams; therefore I am a failure"); dichotomous, or black-and-white thinking (e.g., "If I get above 80% on this exam I am a success, otherwise I am a failure"); and arbitrary inference (e.g., "He did not smile at me; therefore he dislikes me"). Other models have highlighted the role of maladaptive attributional processes (e.g., Alloy, Abramson, Metalsky, & Hartlage, 1988), self-regulatory mechanisms (e.g., Pyszczynski & Greenberg, 1987), and social comparison processes (e.g., Swallow & Kuiper, 1988) in moderating depressive phenomenology.

Depressive thinking processes, in turn, are thought to reflect the operation of enduring structural components of the information-processing system. Self-structures (or "schemata") have received particular emphasis in this regard. Self-schemata are clusters of experientially derived self-referent information, organized around general themes, that guide the processing of incoming data and facilitate the retrieval of schema-congruent information. Schematic information is stored in long-term memory in the form of general propositions, beliefs, assumptions, and judgments, including rules for self-evaluation. Individuals can possess a number of different self-schemata, most of which remain latent until activated by thematically related events. According to cognitive-behavioral accounts, depression is associated with the activation of self-schemata organized around predominantly negative themes. These negative self-schemata may comprise constellations of unfavorable propositions about the self (e.g., "I have always failed"), unflattering self-appraisals (e.g., "I am inferior"), and rigid, absolutistic rules for self-evaluation (e.g., "If I fail partly, then I am a complete failure").

The ultimate goal of cognitive-behavioral therapy is to effect change at the structural level of cognition. This goal reflects the theoretical assumption that structural change will precipitate concomitant change in dysfunctional information processing and negative automatic thoughts. Importantly, CBT itself generally proceeds in a "top-down" fashion. As such, early phases of CBT typically are devoted to identifying, monitoring, and modifying negative automatic thoughts. Subsequent treatment efforts may focus on identifying and modifying dysfunctional information processing. Later stages of therapy often entail work targeting underlying negative self-schemata.

ASSESSMENT OF UNIPOLAR
DEPRESSION IN CBT

Before we turn to a consideration of specific intervention procedures, it may be helpful to review cognitive-behavioral approaches to clinical assessment. In CBT, as in other treatment modalities, assessment plays an important role in case formulation, as well as in the selection and implementation of specific treatment strategies. Within the cognitive-behavioral framework, clinically useful assessments should provide measures of relevant cognitive constructs (e.g., automatic thoughts, logical distortions, self-schemata), as well as indices of characteristic behavioral responses. In addition, general measures of mood, particularly those tapping depressive severity, represent an integral component of responsible assessment. Here we highlight representative methods for evaluating each of these dimensions of the clinical picture.

General Measures of Depressive Symptomatology

Although not uniquely associated with cognitive-behavioral formulation and treatment, general measures of depression play an important role in CBT.

Specifically, they provide a baseline index of depressive severity against which to monitor subsequent therapeutic progress. Furthermore, general depression measures can be used to identify and to flag important clinical issues (e.g., suicidality) that otherwise may go unprobed or unreported. This is particularly useful when these measures are employed on a regular session-by-session basis.

The Beck Depression Inventory (BDI; Beck, Ward, Mendelson, Mock, & Erbaugh, 1961) is probably the best known and most widely used general measure of depressive functioning. Its 21 items, each rated for intensity on a scale from 0 to 3, reflect attitudes and symptoms frequently displayed by depressed patients (e.g., low mood, pessimism, sense of failure, suicidal wishes, irritability, social withdrawal, loss of appetite, loss of libido). BDI scores falling between 10 and 18 are thought to reflect mild to moderate levels of depression; scores of 19 to 29 suggest moderate to severe distress; and scores of 30 or above probably indicate severe levels of depression (Beck & Beamesderfer, 1974). It is important to note, however, that the BDI was designed to be a measure of the severity of depressed mood. As such, it is most appropriately employed with individuals already diagnosed with depression. Because BDI scores can be inflated for reasons other than clinical depression (e.g., bereavement, chronic low self-esteem), its use as a diagnostic tool is typically unwarranted (Williams, 1992). The BDI's popularity owes much, no doubt, to its ease of administration and scoring, as well as to its solid psychometric properties (for a review see Beck, Steer, & Garbin, 1988).

The Hamilton Rating Scale for Depression (HRSD; Hamilton, 1967) is another useful measure of depressive severity, tapping the affective, cognitive, behavioral, and vegetative components of depression. Unlike the BDI, however, the HRSD is an observer-rated scale. Its 17 items are scored by one or two trained observers on the basis of what they know about the patient's mental state, supplemented by a clinical interview. Each item is a symptom (e.g., guilt, insomnia, gastrointestinal distress), rated in most cases on a scale from 0 (*absent*) to 4 (*severe*). Ratings are totaled for a maximum score of 50. Overall, HRSD scores of 14 or above are considered clinically significant (Knesevich, Biggs, Clayton, & Ziegler, 1977). Although more time-consuming to administer than the BDI (and therefore less useful for session-by-session tracking), the HRSD has the advantage of providing an index of depression that is potentially less vulnerable to self-presentational biases. Furthermore, like the BDI, the HRSD's psychometric properties are sound (Rehm, 1981).

Behavioral Assessment of Depression

In CBT, the primary goal in conducting behavioral assessments is to assist therapists as well as patients in building a working formulation by identifying the behavioral patterns that may be contributing to the maintenance of the depressive episode. In turn, these data may be used to inform plans for intervention.

One approach to gathering behavioral information involves asking patients to keep daily records of their activities. These records may include information about patients' feelings as well as their behavior in a variety of everyday situations. More specifically, they can provide valuable insights into the spontaneous coping strategies that patients employ and their characteristic response styles. Furthermore, in cases where presenting complaints focus on particular behavioral excesses or deficits, daily records provide a means of tracking these targets and monitoring progress.

Behavioral interviews represent another source of information about patients' characteristic behavior patterns. Although lacking the immediacy of information obtained via daily diaries, interviews have the advantage of flexibility and scope. For instance, behavioral interviews need not be limited to information provided by the patient, but may incorporate the observations of family members or friends. In addition, behavioral interviews may be used to conduct functional analyses of problematic behavioral patterns—for example, by probing the antecedents or consequences of target difficulties. Further, behavioral skills (e.g., assertiveness, self-reinforcement) may be assessed on the basis of both in-session and out-of-session evidence. Williams (1992) has provided a useful and comprehensive protocol for general behavioral assessment interviews that interested readers may wish to consult.

Finally, behavioral information may be culled from self-report inventories focusing specifically on patients' perceptions of their own patterns of behavior in various circumstances. One such measure, the Pleasant Events Schedule (PES; MacPhillamy & Lewinsohn, 1971), is a scale that provides an index of the frequency with which patients engage in 320 activities commonly considered enjoyable and the emotional impact of doing so. As such, the PES is thought to provide an index of the amount of positive reinforcement to which patients are exposed. The Coping Strategies Scale (Beckham & Adams, 1984) is another example. This scale presents patients with 139 different strategies for coping with depression, stress, and illness. Patients state whether they engaged in each of these behaviors over the preceding 2 weeks and whether they felt better, worse, or the same after doing so. For interested readers, Hammen and Krantz (1985) have provided a thoughtful review of several other behavioral self-report measures for depression.

Measures of Depressive Cognition

Given CBT's emphasis on identifying and modifying dysfunctional patterns of thought, it stands to reason that the measurement of cognition should represent a central feature of cognitive-behavioral assessment of depression. At the same time, researchers and clinicians have wrestled with the conceptual and methodological difficulties inherent in attempts to measure cognitive variables in a valid, clinically meaningful fashion. Nevertheless, progress has been made. Earlier, we distinguished among three types of cognitive variables: automatic thoughts, thinking processes, and cognitive structures. Elsewhere (Segal & Swallow, 1994), we have reviewed representative strategies for assessing cognition at each of these three levels. Here we provide a brief synopsis of this work.

Strategies for assessing automatic thoughts typically fall into one of two categories: self-report questionnaires and "on-line" procedures. The Automatic Thoughts Questionnaire (ATQ; Hollon & Kendall, 1980) is one prominent self-report measure. The ATQ taps the frequency with which 30 depression-related thoughts (e.g., "I don't think I can go on," "No one understands me") have "popped" into the patient's head during the past week. Other self-report questionnaires tap specific thematic components of depressive automatic thinking (e.g., the Hopelessness Scale [Beck, Weissman, Lester, & Trexler, 1974]; the Beck Self-Concept Test [Beck, Steer, Epstein, & Brown, 1990]). Alternatively, automatic thinking can be assessed using less structured on-line strategies. The Daily Record of Dysfunctional Thoughts (Beck, Rush, Shaw, & Emery, 1979), on which patients record their automatic thoughts in situations that precipitate unpleasant emotions, is one such instrument. Other popular on-line strategies include the think-aloud procedure (Genest & Turk, 1981), thought listing (Cacioppo & Petty, 1981), and random thought sampling (Hurlburt, 1979).

Several measures have been developed to assess dysfunctional cognitive processes in depression. The Cognitive Bias Questionnaire (CBQ; Hammen & Krantz, 1976) is one example. The CBQ requires subjects to project themselves into six problematic situations and, for each, to select one of four possible response alternatives most closely resembling their own response.

The response alternatives are designed to reflect both distorted (e.g., over-generalized, personalized) and nondistorted thinking. As such, the CBQ provides an index of the frequency with which depressed individuals may engage in distorted thinking. As another example, the Cognitive Response Test (CRT; Watkins & Rush, 1983) is a more open-ended measure of dys-functional depressive thinking. Here subjects are asked to respond to incom-plete sentences (e.g., "When I consider being married, my first thought is . . .") with the first thought that comes to mind. Responses are categorized (e.g., irrational view of self, irrational view of other) on the basis of stand-ardized scoring criteria to yield several indices of irrational depressive thinking.

Assessing the structural components of depressive cognition poses one of the more difficult challenges for cognitively oriented researchers. Currently, the dominant approach involves tapping the core assumptions, beliefs, and rules governing self-evaluation that, in theory, constitute an element of schematic self-representation. The Dysfunctional Attitude Scale (DAS; Weissman & Beck, 1978) is used frequently for this purpose. The DAS is a 40-item inventory that provides an index of the extent to which individuals endorse depressogenic beliefs and attitudes. Most typically, these attitudes reflect concerns about social approval (e.g., "My value depends on what others think of me") and perfectionistic standards of performance ("If I fail partly, it is as bad as being a complete failure"). Difficulties with the use of a self-report measure to assess theoretically latent constructs have dampened enthusiasm for the DAS as a measure of depressive vulnerability. However, these difficulties have stimulated researchers to begin employing paradigms borrowed from cognitive psychology to assess the schema construct in depression (see Segal, 1988, for a detailed discussion of this work). The routine clinical application of these procedures represents an exciting pros-pect that must at present await theoretical and methodological refinement.

GENERAL FEATURES OF CBT

Having briefly reviewed representative assessment strategies, we now turn to a more detailed consideration of cognitive-behavioral treatment of depression. In this section, we consider some general characteristics of CBT. This is followed by a discussion of behavioral and cognitive intervention strategies.

Collaborative Empiricism

CBT distinguishes itself from many other psychotherapeutic approaches in its insistence upon *collaborative empiricism* as the modus operandi. This term highlights two important features of CBT. First, cognitive-behavioral therapists seek to establish collaborative working alliances with their patients. Therapists and patients work together to identify and track target problems, to generate strategies for change, and to execute and evaluate these strategies. Second, therapists encourage patients to view their thoughts as scientific hypotheses that can be tested empirically. As such, cognitive change is presumed to take place, at least in part, as patients, in collaboration with their therapists, repeatedly generate opportunities to compare and contrast their thoughts (expectations, assumptions, beliefs, etc.) with actual outcomes. This "evidence-gathering" approach contrasts with other cognitively oriented therapies, notably rational emotive therapy (RET; Ellis & Dryden, 1987), which emphasizes the role of logical disputation and persuasion in promoting cognitive change.

Use of Questions

A foundational therapeutic skill in CBT relates to use of questioning. Beck et al. (1979) have enumerated a number of important therapeutic functions served by a question-asking orientation. In summary, framing verbalizations in the form of questions may facilitate the process of translating patients' personal axioms into tentative hypotheses, thereby setting the stage for a consideration of self-generated alternatives and subsequent experimentation. In addition, the use of questioning (rather than indoctrination or overly aggressive disputation) can serve to promote a collaborative, respectful therapeutic alliance in which therapists may help patients to focus their concerns, explore the evidence for their beliefs, identify the criteria for their evaluations, and examine the consequences of their actions.

Here-and-Now Focus

CBT has, as one goal, the interruption of the vicious cycle of cognition, mood, and behavior thought to maintain the depressive syndrome. As such, CBT maintains a predominantly here-and-now focus. This stance does not imply a view of historical material as irrelevant or unimportant. Indeed, there is convergent evidence that dysfunctional attitudes and beliefs may arise from negative early experience (Kovacs & Beck, 1978; for a recent review, see Brewin, Andrews, & Gotlib, 1993). Furthermore, and as we will elaborate later, exploring the developmental antecedents of dysfunctional thinking represents one approach to promoting schematic change. In CBT, however, emphasis is placed on identifying and addressing the cognitive components that play a role in maintaining depressive functioning. Consequently patients' current concerns generally constitute the "raw material" for therapeutic attention. In this regard, it should be noted that events transpiring within the therapy session itself (e.g., the patient's thoughts or feelings about the therapist, occurring quite literally in the here and now) may constitute a highly relevant clinical focus (see Safran & Segal, 1990, for a detailed discussion of interpersonal process in CBT).

Use of Homework

In CBT, therapists and patients typically work together to generate assignments that patients can carry out between sessions. In early sessions, homework may involve the maintenance of daily records of mood, behavior, and/or dysfunctional thoughts. Alternatively, and in keeping with CBT's emphasis on empiricism, homework assignments may take the form of behavioral experiments designed to test the validity of patients' thoughts, beliefs, or assumptions. Under circumstances in which a new behavioral skill is being developed (e.g., assertiveness), homework may involve the strategic real-life application of these skills. Whatever their form, homework assignments constitute an integral component of CBT. Indeed, the tendency to complete homework assignments has been linked to superior therapeutic response (Neimeyer & Feixas, 1990). Furthermore, there is also evidence to suggest that those therapists who regularly take up and review homework assignments obtain better clinical outcomes than those who fail to do so (Burns & Nolen-Hoeksema, 1991; Williams, 1992).

Short-Term Orientation

Finally, CBT is generally conducted on a short-term basis. Standard treatment protocols (e.g., Beck et al., 1979) recommend up to 20 sessions for treating individuals with major unipolar depression. The short-term focus establishes clear temporal parameters for therapy that can facilitate the motivation of both patient and therapist to maintain a problem-centered orientation. In addition, it increases the importance of a clear formulation on the part of the therapist and requires a higher degree of patient suitability than longer-term approaches (Safran, Segal, Shaw, & Vallis, 1990). This suitability issue will be addressed in greater detail in a later section of the chapter.

BEHAVIORAL INTERVENTION STRATEGIES

As a rule, CBT focuses on cognitive variables as targets of therapeutic change. Cognitive change, however, can be mediated by interventions targeting the behavioral components of depressive functioning. These behavioral interventions may serve the larger goal of cognitive change in several ways. As one example, behavioral change, in and of itself, may interrupt the vicious cognition-affect-behavior cycle described earlier, thereby effecting synchronous change at the affective and cognitive levels. Further, behavioral interventions may address the immobilization typical of severely depressed patients, particularly in early phases of treatment. Increasing levels of activity, in turn, may stimulate the "flow" of automatic thoughts, which can then be addressed via cognitive strategies. In addition, behavioral activation may provide evidence that can be marshalled against self-defeating thoughts such as "I can't do anything." Similarly, in cases in which depression is maintained by avoidant patterns (e.g., social withdrawal), behavioral interventions (e.g., exposure tasks) may serve to desensitize as well as provide evidence against catastrophic expectations (e.g., "Other people will laugh at me").

Thus, unlike strictly behavioral approaches to the treatment of depression, CBT employs behavioral strategies with the ultimate goal of addressing depression-related cognitions. In the following sections, we highlight representative behavioral strategies. It should be emphasized that the selection of particular interventions in CBT should be guided by the therapist's conceptual formulation of the case. The willy-nilly application of "techniques" is a caricature of CBT and reflects a misunderstanding of its conceptual foundations.

Representative Strategies

Activity Scheduling. As noted above, behavioral activation can represent an important therapeutic goal, particularly in early phases of treatment.

Clinicians can improve the likelihood of effective behavioral activation by working with patients to establish an activity schedule (see Lewinsohn & Graf, 1973). The first step in this process usually involves obtaining a baseline measure of patients' activities and corresponding moods. In the next phase, patients enumerate the tasks, the responsibilities, and especially the pleasant activities that they want to integrate into their schedules. Following this, a daily schedule can be worked out in which patients designate specific time slots for engaging in selected activities. These activities should include both pleasure- and mastery-related events. At this point, it can be helpful to have patients predict the amount of pleasure and/or mastery they expect to derive from each of the scheduled activities. In addition, obstacles to the successful completion of these activities should be anticipated and addressed, with contingency plans being made where possible. Finally, patients should be instructed to monitor their behavior, noting the actual degree of pleasure and/or mastery they derived from the scheduled activities. These actual pleasure and mastery ratings can be compared to patients' earlier ratings in order to obtain an index of the accuracy of their predictions.

Graded Task Assignments. In selecting and scheduling pleasant events and mastery tasks, it is important for therapists to attempt to maximize the likelihood of successful completion. As noted above, anticipating and dealing proactively with potential obstacles is one means of doing so. Another approach involves grading tasks such that patients start with the easiest and then move on to greater challenges. Tasks may be simplified by being broken down into smaller units. For example, whereas cleaning the house may represent an overwhelming prospect for a seriously depressed patient, smaller components of the task, like making the bed, may be more manageable. After the patient has made the bed successfully, other components of the larger task may be undertaken.

Self-Reinforcement. Rewarding oneself for successfully accomplishing certain goals can represent an effective means of increasing levels of behavioral activation and of maintaining these gains. In addition, for depressed individuals who view themselves as unworthy, self-reinforcement may represent counterattitudinal behavior and, as such, promote change at the cognitive level. Therapists can encourage self-reinforcement by (a) providing a compelling rationale; (b) encouraging patients to establish specific, attainable goals with clearly defined performance criteria; (c) identifying activities that patients construe as reinforcing; (d) instructing patients to engage in reinforcing activities immediately after meeting their goals; and (e) monitoring patients' progress.

COGNITIVE INTERVENTION STRATEGIES

Once patients are mobilized appropriately, therapeutic efforts can begin to focus more specifically on cognitive targets. In this section, we describe some representative strategies for addressing depression-related thinking patterns. First, we focus on techniques for addressing negative automatic thoughts and their corresponding cognitive distortions. Next, we consider strategies for dealing with the core beliefs, attitudes, and assumptions hypothesized to play a foundational role in the onset and maintenance of depressive episodes.

Strategies Targeting Automatic
Thoughts and Cognitive Distortions

Designing Experiments. As noted earlier, one of CBT's distinguishing characteristics is its emphasis on empiricism as a modus operandi. In line with this approach, therapists typically encourage patients to regard their automatic thoughts as scientific hypotheses that then can be subjected to empirical (rather than strictly logical) examination. Automatic thoughts reported in the form of propositions (e.g., "Everyone I know dislikes me") can usually be tested quite readily and, as such, make ideal hypotheses. However, automatic thoughts frequently are expressed in the form of questions (e.g., "What do people think of me?"). In most cases, such queries can be translated into propositions via appropriate probes (e.g., "Do you have any thoughts about what the people you know think of you?" "What runs through your mind as you consider that question?").

Designing effective experiments can require a good deal of creativity and ingenuity on the part of both therapist and patient. One means of generating ideas for experiments involves considering, a priori, the type of evidence that could either support or disconfirm the hypothesis in question. To test the thought "Everyone I know dislikes me," for example, therapists and patients might first consider how people generally signal their dislike for another person (e.g., they might fail to return a greeting). Next, an experiment could be designed in which, say, patients would greet a random sample of acquaintances and take note of whether the greetings were reciprocated. A series of such experiments could help weaken the subjective plausibility of patients' negative automatic thoughts and provide evidence for more reasonable alternatives (e.g., "Many if not most of the people I know seem to respond to me in a favorable manner").

Operationalizing Negative Constructs. Automatic thoughts in depression often have an absolute, black-and-white quality. Examples of such thoughts are "I am a failure," "I am a bad parent," and "I am a stupid person." The constructs (e.g., failure, bad parent, stupid person) that feature so prominently in these negative automatic thoughts allow little sense of gradation and, as such, can generate intensely negative affect. One means of introducing some sense of gradation involves working with patients to operationalize these negative constructs. As a first step, patients are asked to provide specific definitional criteria for the construct in question (e.g., "A failure is someone who completely fails on everything he or she does"). Next, therapists can work with patients to construct a Likert-type scale (e.g., a "failure" scale) that patients can use to rate the extent to which they, and other people they know, meet the definitional criteria identified earlier. Most typically, these ratings will fall into the intermediate range (i.e., denoting that the patient has done poorly on some things but not on everything). As a result, patients will find that they do not meet their own criteria for the negative label. More reasonable self-referent thoughts can then be considered (e.g., "I have done well on some things and done poorly on other things"; "I am not a failure but a human being who, like everyone else, has strengths as well as weaknesses"). Patients can be trained to practice this approach whenever they notice themselves thinking in terms of these absolute negative constructs.

Consequential Analysis. Depressed patients often exhibit dramatic downward mood shifts in response to what appear to be relatively benign automatic thoughts. Consequential analysis (also known as the inverted arrow technique) can be a useful means of eliciting the underlying fears, thoughts, or assumptions that may be generating the disproportionate affective response. When employing this technique, therapists guide patients through a series of "What if?" questions. To illustrate, a depressed patient might report the automatic thought "I feel anxious." When asked about the potential consequences of feeling anxious ("So what if you are anxious?"), the patient might respond, "It means something's wrong with me." The consequences of this, in turn, might be "I'm inferior," "No one will want to be with me," "I'll be rejected," or ultimately, "I will always be alone." Working with patients to make these links explicit can help them get a better understanding of their affective discomfort and reinforce the relationship between thoughts and feelings. Furthermore, the underlying assumptions (e.g., "When people feel anxious it means there is something wrong with them") can themselves be translated into hypotheses that may then be subjected to empirical testing.

Reattribution. As noted earlier, automatic thinking in depression is often associated with maladaptive patterns of attribution. In particular, depressed patients tend to account for negative events in terms of internal, stable, and global factors (Alloy et al., 1988). As such, they typically need to be led to consider a wider range of attributional possibilities. Williams (1992) has described a procedure in which patients imagine a hypothetical negative event (e.g., a friend passes by on the street and ignores them) and describe their naturally occurring attributions (e.g., "I've offended her," "I'm a boring, insignificant person"). Reasonable alternative explanations can then be generated and evaluated with respect to plausibility (e.g., she was in a hurry, she was daydreaming). This technique can be rehearsed using actual events with an ultimate goal of enabling patients to (a) identify and monitor their dysfunctional attributional patterns, and (b) develop proficiency in generating reasonable alternative accounts of troubling events.

Strategies Targeting Dysfunctional Core Beliefs

Changes at the level of automatic thoughts and cognitive distortions can effect rapid and marked symptomatic improvement. However, remission is likely to be short-lived when therapy has failed to address the enduring beliefs, rules, and attitudes that underlie depressive phenomenology. Thus, whereas early stages of CBT focus primarily on behavioral activation and change at the level of automatic thoughts, later sessions typically are devoted to addressing these more enduring cognitive elements.

Historical Exploration. Despite its predominantly here-and-now orientation, cognitive-behavioral theorists generally concur that dysfunctional
core beliefs or rules have their origins in early experience. Examining the
developmental roots of these beliefs can serve to weaken their hold in
several ways. Most importantly, historical explorations can promote decentering—a process through which individuals, as it were, step outside
of their immediate experience to view themselves constructing reality.
Decentering "fosters a recognition that the reality of the moment is not
absolute, immutable, or unalterable, but rather something that is being
constructed" (Safran & Segal, 1990, p. 117). By examining how they have
come to believe what they do, patients may come to regard their beliefs in
a more tentative, less axiomatic fashion.

Furthermore, dysfunctional beliefs often derive from distorted interpretations of painful early experiences. In reviewing those circumstances, patients
may recognize these errors or distortions and work to revise them. To
illustrate, an individual with the core belief "If someone criticizes me then
it means that I am a bad person" reported memories of being harshly
criticized and punished by her father. In exploring these circumstances, the
patient recalled attributing the father's attacks to her own badness because,
as a child, she could conceive of no other explanations for his hostile
behavior. Her core belief was weakened when, as an adult, she was able to
make alternative attributions for her father's behavior (e.g., he was under
financial and personal pressure, had difficulty showing affection, was an
ineffective father).

Cost-Benefit Analysis. As core dysfunctional beliefs are identified and
challenged, therapists may be surprised to discover that patients can be
reluctant to give them up. Often this is due to the fact that the beliefs or
rules have served a self-protective function or provided patients with some
important benefits. To illustrate, perfectionistic core beliefs (e.g., "If you
can't do something perfectly, then don't bother doing it at all") can
motivate impressive achievements. Patients are often loath to tamper with
such beliefs, fearing that doing so may result in mediocrity or failure. In
such cases, the costs and the benefits of maintaining such a belief system
can be enumerated and compared. Similar cost-benefit analyses should be
conducted on alternative but more reasonable beliefs (e.g., "It's good to
do as well as possible, but I can still enjoy something even if it's not
perfect").

Rule-Breaking Experiments. Dysfunctional core beliefs are commonly articulated in the form of general rules (e.g., "To be average is to be a contemptible nobody," "People will reject you if you make a mistake"). Unfortunately, depressed individuals rarely, if ever, expose themselves to the possibility of disconfirming evidence. Another approach to addressing these beliefs, therefore, is to design experiments in which patients deliberately seek out opportunities to break these fundamental rules, and note the outcomes. Burns (1981) has provided a good example of an experiment designed to test the perfectionistic notion that being average leads to mediocrity and rejection. Here, patients are asked to make an effort to be as average as possible for a given period of time (e.g., 1 week). Patients typically discover, contrary to expectation, that this experience has no untoward effects; many even find it enjoyable. The ultimate goal, of course, is to weaken core beliefs by providing disconfirming evidence.

STRATEGIES FOR PATIENT SELECTION

Not all depressed patients benefit uniformly from a short-term course of CBT. Thus it is important—from both a therapeutic and a resource management perspective—to evaluate whether a particular patient is suitable for this approach. One method of patient selection, outlined by Safran et al. (1990), involves evaluating prospective patients on 10 specific suitability criteria derived from previous work on patient selection and from a consideration of the important tasks and goals in short-term CBT. These criteria include (a) patients' ability to access and report their automatic thoughts; (b) patients' awareness of their emotions, and their ability to differentiate among their emotional experiences; (c) patients' acceptance of personal responsibility for therapeutic change; (d) patients' compatibility with the rationale for CBT; (e) patients' potential for establishing a good therapeutic alliance with the therapist on the basis of in-session evidence and out-of-session evidence, including previous therapy; (f) the chronicity of the patients' presenting problems; (g) the extent to which patients mobilize security operations that would threaten to block self-exploration; (h) patients' ability to maintain a problem-focused orientation; and (i) patients' general sense of optimism regarding therapy.

Safran, Segal, Vallis, Shaw, and Samstag (1993) recently have described a semistructured suitability interview procedure, called the Suitability for

Short-Term Cognitive Therapy (SSCT) interview. The SSCT procedure typically involves a 1-hour interview in which patients are appropriately probed and rated on each of the 10 criteria listed above. In support of the validity of this procedure, Safran et al. (1993) have found that scores on the SSCT reliably predict outcome of short-term CBT on a variety of measures, including both patient and therapist reports. These data suggest that the SSCT interview procedure represents a promising and timely response to the difficult but increasingly critical issue of patient selection.

CONCLUDING COMMENTS

Our aim in this chapter is to provide readers with a state-of-the-art overview of CBT. We have reviewed the theoretical underpinnings of CBT, described relevant assessment procedures, highlighted some of the distinctive features of CBT, and detailed representative strategies for intervention and patient selection. Having done so, we must point out that CBT is a continually evolving modality of treatment. Advances at the theoretical level continue to generate innovations in both how we assess and how we treat unipolar depression. In addition, recent years have witnessed steadily growing interest in integrating the constructs and procedures of CBT with those of other theoretical orientations (Hammen, 1992; Segal & Blatt, 1993). Although these trends are to be encouraged, it is also important that CBT retain its emphasis on empiricism, both as a modus operandi and as the ultimate standard for evaluating the soundness of its theoretical constructs and the efficacy of its interventions.

REFERENCES

Alloy, L. B., Abramson, L. Y., Metalsky, G. I., & Hartlage, S. (1988). The hopelessness theory of depression: Attributional aspects. *British Journal of Clinical Psychology, 27,* 5-21.

Beck, A. T. (1967). *Depression: Clinical experimental and theoretical aspects.* New York: Harper & Row.

Beck, A. T., & Beamesderfer, A. (1974). Assessment of depression: The depression inventory. In P. Pichot (Ed.), *Modern problems in pharmacopsychiatry* (pp. 151-169). Basel, Switzerland: Karger.

Beck, A. T., Rush, P. J., Shaw, B. F., & Emery, G. (1979). *Cognitive therapy of depression.* New York: Guilford.

Beck, A. T., Steer, R. A., Epstein, N., & Brown, G. (1990). Beck Self-Concept Test. *Psychological Assessment, 2,* 191-197.

Beck, A. T., Steer, R. A., & Garbin, M. G. (1988). Psychometric properties of the Beck Depression Inventory: Twenty-five years of evaluation. *Clinical Psychology Review, 8,* 77-100.

Beck, A. T., Ward, C. H., Mendelson, M., Mock, J., & Erbaugh, J. (1961). An inventory for measuring depression. *Archives of General Psychiatry, 4,* 561-571.

Beck, A. T., Weissman, A., Lester, D., & Trexler, L. (1974). The measurement of pessimism: The Hopelessness Scale. *Journal of Consulting and Clinical Psychology, 42,* 861-865.

Beckham, E. E., & Adams, R. L. (1984). Coping behavior in depression: Report on a new scale. *Behavior Research and Therapy, 22,* 71-75.

Blackburn, I. M., Eunson, K. M., & Bishop, S. (1986). A two year naturalistic follow-up of depressed patients treated with cognitive therapy, pharmacotherapy and a combination of both. *Journal of Affective Disorders, 10,* 67-75.

Brewin, C. R., Andrews, B., & Gotlib, I. H. (1993). Psychopathology and early experience: A reappraisal of retrospective reports. *Psychological Bulletin, 113,* 82-98.

Burns, D. D. (1981). *Feeling good: The new mood therapy.* New York: Signet.

Burns, D. D., & Nolen-Hoeksema, S. (1991). Coping styles, homework assignments and the effectiveness of cognitive behavioral therapy. *Journal of Consulting and Clinical Psychology, 59,* 564-578.

Cacioppo, J. T., & Petty, R. E. (1981). Social psychological procedures for cognitive response assessment: The thought-listing technique. In T. V. Merluzzi, C. R. Glass, & M. Genest (Eds.), *Cognitive assessment* (pp. 309-342). New York: Guilford.

de Jong, R., & Verhage, J. (1985). Quality of life and depression: Research for O.D. practice. *Organization Development Journal, 3,* 27-29.

Elkin, I., Shea, M. T., Watkins, J. T., Imber, S. D., Sotsky, S. M., Collins, J. F., Glass, D. R., Pilkonis, P. A., Leber, W. R., Docherty, J. P., Fiester, S. J., & Parloff, M. B. (1989). NIMH treatment of depression collaborative research program: General effectiveness of treatments. *Archives of General Psychiatry, 46,* 971-983.

Ellis, A., & Dryden, W. (1987). *The practice of rational-emotive therapy.* New York: Springer.

Evans, M. D., Hollon, S. D., DeRubeis, R. J., Piasecki, J., Grove, W. M., Garvey, M. J., & Tuason, V. B. (1992). Differential relapse following cognitive therapy and pharmacotherapy for depression. *Archives of General Psychiatry, 49,* 802-808.

Genest, M., & Turk, D. C. (1981). Think-aloud approaches to cognitive assessment. In T. V. Merluzzi, C. R. Glass, & M. Genest (Eds.), *Cognitive assessment* (pp. 233-269). New York: Guilford.

Gilbert, P. (1991). *Depression: The evolution of powerlessness.* New York: Guilford.

Hamilton, M. (1967). Development of a rating scale for primary depressive illness. *British Journal of Social and Clinical Psychology, 6,* 278-296.

Hammen, C. L. (1992, June). *Cognition and psychodynamics: A modest proposal.* Paper presented at the World Congress of Cognitive Therapy, Toronto.

Hammen, C. L., & Krantz, S. E. (1976). Effects of success and failure on depressive cognitions. *Journal of Abnormal Psychology, 85,* 577-586.

Hammen, C. L., & Krantz, S. E. (1985). Measures of psychological processes in depression. In E. E. Beckham & W. R. Leber (Eds.), *Handbook of depression: Treatment, assessment, and research* (pp. 408-444). Homewood, IL: Dorsey.

Hollon, S. D., & Kendall, P. C. (1980). Cognitive self-statements in depression: Development of an automatic thoughts questionnaire. *Cognitive Therapy and Research, 4,* 383-396.

Hollon, S. D., & Kriss, M. R. (1984). Cognitive factors in clinical research and practice. *Clinical Psychology Review, 4,* 35-76.

Hurlburt, R. T. (1979). Random sampling of cognitions and behavior. *Journal of Research in Personality, 13,* 103-111.

Keller, M. B., Lavori, P. W., Klerman, G. L., Rice, J., Coryell, W., & Hirschfield, R. M. A. (1986). The persistent risk of chronicity in recurrent episodes of non-bipolar major depressive disorder: A prospective follow-up. *American Journal of Psychiatry, 143,* 24-28.

Knesevich, J. W., Biggs, J. T., Clayton, P. J., & Ziegler, V. E. (1977). Validity of the Hamilton Rating Scale for Depression. *British Journal of Psychiatry, 131,* 49-52.

Kovacs, M., & Beck, A. T. (1978). Maladaptive cognitive structures in depression. *American Journal of Psychiatry, 135,* 525-533.

Lewinsohn, P. M., & Graf, M. (1973). Pleasant activities and depression. *Journal of Consulting and Clinical Psychology, 41,* 261-268.

MacPhillamy, D. J., & Lewinsohn, P. M. (1971). *Pleasant events schedule.* Unpublished manuscript, University of Oregon.

Minkoff, K., Bergman, E., Beck, A. T., & Beck, R. (1973). Hopelessness, depression, and attempted suicide. *American Journal of Psychiatry, 130,* 455-459.

Murphy, G. E., Simons, A. D., Wetzel, R. D., & Lustman, P. J. (1984). Cognitive therapy and pharmacotherapy: Singly and together in the treatment of depression. *Archives of General Psychiatry, 41,* 33-41.

Neimeyer, R., & Feixas, G. (1990). The role of homework and skill acquisition in the outcome of group cognitive therapy for depression. *Behavior Therapy, 21,* 281-292.

Paykel, E. S. (1989). The background: Extent and nature of the disorder. In K. Herbst & E. S. Paykel (Eds.), *Depression: An integrative approach.* London: Heinemann Medical Press.

Pyszczynski, T., & Greenberg, J. (1987). Self-regulatory perseveration and the depressive self-focusing style: A self-awareness theory of the development and maintenance of depression. *Psychological Bulletin, 102,* 122-138.

Rehm, L. P. (1981). *Behavior therapy for depression.* New York: Academic Press.

Safran, J. D., & Segal, Z. V. (1990). *Interpersonal process in cognitive therapy.* New York: Basic Books.

Safran, J. D., Segal, Z. V., Shaw, B. F., & Vallis, T. M. (1990). Patient selection for short-term cognitive therapy. In J. D. Safran & Z. V. Segal (Eds.), *Interpersonal process in cognitive therapy* (pp. 229-237). New York: Basic Books.

Safran, J. D., Segal, Z. V., Vallis, T. M., Shaw, B. F., & Samstag, L. W. (1993). Assessing patient suitability for short-term cognitive therapy with an interpersonal focus. *Cognitive Therapy and Research, 17,* 23-38.

Segal, Z. V. (1988). Appraisal of the self-schema construct in cognitive models of depression. *Psychological Bulletin, 103,* 147-162.

Segal, Z. V., & Blatt, S. J. (1993). *The self in emotional distress: Cognitive and psychodynamic perspectives.* New York: Guilford.

Segal, Z. V., & Swallow, S. R. (1994). Cognitive assessment of unipolar depression: Measuring products, processes and structures. *Behaviour Research and Therapy, 32,* 147-158.

Simons, A. D., Murphy, G. E., Levine, J. E., & Wetzel, R. D. (1986). Cognitive therapy and pharmacotherapy for depression: Sustained improvement over one year. *Archives of General Psychiatry, 43,* 43-49.

Swallow, S. R., & Kuiper, N. A. (1988). Social comparison and negative self-evaluations: An application to depression. *Clinical Psychology Review, 8,* 55-76.

Watkins, J. T., & Rush, A. J. (1983). Cognitive Response Test. *Cognitive Therapy and Research, 7,* 425-436.

Weissman, A. N., & Beck, A. T. (1978). *Development and validation of the Dysfunctional Attitude Scale: A preliminary investigation.* Paper presented at the annual meeting of the American Education Research Association, Toronto.

Williams, J. M. R. (1992). *The psychological treatment of depression.* New York: Routledge.

11

A Course for the Treatment
of Depression Among Adolescents

HYMAN HOPS

PETER M. LEWINSOHN

PREVALENCE OF DEPRESSIVE
DISORDERS AMONG ADOLESCENTS

Over the past decade, following the groundbreaking contributions of Carlson and her colleagues (e.g., Carlson & Strober, 1978), Cytryn and McKnew (1972), Puig-Antich and his associates (e.g., Puig-Antich, Blau, Marx, Greenhill, & Chambers, 1978), Kovacs (e.g., Kovacs & Beck, 1977), Poznanski and Zrull (1970), and Weinberg and colleagues (e.g., Weinberg, Rutman, Sullivan, Penick, & Dietz, 1973), an increasing number of epidemiologic studies have reliably identified depressive disorders among children and adolescents using adult criteria (e.g., Kashani et al., 1987; Lewinsohn, Hops, Roberts, Seeley, & Andrews, 1993; McGee et al., 1990; Velez, Johnson, & Cohen, 1989; Whitaker et al., 1990). A review of these studies (e.g., Gotlib & Hammen,

AUTHORS' NOTE: This research was supported by Grant No. MH41278 from the National Institute of Mental Health. The authors wish to acknowledge the contribution of Pam Clark in the preparation of this manuscript.

1992) indicates that whereas the prevalence of major depressive disorder is less than 2% among children up to age 12, there is a dramatic increase in the rates with the onset of adolescence. This increase in the prevalence coincides with a dramatic shift in the proportion of males and females meeting criteria. Up to age 11, males have slightly higher prevalence rates; after age 12, females decisively outnumber males (2:1). One of the most recent studies, and perhaps the largest study conducted among an adolescent high school population (Lewinsohn et al., 1993), found the point-prevalence rates for unipolar depression to be 2.9%, with females (3.8%) outnumbering males (2.0%) nearly 2 to 1, approximating the rates found in studies of adults (Robins & Regier, 1991). These rates were relatively consistent in a 1-year follow-up. Moreover, reports of lifetime depressive disorder, even among this young age group, were approximately 20%, with females' rate doubling that of males, 27.2% versus 12.9%, respectively. It is also important to note that nearly half of those adolescents experiencing an episode of depression were also experiencing a second disorder (Lewinsohn et al., 1993). The most frequent were anxiety (18%), substance use (14%), and disruptive behavior (8%).

Taken together, these data indicate that clinical depression occurs at rates comparable to those observed with adults (Robins & Regier, 1991) and appears to be perhaps the most significant psychological problem today. Fewer than 30% receive treatment (Keller, Lavori, Beardslee, Wunder, & Ryan, 1991; Rohde, Lewinsohn, & Seeley, 1991).

TREATMENT OF DEPRESSION
AMONG ADOLESCENTS

Unfortunately, the development of empirically validated treatment strategies and controlled treatment outcome studies has not kept pace with the number of epidemiologic studies and studies examining the correlates of depression in this age group (e.g., Hops, Lewinsohn, Andrews, & Roberts, 1990). Initial investigations were primarily of single-subject design (e.g., Frame et al., 1982) and showed that cognitive-behavioral techniques could be adapted for use with this age group. Several experimental control group studies have also been conducted (e.g., Kahn, Kehle, Jenson, & Clark, 1990; Reynolds & Coats, 1986; Stark, Reynolds, & Kaslow, 1987). More recently, comprehensive treatment manuals have been prepared on the basis of theoretical perspectives such as behavioral-cognitive (Stark, 1990) and interpersonal

(Moreau, Mufson, Weissman, & Klerman, 1991). Still, few of these studies have used experimental-control group designs with both self-report questionnaire data and standardized diagnostic interviews as evaluative instruments. Kazdin (1989) has recently suggested that different individuals may be identified by these two assessment methods. To the extent that Kazdin's assertion is validated, the differences may have significant implications for treatment outcome studies.

THE COPING WITH DEPRESSION
COURSE FOR ADOLESCENTS

At the Oregon Research Institute and at the University of Oregon, we have been involved in a long-term longitudinal study assessing the effectiveness of a treatment program that has several unique characteristics.

First, the treatment is based on a comprehensive conceptual model developed by Lewinsohn and his colleagues (Lewinsohn, Hoberman, Teri, & Hautzinger, 1985) that attempts to integrate various theoretical approaches. For example, the model suggests that behavioral, cognitive, social interactional, and other situational variables play an important and interactive role in the development and maintenance of depressive disorders. Within this framework, depression is conceptualized as the end result of environmentally initiated changes in behavior, affect, and cognitions. Situational factors are seen as potential precipitates of the process, and cognitive factors behave as moderators of environmental effects. Consequently an effective treatment should contain components that match the possible range of contributing factors as well as the multiplicity of the cognitive-behavioral problems shown by depressed adolescents.

Second, the program is a downward extension of the adult Coping With Depression (CWD) course developed by Lewinsohn and colleagues (Lewinsohn, Antonuccio, Steinmetz, & Teri, 1984), which has been shown to be effective in alleviating depression in a series of studies with adults (e.g., Hoberman, Lewinsohn, & Tilson, 1988; Steinmetz, Lewinsohn, & Antonuccio, 1983). Thus the program has an empirical base. Given that research has suggested that variables covarying with depression among adults and adolescents are similar (e.g., Hops et al., 1990; Lewinsohn et al., 1994), it seems reasonable to assume that treatment components shown to be effective with adults would, with some modifications, prove to be effective with adolescents as well.

Third, the format of the intervention is designed to be developmentally appropriate for an adolescent population. Classroom-like features and program components such as cartoons and other characteristics that are popular with adolescents are used throughout. Workbooks are provided that include exercises and call for behaviors similar to those characteristic of the school setting, but, hopefully, without some of the pressures usually associated with schools.

Fourth, in concert with its appropriateness for adolescents and in acknowledgment of the social interactional aspects of depressive disorder, parental involvement is included. Providing treatment for specific problems within a social interactional or systems context has characterized much of behavioral family therapy (e.g., Dadds, Schwartz, & Sanders, 1987; Patterson, 1982). The behavioral model assumes that individual difficulties are being maintained by the social environment. Consequently its involvement in the therapeutic process is critical if long-term gains are to be made. Recent efforts at treating depression have also emphasized the social context across theoretical paradigms (e.g., Gotlib & Colby, 1987; Jacobson, Fruzzetti, Dobson, Whisman, & Hops, 1993; Klerman, Weissman, Rounsaville, & Chevron, 1984; Lewinsohn, Clarke, Hops, Andrews, & Williams, 1990). Some of the earliest attempts to involve spouses in the treatment of depressed persons were carried out by Lewinsohn and his colleagues (Lewinsohn & Atwood, 1969; Lewinsohn & Shaffer, 1971). Similarly, McLean, Ogston, and Grauer (1973) used behavioral conjoint marital therapy to effectively reduce the level of depressed mood and aversive interaction between couples. In more recent work, O'Leary and Beach (1990) and Jacobson, Dobson, Fruzzetti, Schmaling, and Salusky (1991) found that behavioral marital therapy was effective in reducing levels of depression as well as in improving marital satisfaction. Thus it seems logical that treatment for depressed adolescents should involve members of their families.

Fifth, treatment is based on a life skills remediation approach, suggesting that depressive disorders may be due to problems in coping with aversive events that occur on a regular basis in the natural environment and that learning to cope more effectively with these events should reduce depression as well as the likelihood of further episodes.

Sixth, selection and outcome criteria include both self-report data and the most current standardized psychiatric interviews, such as the Kiddie-SADS (K-SADS; Puig-Antich & Chambers, 1983), which provide *DSM-III-R* (American Psychiatric Association, 1987) diagnoses. Thus treatment effectiveness can be evaluated and compared across studies using similar or different treatment methods.

CWD-A TREATMENT FORMAT
AND COMPONENTS

The basic rationale underlying the course that is provided to the depressed adolescents is that depression is a function of deficits in specific skills that are critical for coping with life's aversive events and for maximizing positive outcomes. Thus improvement in their coping repertoires should enhance their ability to adjust successfully. This rationale is repeated throughout the course to emphasize the need for the adolescents to practice the skills taught in the classroom as well as in extratherapeutic settings. Classes are held twice weekly for 8 weeks, and adolescents are provided with homework to encourage their practice of the skills learned. Each group of 4 to 8 adolescents has a group leader who introduces the materials, assigns and checks homework assignments, and otherwise facilitates the discussion. Workbooks are provided to each teen; they contain brief readings, examples of depressogenic thoughts, forms for completing assignments, and structured learning tasks.

An important feature of the course is that the components are arranged hierarchically so that the basic skills taught earlier form the necessary foundation for the teaching of more complex skills introduced later on.

Adolescent Components

Self-monitoring and Self-reinforcement. Rehm (1977) has suggested that depression is the consequence of deficiencies in various self-control strategies including self-monitoring, self-evaluation, and self-reinforcement. Stark et al. (1987) found self-control procedures to be effective in reducing depressive symptoms reported by adolescents. In the CWD-A course, adolescents are taught to monitor their mood from the outset to provide a baseline from which they can evaluate their improvement. They are also taught to provide reinforcers following successful gains in mood reduction.

Social Skills Training. Deficits in social skills have been consistently demonstrated among depressed individuals for nearly two decades (e.g., Libet & Lewinsohn, 1973). Consequently a solid foundation is given in the skills required to enter into more complex social interactions, and these skills are staggered throughout the course as the building blocks for later training in conflict resolution skills. They include conversation techniques, planning social activities, and strategies of friendship making.

Increasing Pleasant Activities. A hallmark assumption of all behavioral approaches to the treatment of depressed individuals is that relatively low rates of positive reinforcement are the prerequisite conditions that trigger depressive episodes (see Lewinsohn, Biglan, & Zeiss, 1976). Consequently depressed adolescents are urged to increase the number of pleasant activities that they engage in. These include both positive social interactions and nonsocial activities. To assist them toward this end, they are taught to set realistic goals, develop a plan and a contract for behavior change, and reward themselves at each successful step along the way.

Anxiety Reduction. The overlap and the strong association between anxiety and depression have been noted frequently among adults (e.g., Maser & Cloninger, 1990) and children and adolescents (Kendall, this volume; Lewinsohn et al., 1993). Anxiety may interfere with learning new skills, interfere with responding in social situations, and reduce the enjoyability of pleasant activities. Adolescents are given initial training with the Jacobson (1929) procedure involving alternatively tensing and relaxing major muscle groups, and finally with a less conspicuous method (Benson, 1975) for use in more public settings. The skills are taught early to provide adolescents with an initial success experience.

Reducing Depressogenic Cognitions. Following the work of Beck and his colleagues (e.g., Beck, Rush, Shaw, & Emery, 1979), Ellis and Harper (1961), and Kranzler (1974), the CWD-A course includes several sessions designed to identify, challenge, and change negative thoughts and irrational beliefs. Depressogenic cognitions have been shown to be associated with depression, and although their etiologic role has not been clearly determined, successful interventions using cognitive methods have been demonstrated with adults (Jacobson et al., 1993). To appeal to adolescents, cartoon characters such as Garfield the Cat, Bloom County, and Calvin & Hobbes are used to illustrate depressogenic thinking, and participants are asked to come up with more constructive thoughts as counters.

Communication, Negotiation, and Problem-Solving Skills. Given the evidence for the use of coercive behavior among the depressed (Biglan et al., 1985; Hops et al., 1987), an important component of treatment focuses on procedures to teach depressed people how to elicit behavior change in others in a more direct, nonaversive, and productive fashion. Behaviors that are incompatible with coercion include assertiveness, effective communication, negotiation, and problem solving. Current behavioral family interventions for adolescents such as those of Alexander and Parsons (1973), Forgatch and Patterson (1989), Patterson and Forgatch (1987), and Robin and Foster (1989) promote full-scale training in communication, negotiation, and problem-solving skills for both adolescents and their parents. Adolescents have the capacity for understanding the rationale and entering into successful negotiations, a critical element for this age group. As adolescents enter that period of life in which they begin to assert their independence from parental control, negotiation and successful conflict resolution between parent and adolescent become increasingly important.

As a prerequisite to successful negotiation, clear forms of communication are also necessary. Parents and adolescents need to be taught how to listen, paraphrase, and respond in kind. Only after this is done can they be taught to successfully negotiate changes in the behavior of other family members. Problem solving is the final step in this process. Family brainstorming, in which parents and adolescents offer suggestions for resolving issues without fear of reprisal, is a process in which compromise is emphasized and reinforced. The combination of these skills teaches all family members more constructive ways of interacting such that negative and coercive exchanges are no longer necessary to achieve results. Sanders, Dadds, Johnston, and Cash (1992) found that effective family problem solving discriminated between depressed and nondepressed clinic children and nonclinic children.

Six sessions are devoted to the demonstration and role playing of these activities as the focus shifts from communication, to negotiation, and then to problem solving. All of these procedures are then practiced during two *joint* parent-adolescent sessions attended by all adolescents and parents in the two groups. The parent and adolescent leaders act as facilitators and reinforcers during these sessions.

Future Planning. The final two sessions are designed to teach the adolescents how to use the newly acquired skills to anticipate and be prepared to cope with future problems. The goal of the course is to prevent relapse from occurring. Possible stressful situations that may arise in the future are listed and methods of coping with each are identified. Finally, each participant develops a written, personalized "emergency plan" detailing the steps he or she will take if there is a recurrence of depressive feelings. The plan includes what components learned in the course could be used to cope with the individual problems as they arise.

Parent Component

Parents participate in a parallel course meeting weekly for 2-hour sessions with a group leader (Lewinsohn, Rohde, Hops, & Clarke, 1991). Parents are provided information about the adolescent course and the skills that are taught to them, with the expectation that they will provide support and reinforcement for the activities required by the course and new skills observed in the home. Parents are also taught communication, negotiation, and problem-solving skills identical to those taught to the adolescents. Finally, two joint lessons are held during which each parent-adolescent dyad or triad practices the skills on issues salient to each family. As with the other components, homework is provided in which each family is asked to complete a contract and try it out. Workbooks are provided parents to guide them through the sessions.

Booster Sessions

Given the high rate of relapse for depressive disorders in adolescence (21.8% for females and 9.6% for males) found in community samples (Lewinsohn et al., 1993), procedures aimed at relapse prevention are clearly needed. Booster sessions were developed using future-planning sessions as a model. The model is consistent with the literature on relapse prevention in addictive disorders (e.g., Marlatt & Gordon, 1985).

The booster sessions were designed to assist the teens in maintaining gains made during the course. The procedures are as follows. The therapist reviews a series of assessments that are part of the booster protocol and determines the level of the adolescent's functioning. The therapist then meets with the adolescent and parent to obtain further information about the adolescent's current situation. Depending upon whether any deterioration has occurred, the therapist makes recommendations about changes in teens' and parents' behavior, such as reinstituting components of the course that might be of greatest use in overcoming relapses or difficulties. The therapist may also assign homework if necessary. A second weekly meeting is scheduled by the therapist with the adolescent and/or family a second time to evaluate whether homework was carried out, to review the situation again, and to make further recommendations. Distinct from the group format of the regular course, the boosters are conducted on an individual basis and are customized for each adolescent. The goal of the sessions is to continue to assist the adolescents to self-monitor their own behavior, thoughts and feelings, and environment and to reinstitute program components whenever there has been a significant deterioration in their adjustment.

TREATMENT OUTCOME STUDIES

Preliminary Study

In our initial study of the above-mentioned treatment program, which is described in greater detail in Lewinsohn et al. (1990), 59 adolescents meeting RDC/*DSM-III* (American Psychiatric Association, 1980) criteria for major depressive disorder or intermittent depression were randomly assigned to one of three treatment groups: (a) adolescents only ($n = 21$); (b) adolescents plus parents ($n = 19$); and (c) a waiting-list control group ($n = 19$). Parents involved in the second group were enrolled in an independent treatment condition, meeting once weekly for 8 weeks, during which they were provided information on depression among adolescents and the possible contributing factors and instructed on how to be supportive during this period. In addition, they were brought together with the adolescents for two of the treatment sessions, during which they practiced their conflict resolution skills.

Method. Adolescents were involved in 16 biweekly treatment sessions over a period of 8 weeks. Parents met weekly for 8 weeks in independent sessions. Assessments were conducted at intake, post treatment, and at 1-, 6-, 12- and 24-month follow-ups. Both parents and adolescents completed comprehensive questionnaires and diagnostic interviews.

Results. Planned comparisons following significant multivariate analyses showed that adolescents in both treatment conditions improved on the BDI and that a significant number showed a decrease in depressive symptoms, no longer meeting *DSM-III* criteria for unipolar depression. BDI scores decreased from a mean of 21.5 to 8.3 compared to the waiting-list controls, who maintained their initial levels (23.8 vs. 20.47). Similarly, 57.1% of the adolescent-only group and 52.4% of the adolescent-plus-parent group still met diagnostic criteria at posttreatment. This contrasted with 94.7% of the wait-list group. Over the 24 months of follow-up, the rate of recovery showed marked increases, with only 17% still meeting criteria after 6 months, and these gains were maintained over the rest of the 2-year period. Clearly, both treatments significantly influenced depressive symptoms among the treated adolescents in a way that was maintained over time. We were surprised to find that the adolescents-plus-parent group was not superior to the group in which adolescents were treated alone. The single significant difference between the two groups was a lower score on the Child Behavior Checklist (Achenbach & Edelbrock, 1983) reported by the involved parents.

Predictors of Outcome. To further examine which pretreatment variables may have been contributing to successful outcome, data from 37 of the 40 treated subjects were entered into discriminant function and regression analysis (Clarke, Hops, Lewinsohn, Andrews, & Seeley, 1992). In the former, we tried to discriminate between those that recovered and those that did not, using diagnostic criteria. In the regression analyses, we examined variables that were associated with the residual pre- to post-treatment change on the BDI.

Interestingly, the results differed considerably depending upon the dependent variable used. Recovery was associated with lower BDI scores, lower anxiety scores, higher enjoyment and frequency of pleasant activities, and more rational thoughts; the final canonical correlation was .63. In contrast, the best predictors of the residualized BDI scores were a greater number of past psychiatric diagnoses, parent involvement in treatment, and younger age at onset of the first depressive episode; the multiple correlation was .84. Finer analyses of the data suggested that the recovered subjects were somewhat less severely depressed than those that did not recover. The results of the BDI analyses, save for the parent involvement, were in unpredicted directions. These data suggest that both diagnostic and continuous data may be necessary to fully interpret the outcome of interventions.

Treatment Replication

A second test of the efficacy of the treatment program was conducted on 96 adolescents meeting *DSM-III-R* (American Psychiatric Association, 1987) criteria for MDD or dysthymia (Lewinsohn, Clarke, Rohde, Hops, & Seeley, in press). For this trial, the course protocol was rewritten so that the components were laid out in a more systematic, hierarchical fashion, and basic skill building occurred prior to more complex skills. For example, communication skills were established prior to conflict resolution skills because the former are basic prerequisites for successful negotiation, which requires effective sending and receiving of messages and paraphrasing. The course was made more developmentally appropriate, adding components such as cartoons that would appeal to the adolescent. In this study, we examined the power of the boosters to prevent relapse and maintain the adolescents' gains. The 96 adolescents were randomly assigned to treatment conditions similar to those in the initial study.

Results. The results were quite similar to those of the initial study. The two treatment groups showed significantly greater improvement than the waiting-list control group, both in recovery rates and in decreases in BDI scores. Sixty-seven percent of the treated adolescents no longer met criteria at posttreatment compared to only 48% of the waiting-list subjects. Further, there were no significant differences in recovery or relapse rates in the three follow-up conditions or by gender. By 12 months and 24 months post treatment, 81.3% and 97.5% of the adolescents, respectively, had recovered.

Effect of booster conditions. We did not find a significant effect of our booster conditions. In retrospect, it would appear that it would have been difficult to surpass the recovery rates associated with the basic treatment model. The long 4-month delay between the end of treatment and the beginning of the booster conditions may have been too long to have had an impact, and adolescents needing assistance may have ventured elsewhere. Several improvements could be made to the booster condition to add to its apparent minimal effectiveness. These include (a) a more individualized commitment from each group leader at the end of the formal classes to change the emphasis from prevention to a continuation of treatment; (b) beginning the boosters earlier so as to maintain the relationship with the group leader; (c) adjusting the frequency prescriptively—that is, depending upon the adolescent's level of adjustment; (d) providing boosters only to those who are experiencing depressive symptoms; (e) having boosters begin at monthly intervals and fading them as appropriate for the individual teen; and (f) using some form of group booster to reduce cost and maintain the group atmosphere of the classes.

Taken together, these results suggest that the two treatment conditions are both powerful additions to our clinical armamentarium. However, the puzzling aspect of the results is the lack of a significant effect for the parental addition.

ISSUES FOR FUTURE RESEARCH

The major issue that remains for future studies to explore is the lack of impact of the parenting course, and clearly the protocol we developed for use with the parents needs to be reexamined. Several options need to be considered. Perhaps we should have allowed more time for the joint sessions and seen each family unit individually. Another possibility is that we need to consider the depressive symptomatology in the parents and determine how much specific assistance each of them requires, similar to that provided to their adolescents (see Hops, 1992). Another possibility is that the parent course needs to include more focus on parenting skills. Previous research has shown that depressed mothers may not be sufficiently skilled in being assertive and making specific demands of their offspring (e.g., Radke-Yarrow, 1990). As children become adolescents, the challenge they pose may become even more intimidating to such parents. Although the process of communication, negotiation, and problem solving is vital to establishing and maintaining positive family relationships, within that context it is also necessary for parents to monitor and set limits on their adolescents' behavior, backing them up with specific and effective consequences. Consequently parents should be encouraged and reinforced in setting precise contingencies and enforcing them in a direct way. Clearly, these and other similar issues require further exploration. In this way, the impact of the CWD-A could be enhanced.

REFERENCES

Achenbach, T. M., & Edelbrock, C. S. (1983). *Manual for the Child Behavior Checklist and Revised Child Behavior Profile.* Burlington: University of Vermont, Department of Psychiatry.

Alexander, J. F., & Parsons, B. V. (1973). Short-term behavioral intervention with delinquent families: Impact on family process and recidivism. *Journal of Abnormal Psychology, 81,* 219-225.

American Psychiatric Association. (1980). *Diagnostic and statistical manual of mental disorders (DSM-III)* (3rd ed.). Washington, DC: Author.

American Psychiatric Association. (1987). *Diagnostic and statistical manual of mental disorders (DSM-III-R)* (3rd ed., rev.). Washington, DC: Author.

Beck, A. T., Rush, A. J., Shaw, B. F., & Emery, G. (1979). *Cognitive therapy of depression.* New York: Guilford.

Benson, H. (1975). *The relaxation response.* New York: William Morrow.

Biglan, A., Hops, H., Sherman, L., Friedman, L. S., Arthur, J., & Osteen, V. (1985). Problem-solving interactions of depressed women and their husbands. *Behavior Therapy, 16,* 431-451.

Carlson, G. A., & Strober, M. (1978). Affective disorders in adolescence: Issues in misdiagnosis. *Journal of Clinical Psychiatry, 39,* 63-66.

Clarke, G. N., Hops, H., Lewinsohn, P. M., Andrews, J. A., & Seeley, J. R. (1992). Cognitive-behavioral group treatment of adolescent depression: Prediction of outcome. *Behavior Therapy, 23,* 341-354.

Cytryn, L., & McKnew, D. H. (1972). Proposed classification of childhood depression. *American Journal of Psychiatry, 129,* 140-155.

Dadds, M. R., Schwartz, S., & Sanders, M. R. (1987). Marital discord and treatment outcome in behavioral treatment of child conduct disorders. *Journal of Consulting and Clinical Psychology, 55,* 396-403.

Ellis, A., & Harper, R. A. (1961). *A guide to rational living.* Hollywood, CA: Wilshire.

Forgatch, M. S., & Patterson, G. R. (1989). *Parents and adolescents living together—Part 2: Family problem solving.* Eugene, OR: Castalia.

Frame, C., Matson, J. L., Sonis, W. A., Falkov, M. J., & Kazdin, A. E. (1982). Behavioral treatment of depression in a prepubertal child. *Behavior Therapy and Experimental Psychiatry, 13,* 239-243.

Gotlib, I. H., & Colby, C. A. (1987). *Treatment of depression: An interpersonal systems approach.* New York: Pergamon.

Gotlib, I. H., & Hammen, C. L. (1992). *Psychological aspects of depression: Toward a cognitive-interpersonal integration.* New York: John Wiley.

Hoberman, H. M., Lewinsohn, P. M., & Tilson, M. (1988). Group treatment of depression: Individual predictors of outcome. *Journal of Consulting and Clinical Psychology, 56,* 393-398.

Hops, H. (1992). Parental depression and child behaviour problems: Implications for behavioural family intervention. *Behaviour Change, 9,* 126-138.

Hops, H., Biglan, A., Sherman, L., Arthur, J., Friedman, L., & Osteen, V. (1987). Home observations of family interactions of depressed women. *Journal of Consulting and Clinical Psychology, 55,* 341-346.

Hops, H., Lewinsohn, P. M., Andrews, J. A., & Roberts, R. E. (1990). Psychosocial correlates of depressive symptomatology among high school students. *Journal of Clinical Child Psychology, 19,* 211-220.

Jacobson, E. (1929). *Progressive relaxation.* Chicago: University of Chicago Press.

Jacobson, N. S., Dobson, K., Fruzzetti, A. E., Schmaling, K. B., & Salusky, S. (1991). Marital therapy as a treatment for depression. *Journal of Consulting and Clinical Psychology, 59,* 547-557.

Jacobson, N. S., Fruzzetti, A. E., Dobson, K., Whisman, M., & Hops, H. (1993). Couple therapy as a treatment for depression: II. The effects of relationship quality and therapy on depressive relapse. *Journal of Consulting and Clinical Psychology, 61,* 516-519.

Kahn, J. S., Kehle, T. J., Jenson, W. R., & Clark, E. (1990). Comparison of cognitive-behavioral, relaxation, and self-modeling interventions for depression among middle-school students. *School Psychology Review, 19,* 196-211.

Kashani, J. H., Beck, N. C., Hoeper, E. W., Fallahi, C., Corcoran, C. M., McAlister, J. A., Rosenberg, T. K., & Reid, J. C. (1987). Psychiatric disorders in a community sample of adolescents. *American Journal of Psychiatry, 144,* 584-589.

Kazdin, A. E. (1989). Identifying depression in children: A comparison of alternative selection criteria. *Journal of Abnormal Child Psychology, 17,* 437-454.

Keller, M. B., Lavori, P. W., Beardslee, W. R., Wunder, J., & Ryan, N. (1991). Depression in children and adolescents: New data on "undertreatment" and a literature review on the efficacy of available treatments. *Journal of Affective Disorders, 21,* 163-171.

Klerman, G. L., Weissman, M. M., Rounsaville, B. J., & Chevron, E. (1984). *Interpersonal psychotherapy of depression.* New York: Basic Books.

Kovacs, M., & Beck, A. T. (1977). The wish to die and the wish to live in attempted suicides. *Journal of Clinical Psychology, 33,* 361-365.

Kranzler, G. (1974). *You can change how you feel.* Eugene, OR: RETC.

Lewinsohn, P. M., Antonuccio, D., Steinmetz, J., & Teri, L. (1984). *The coping with depression course: A psychoeducational intervention for unipolar depression.* Eugene, OR: Castalia.

Lewinsohn, P. M., & Atwood, G. (1969). Depression: A clinical research approach. The case of Mrs. G. *Psychotherapy: Theory, Research and Practice, 6,* 166-171.

Lewinsohn, P. M., Biglan, A., & Zeiss, A. (1976). Behavioral treatment of depression. In P. Davidson (Ed.), *Behavioral management of anxiety, depression, and pain* (pp. 91-146). New York: Brunner/Mazel.

Lewinsohn, P. M., Clarke, G. N., Hops, H., Andrews, J., & Williams, J. (1990). Cognitive-behavioral treatment for depressed adolescents. *Behavior Therapy, 21,* 385-401.

Lewinsohn, P. M., Clarke, G. N., Rohde, P., Hops, H., & Seeley, J. R. (in press). A cognitive-behavioral approach to the treatment of adolescent depression. In E. Hibbs & P. Jensen (Eds.), *Psychosocial treatment research of child and adolescent disorders.*

Lewinsohn, P. M., Hoberman, H., Teri, L., & Hautzinger, M. (1985). An integrative theory of depression. In S. Reiss & R. Bootzin (Eds.), *Theoretical issues in behavior therapy* (pp. 331-359). New York: Academic Press.

Lewinsohn, P. M., Hops, H., Roberts, R. E., Seeley, J. R., & Andrews, J. A. (1993). Adolescent psychopathology: I. Prevalence and incidence of depression and other DSM-III-R disorders in high school students. *Journal of Abnormal Psychology, 102,* 133-144.

Lewinsohn, P. M., Roberts, R. E., Seeley, J. R., Rohde, P., Gotlib, I. H., & Hops, H. (1994). Adolescent depression: II. Psychosocial risk factors. *Journal of Abnormal Psychology, 103,* 302-315.

Lewinsohn, P. M., Rohde, P., Hops, H., & Clarke, G. N. (1991). *Parent workbook: The adolescent coping with depression course.* Eugene, OR: Castalia.

Lewinsohn, P. M., & Shaffer, M. (1971). Use of home observations as an integral part of the treatment of depression: Preliminary report and case studies. *Journal of Consulting and Clinical Psychology, 37,* 87-94.

Libet, J., & Lewinsohn, P. M. (1973). Concept of social skill with special reference to the behavior of depressed persons. *Journal of Consulting and Clinical Psychology, 40,* 304-312.

Marlatt, G. A., & Gordon, J. R. (1985). *Relapse prevention: Maintenance strategies in the treatment of addictive behaviors.* New York: Guilford.

Maser, J. D., & Cloninger, C. R. (1990). *Comorbidity in anxiety and mood disorders.* Washington, DC: American Psychiatric Press.

McGee, R., Feehan, M., Williams, S., Partridge, F., Silva, P. A., & Kelly, J. (1990). DSM-III disorders in a large sample of adolescents. *Journal of the American Academy of Child and Adolescent Psychiatry, 29,* 611-619.

McLean, P. D., Ogston, L., & Grauer, L. (1973). Behavioral approach to the treatment of depression. *Journal of Behaviour Therapy and Experimental Psychiatry, 4,* 323-330.

Moreau, D., Mufson, L., Weissman, M. M., & Klerman, G. L. (1991). Interpersonal psychotherapy for adolescent depression: Description of modification and preliminary application. *Journal of the American Academy of Child and Adolescent Psychiatry, 30,* 642-651.

O'Leary, K. D., & Beach, S. R. H. (1990). Marital therapy: A viable treatment for depression and marital discord. *American Journal of Psychiatry, 147,* 183-186.

Patterson, G. R. (1982). *Coercive family process.* Eugene, OR: Castalia.

Patterson, G. R., & Forgatch, M. S. (1987). *Parents and adolescents living together. Part 1: The basics.* Eugene, OR: Castalia.

Poznanski, E. O., & Zrull, J. P. (1970). Childhood depression. *Archives of General Psychiatry, 23,* 8-15.

Puig-Antich, J., Blau, S., Marx, N., Greenhill, L., & Chambers, W. (1978). Prepubertal major depressive disorders: A pilot study. *Journal of the American Academy of Child Psychiatry, 17,* 695-707.

Puig-Antich, J., & Chambers, W. J. (1983). *Schedule for affective disorders and schizophrenia for school age children (6-18).* Pittsburgh: Western Psychiatric Institute and Clinic.

Radke-Yarrow, M. (1990). Family environments of depressed and well parents and their children: Issues of research methods. In G. R. Patterson (Ed.), *Depression and aggression in family interaction* (pp. 169-184). New York: Lawrence Erlbaum.

Rehm, L. P. (1977). A self-control model of depression. *Behavior Therapy, 8,* 787-804.

Reynolds, W. M., & Coats, K. I. (1986). A comparison of cognitive behavioral-therapy and relaxation training for the treatment of depression in adolescents. *Journal of Consulting and Clinical Psychology, 54,* 653-660.

Robin, A. L., & Foster, S. L. (1989). *Negotiating parent-adolescent conflict: A behavioral-family systems approach.* New York: Guilford.

Robins, L. N., & Regier, D. (1991). *Psychiatric disorders in America.* New York: Free Press.

Rohde, P., Lewinsohn, P. M., & Seeley, J. R. (1991). Comorbidity of unipolar depression: II. Comorbidity with other mental disorders in adolescents and adults. *Journal of Abnormal Psychology, 100,* 214-222.

Sanders, M. R., Dadds, M. R., Johnston, B., & Cash, R. (1992). Childhood depression and conduct disorder I: Behavioural, affective and cognitive aspects of family problem solving interactions. *Journal of Abnormal Psychology, 101,* 495-504.

Stark, K. D. (1990). *Childhood depression: School-based intervention.* New York: Guilford.

Stark, K. D., Reynolds, W. M., & Kaslow, N. J. (1987). A comparison of the relative efficacy of self-control therapy and a behavioral problem-solving therapy for depression in children. *Journal of Abnormal Child Psychology, 15,* 91-113.

Steinmetz, J., Lewinsohn, P. M., & Antonuccio, D. (1983). Prediction of individual outcome in a group intervention for depression. *Journal of Consulting and Clinical Psychology, 51,* 331-337.

Velez, C. N., Johnson, J., & Cohen, P. (1989). A longitudinal analysis of selected risk factors for childhood psychopathology. *Journal of the American Academy of Child and Adolescent Psychiatry, 28,* 861-864.

Weinberg, W. A., Rutman, J., Sullivan, L., Penick, E. C., & Dietz, S. G. (1973). Depression in children referred to an educational diagnostic center: Diagnosis and treatment. *Journal of Pediatrics, 83,* 1065-1072.

Whitaker, A., Johnson, J., Shaffer, D., Rapoport, J. L., Kalikow, K., Walsh, B. T., Davies, M., Braiman, S., & Dolinsky, A. (1990). Uncommon troubles in young people. *Archives of General Psychiatry, 47,* 487-496.

Name Index

Friedman, L. S., 77, 242
Friedman, R. M., 206
Fritz, G. F., 141, 157
Fruzzetti, A. E., 233, 242
Fuchs, C. Z., 195, 200, 205, 207
Fung, T., 146-147, 158

Gajdos, G., 125, 133
Gallagher, D., 187, 192, 208
Gammon, G. D., 4, 25, 36
Garber, J., 40-41, 53
Garbin, M. G., 213, 227
Garfinkel, B. D., 19-20, 25-26, 33
Garssen, B., 8, 34
Garvey, M. J., 206, 227
Gatsonis, C., 24-25, 35
Gelder, M., 163, 178
Gelder, M. C., 58, 76
Genest, M., 215, 227
Gilbert, F. S., 60, 78
Gilbert, P., 209, 227
Girodo, M., 63, 78
Gitlin, M., 86, 89, 95
Gitow, A., 66, 77
Glas, D. R., 38, 53
Glasgow, R. E., 63, 78
Glass, C. R., 63, 77-78, 227
Glass, D. R., 58, 80, 205, 227
Glenn, A. I. M., 205
Glennon, B., 110-111, 122
Goeke, K. E., 110, 123
Gold, D. T., 158
Goldfried, M. R., 41, 53, 61, 78
Goldin, J. C., 208
Gonzales, A. C., 164, 179
Gordon, D., 87, 95
Gordon, J. R., 237, 244
Gormally, J., 39, 53
Gorsky, J. M., 64, 77
Gotlib, I. H., 15., 34, 39, 47, 53, 63, 65-67, 78-79, 82-85, 88-89, 94-95, 188, 205, 218, 227, 230, 233, 242-243
Graf, M., 220, 228
Graham, P., 102, 124
Grauer, L., 183, 190, 206, 233, 244
Graziano, A. M., 119, 122
Greenberg, J., 211, 228
Greenberg, M. S., 14, 34, 46, 53

Greenberg, M. T., 95
Greenfeld, S., 96
Greenhill, L., 230, 244
Grossman-McKee, D., 39, 55
Grove, W. M., 206, 227
Grubb, H., 4, 35
Gruen, C. E., 102, 123
Gullone, E., 47, 54

Haaga, D. A. F., 88, 95
Hagopian, L. P., 103, 123
Hakstian, A. R., 188, 190, 197, 206
Hamblin, D., 205
Hamilton, D. I., 99, 122, 213
Hamilton, M., 227
Hammen, C., 38
Hammen, C. L., 53, 55, 60, 78, 82-89, 92-95, 208, 215, 226-227, 230, 242
Hampe, E., 109, 123
Hanna, T., 150, 157
Harper, R. A., 235, 242
Harrell, T. H., 38, 54
Harris, T., 85, 92, 94
Harris, T. O., 89,94
Hart, C. W., 145, 157
Hart, K., 164, 178
Hartlage, S., 211, 226
Hartmann, D. P., 113, 121
Hartney, L. M., 38, 54
Hautzinger, M., 67, 78, 232, 243
Hayman, P. M., 190, 205
Hays, R. D., 96
Hazaleus, S. L., 164, 178
Heath, A. C., 27, 35
Heick, H., 164, 178
Heide, F. J., 142, 157
Heimberg, R., 61, 78, 79
Heimberg, R. G., 58, 63, 66, 77, 78, 79, 188, 205
Hellstrom, K., 129, 133
Helsel, W. J., 105, 123
Heninger, G. R., 3, 33
Herbst, K., 228
Herjanic, B., 17, 34, 102-103, 122
Herjanic, M., 102, 122
Herschberg, S. G., 21, 26, 30, 34
Hersen, M., 4, 7, 25, 35-36, 47, 55, 100, 123, 188, 190, 197, 122, 205, 207

Subject Index

About the Editors

Kenneth D. Craig, Ph.D., is Professor of Psychology in the Department of Psychology at the University of British Columbia. His post-secondary education was at Sir George Williams University (B.A.), the University of British Columbia (M.A.), and Purdue University (Ph.D. in Clinical Psychology, 1964). At the University of British Columbia, he has served as Director of the Graduate Programme in Clinical Psychology on two occasions. His teaching presently focuses upon abnormal psychology and health psychology at the undergraduate level and psychological assessment and supervision in the Psychological Clinic at the graduate level. He has authored numerous research papers and chapters on the psychology of pain and on the anxiety disorders, and his current focus is upon pain in children, assessment of pain in the newborn and infant, and the use of nonverbal measures in understanding pain. His research has won a number of awards, including the Canada Council Killam Research Fellowship. He has been the Editor of the *Canadian Journal of Behavioural Science* and presently is an Associate Editor of the journal *Pain.* He has coedited the following books: *Health enhancement, disease prevention and early intervention: Bio-behavioral perspectives,* and *Advances in clinical behavior therapy.* Recent research grants have come from the Social Sciences and Humanities Research Council of Canada, the Natural Sciences and Engineering Research Council of Canada, the B. C. Health Research Foundation, and the pharmaceutical industry. He is a Fellow of the Canadian

Psychological Association, the American Psychological Association, and the Society for Behavioral Medicine; a founding member of the International Association for the Study of Pain; and a member of the Academy of Behavioral Medicine Research. Service for scientific and professional organizations has included terms as President of the Canadian Psychological Association, President of the British Columbia Psychological Association, and Treasurer of the Social Science Federation of Canada. He presently is President of the Banff International Conferences on Behavioural Science and President of the Canadian Pain Society.

Keith S. Dobson is Professor of Psychology of the University of Calgary, where he is also the Director of the Programme in Clinical Psychology. He is a Professional/Scientific Member of the Department of Psychiatry at Foothills Hospital and a Consulting Psychologist at the Calgary Group District Hospital, Calgary. His research interests focus on the issues of cognition and psychopathology (particularly anxiety and depression), gender issues in psychopathology, cognition and interpersonal relationships, cognitive-behavioral therapies, and professional issues in psychology. He is the editor or co-editor of several volumes, including the *Handbook of Cognitive-Behavioral Therapies, Psychopathology and Cognition,* and *Professional Psychology in Canada.* In addition to conducting research, he has been active in professional psychology, and has served on many committees of several organizations. He is the current chair of the National Professional Psychology Consortium and the immediate Past-President of the Canadian Psychological Association.

About the Contributors

Lynn E. Alden completed her Ph.D. at the University of Illinois at Urbana and her clinical internship at the University of Washington School of Medicine in Seattle, Washington. She is currently a Professor in the Department of Psychology at the University of British Columbia in Vancouver, Canada. She has numerous publications that focus on the integration of cognitive and interpersonal models of psychopathology, particularly as applied to social anxiety and depression. She also has a clinical appointment in the Health Psychology Clinic at University Hospital, UBC, where she is a clinical supervisor in the predoctoral internship program. Her clinical interests center on the integration of cognitive and interpersonal treatment strategies in time-limited psychotherapy. She is a Fellow of the Canadian Psychological Association and is President-elect of the Canadian Council of Professional Programs in Psychology.

Her recent publications include authored and coauthored articles in *Innovations in Clinical Practice, 11th ed., Journal of Personality and Social Psychology,* and *Behavior Therapy.*

Peter J. Bieling obtained an Honors B.Sc. from the University of Victoria and an M.A. from the University of British Columbia in Vancouver, Canada. He is currently completing his doctoral degree in clinical psychology at the University of British Columbia. His major research interests lie in the area of interpersonal factors and depression, particularly in the integration of cognitive and dynamic models of depression. Presently, he is engaged in a study of self-defeating interpersonal patterns associated with sociotropy and autonomy in depressed outpatients. His recent publication includes a coauthored article in *Cognitive Therapy and Research.*

Donald Bakal, Ph.D., is Professor of Psychology at the University of Calgary. His research interests include chronic headache disorders, panic anxiety, and somatization disorders. He recently published *Psychology and Health.*

Erika U. Brady received her undergraduate degree in psychology from Cornell University and is presently a doctoral candidate in the clinical psychology program at Temple University. She is currently completing her clinical internship in the Department of Pediatric Psychology at Children's Seashore House, University of Pennsylvania, located in Philadelphia, Pennsylvania.

Her recent publications include; Comorbidity of anxiety and depression in youth: Treatment implications (1992, with Kendall, Kortlander, and Chansky), *Journal of Consulting and Clinical Psychology, 60,* 869-880 and Comorbidity of anxiety and depression in children and adolescents (1992, with Kendall), *Psychological Bulletin, 111,* 244-255.

Her research interests focus on the impact of comorbidity on treatment outcomes and a developing project involving the relationship of anxiety disorders and attention-deficit hyperactivity disorder in school-aged children.

Stefan Demjen, Ph.D., is a clinical psychologist with the Department of Psychiatry, Foothills Hospital, Calgary, and also an Adjunct Professor with the University of Calgary. His research and clinical interests include pain disorders, anxiety, and depression.

Constance Hammen is Professor of Psychology and Psychiatry at UCLA, where she is presently Director of Clinical Training and Associate Director of the Affective Disorders Clinic at the UCLA Neuropsychiatric Institute. Her research interests include affective disorders in adults, children, and adolescents—examining the cognitive, stress, family, and interpersonal factors that predict course of disorder. Her recent books include *Depression Runs in Families* (1991); *Psychological Aspects of Depression: Toward Cognitive-Interpersonal Integration* (1992, cowritten with Ian Gotlib), and a new textbook, *Abnormal Psychology* (in press, with Philip Kendall).

Her current research projects include a longitudinal study of predictors of depression and adjustment in young women in the transition to adulthood and a study of comorbidity and course of disorder in depressed child outpatients.

Kathlyn Hesson, Ph.D., is a clinical psychologist with the Calgary District Hospital Group. She has research interests in childbirth and has developed a psychobiological framework for understanding the various psychological and physiological events that occur during labor.

Hyman Hops has been a research scientist at the Oregon Research Institute since 1978. During that time, he has been actively involved in studies of families, children, and adolescents in home and school settings. His research interests include the development of social relationships with families and friends, adolescent adjustment and pathology such as substance abuse and depression, and the intergenerational transmission of depressive symptomatology from a social interactional perspective. Prior to 1978, while at the University of Oregon, he was instrumental in the development of prevention and intervention school-based programs for children at risk for behavioral disorders, such as aggression and social withdrawal. Currently, he is engaged in several longitudinal studies of adjustment during the transition from childhood to adolescence and from adolescence to young adulthood. He serves on the editorial boards of *Behavior Research and Therapy, Psychological Assessment,* and the *Journal of Family Psychology.*

Rick E. Ingram is Professor of Psychology at San Diego State University and a core faculty member in the SDSU/UCSD Doctoral Training Program in Clinical Psychology, where he is currently Head of the Experimental Psychopathology Training Track. He received his Ph.D. from the University of Kansas in 1983 and completed a clinical internship at the University of Minnesota. In 1990 he received the American Psychological Association's award for an Early Career Contribution to Psychology, and in 1988 he received the Association for the Advancement of Behavior Therapy's new Researcher Award. In a recent international citation analysis reported at the 25th International Congress of Psychology he was ranked 24th among the 50 highest impact authors. He served as an Associate Editor for *Cognitive Therapy and Research* from 1986 to 1993 and as the Program

Chair for the 1990 meeting of the Association for the Advancement of Behavior Therapy. He has edited *Information processing approaches to clinical psychology* (1986) and *Contemporary psychological approaches to depression* (1990) and co-authored *The psychology of personal adjustment* with Dennis Saccuzzo (1992). He is presently coauthoring *Cognitive vulnerability to depression* with Jeanne Miranda, which is scheduled for publication in 1995. His current theoretical and empirical work focuses on the use of information, processing theoretical constructs and methodologies to understand depression, and on cognitive vulnerability to depression. He is currently funded by a grant from the National Institute of Mental Health.

Philip C. Kendall, Ph.D., ABPP, is Professor of Psychology and Head of the Division of Clinical Psychology at Temple University in Philadelphia, where he also serves as the Director of the Child and Adolescent Anxiety Disorders Clinic. He is an Associate Editor for the *Journal of Consulting and Clinical Psychology* and Editor of the journal *Cognitive Therapy and Research.* Recent journal articles have appeared in *Journal of Consulting and Clinical Psychology* and *Abnormal Psychology.* He recently coauthored *Abnormal Psychology* (1995) with Connie Hammen and *Cognitive-behavior therapy for impulsive children* (1993) with Lauren Braswell. He was a Fellow at the Center for Advanced Studies in the Behavioral Sciences and has served as President of the Association for the Advancement of Behavior Therapy. His research interests lie in the assessment and treatment of anxiety disorders in youth, with a special focus on the cognitive, behavioral, and familial factors that contribute to successful treatment outcome.

Peter M. Lewinsohn is a research scientist at Oregon Research Institute. In addition, he is Adjunct Professor of Psychiatry at Oregon Health Sciences University and Emeritus Professor of Psychology at the University of Oregon. He is currently engaged in a longitudinal study focused on the psychosocial antecedents and consequences of adolescent depression. He and his associates were responsible for the development of the Coping With Depression Course. Some of his recent publications include coauthored articles in the *Journal of Abnormal Psychology, Journal of Consulting and Clinical Psychology,* and the *Journal of the American Academy of Child and Adolescent Psychiatry.*

Kenneth G. A. Meleshko obtained his B.A. at the University of Alberta in Edmonton, Canada, and received his M.A. and Ph.D. from the University of British Columbia in Vancouver. He completed his internship at Alberta Hospital, Edmonton, and is currently with the Young Offender Outpatient Unit of Alberta Hospital, Edmonton. He has a continuing interest in interpersonal aspects of anxiety and depression and is currently examining the specificity of maladaptive interpersonal patterns in depression and anxiety. His other research interests are in the area of forensic psychology and are related to the assessment and treatment of young offenders. His most recent publication is a coauthored article in the *Journal of Personality and Social Psychology.*

Thomas H. Ollendick, Ph.D., is Professor of Psychology and Director of Clinical Training at Virginia Polytechnic Institute and State University in Blacksburg, Virginia. He has authored numerous research papers and chapters on the assessment and treatment of childhood anxiety and phobic disorders as well as other disorders of childhood and adolescence. He is the coauthor or coeditor of several books, including *Clinical behavior therapy with children, Handbook of child psychopathology, Child behavioral assessment: Principles and procedures, Enhancing children's social skills, Children's phobias: A behavioural perspective,* and *School refusal: Recent advances in assessment and treatment.* In addition, he coedits the *Advances in Clinical Child Psychology* series with Ron Prinz. A Fellow in the Division of Clinical Psychology and Experimental Analysis of Behavior of the American Psychological Association, he is the Past-President of its Section on Clinical Child Psychology and currently serves as the representative of the Section to the Division of Clinical Psychology. He has also served as Coordinator of Convention Activities and Representative-at-Large for the Association for the Advancement of Behavior Therapy (AABT) and is presently serving as its President.

Lynn P. Rehm received his Ph.D. from the University of Wisconsin-Madison and did his internship at the VA Medical Center in Milwaukee. He has been on the faculties of UCLA-Neuropsychiatric Institute in Psychiatry; University of Pittsburgh in Psychology and Psychiatry; and the University of Houston, Psychology Department. He was Director of Clinical Training at Pittsburgh and Houston and is currently Professor of Psychology at Houston. His research centers on theory, psychopathology, and treatment of depression in adults and children. He has made scientific presentations and given clinical workshops on self-management therapy nationally and internationally. He is the editor of *Behavior therapy for depression: Present status and future directions* (1981) and coeditor of *Psychological research, public policy and practice* (1985). His recent publications include *A memory model of depression* (with May Naus) and *Cognitive and behavioral predictors of response to treatments for depression* (with Stephanie Rude). He is a Diplomat of the American Board of Professional Psychology and Behavioral Psychology and a Fellow of the American Psychological Association in its clinical and psychotherapy divisions.

Vanessa L. Malcarne is Assistant Professor of Psychology at San Diego State University. She is also a core faculty member in the behavioral medicine and experimental psychopathology training tracks of the San Diego State University/University of California, San Diego Doctoral Training Program in Clinical Psychology. She received her Ph.D. from the University of Vermont in 1989 and joined the faculty at SDSU in 1990. She serves on the Editorial Board of *Cognitive Therapy and Research* and as a reviewer for a variety of other journals. Her publications and presentations to date have focused on child psychopathology and child/adult adjustment to stressors, particularly chronic illness. Her current research continues to focus on prediction of adjustment to chronic illness, with emphasis on gender, ethnic identity/acculturation, and developmental level as factors influencing the adjustment process. Her research on adjustment to rheumatic disease is currently funded by a grant from the UCSD Multipurpose Arthritis and Musculoskeletal Diseases Center/National Institutes of Health.

Stanley J. Rachman is Professor of Psychology, University of British Columbia, and formerly Professor of Abnormal Psychology at the Institute of Psychiatry (University of London). His research interests are psychology of fear, obsessions and compulsions, emotional processing, and the application of psychology to health and medical problems. His recent books are *Fear and courage* (2nd ed., 1990) and *Obsessive-compulsive disorders* (1993, with P. DeSilva).

Zindel V. Segal, Ph.D., is Head of the Cognitive Behaviour Therapy Unit at the Clarke Institute of Psychiatry in Toronto and Associate Professor in the Departments of Psychiatry and Psychology at the University of Toronto.

He received his Ph.D. from Queen's University in Kingston, Ontario. His research interests have been primarily focused in the area of cognitive models of psychopathology. These have included studies of self-representation in depressed patients before and after cognitive behavior therapy, along with the development of priming paradigms for the activation of hypothesized latent cognitive risk factors in the remitted state. He is currently involved in developing a treatment for the prevention of depressive relapse that emphasizes training in attentional control, as part of a broader CBT package. In addition to these academic pursuits, he is the past director of the CPA/APA accredited Predoctoral Internship Training Program at the Clarke Institute, and is the Associate Head of the Program in Psychotherapy for the Department of Psychiatry at the University of Toronto.

Richard M. Suinn, is Professor of Psychology at Colorado State University, Fort Collins. His research interests include stress management, Asian acculturation, and counseling/clinical sport psychology. He was President of the Association for the Advancement of Behavior Therapy (1993); Board of Directors, American Psychological Association (1990-1993); Board of Directors, American Board of Behavioral Psychology; Board of Directors, Asian American Psychological Association (1983-1988); and Mayor, City of Fort Collins (1979).

He is the author of Anxiety Management Training (AMT), a brief therapy method for the control of anxiety or anger. For 20 years, he was Head of the Department of Psychology. He has served on the U.S. Olympic Committee's Sport Psychology Committee as psychologist for four Olympic teams. Currently he is the team psychologist for the U.S. Shooting Team. He has been on several editorial boards, including those of the *Journal of Consulting and Clinical Psychology,* the *Journal of Counseling Psychology,* the *Journal of Behavioral Medicine, Behavior Therapy, Clinical Psychology,* and *Professional Psychology.* He has been a Visiting Professor in Mexico, Peoples Republic of China, and Japan. He is the author of seven books, including *Seven steps to peak performance* and *Anxiety management training,* over 100 articles, and tests of mathematics anxiety, test anxiety, and acculturation. He was the 1993 recipient of the APA Career Contribution to Education and Training Award.

Stephen R. Swallow, Ph.D., is a psychologist on the Cognitive Behaviour Therapy Unit at the Clarke Institute of Psychiatry in Toronto and Assistant

Professor in the Department of Psychiatry at the University of Toronto. He received his Ph.D. in clinical psychology from the University of Western Ontario in London, Ontario, in 1990. Since coming to the Clarke Institute in 1991, he has divided his time between academic pursuits and clinical practice. His research has focused primarily on the cognitive and social cognitive mechanisms hypothesized to mediate the depressive response. In addition, he has authored or coauthored papers on cognitive assessment, clinical research methodology, and the integration of cognitive behavioral and ethologically derived formulations of depression. He has acted as reviewer for a number of granting agencies and scientific journals and currently serves on the editorial board of *Cognitive Therapy and Research.* He contributes to the clinical training of psychology interns and psychiatry residents and has held sessional teaching posts at York University, Toronto, and Redeemer College, Ancaster, Ontario. In his clinical work, he provides short-term cognitive behavior therapy to individuals suffering from depression and coordinates a cognitively-oriented relapse prevention program for groups of formerly depressed adults.